37INK

SIMON &
SCHUSTER

ALSO BY NICHOLAS GRIFFIN

THE YEAR *of*

DANGEROUS DAYS

Riots, Refugees, and Cocaine in Miami 1980

NICHOLAS GRIFFIN

37INK

SIMON & SCHUSTER

New York   London   Toronto   Sydney   New Delhi

37 INK

SIMON &
SCHUSTER

Simon & Schuster, Inc.
1230 Avenue of the Americas
New York, NY 10020

First 37 INK / Simon & Schuster hardcover edition July 2020

37 INK / SIMON & SCHUSTER and colophon are trademarks of Simon & Schuster, Inc.

For information about special discounts for bulk purchases, please contact Simon & Schuster Special Sales at 1-866-506-1949 or business@simonandschuster.com.

The Simon & Schuster Speakers Bureau can bring authors to your live event. For more information or to book an event, contact the Simon & Schuster Speakers Bureau at 1-866-248-3049 or visit our website at www.simonspeakers.com.

Interior design by Carly Loman

Manufactured in the United States of America

10   9   8   7   6   5   4   3

Library of Congress Cataloging-in-Publication Data is available.

ISBN 978-1-5011-9102-2
ISBN 978-1-5011-9104-6 (ebook)

To Adriana, Tomás, and Eva—my loves

CONTENTS

PART 3

PART 4

AUTHOR'S NOTE

When it comes to South Florida's local terminology, I have opted to go with 1980's usage rather than today's. 2020's Miami-Dade County is referred to as Dade County. Today's Miami-Dade Police Department was once the PSD (Public Safety Department), etc.

It is important to note that this is a book based on interviews and public records. No names have been changed. All exchanges that occurred in the context of the trial of the police officers involved in the death of Arthur McDuffie were directly quoted from either trial transcripts, television recordings of the trial, or direct quotations carried in local newspapers. Outside of the context of the trial, scenes and conversations have been reconstructed from statements made by individuals featured in the book at public events and/or in the course of interviews and have been reconstructed from **recordings**, memory or notes, to the best of my ability.

PROLOGUE

At noon, amid light traffic on the Florida Turnpike, a black Audi swerved at high speed attempting to outrun a Pontiac Grand Prix. The cars careened toward the end of the highway, where it dovetailed into Miami's main thoroughfare, US 1, used by suburban southern Dade County to connect to the city. A man with thick sideburns leaned out the window of the Pontiac holding a revolver. He'd already blown out the back windshield of the Audi and sunk four more bullets into its chassis. Returning fire amid the shattered glass on the back seat of the Audi was a young man with a smudge of a mustache and long, dark hair whipping in the wind. Wearing a white dress shirt and crisp black slacks, he used both hands to fire an Ingram MAC-10 fitted with a suppressor.

Bewildered witnesses numbered in the dozens as the two cars decelerated and entered US 1. At the corner of Caribbean Boulevard the cars slowed long enough for a man to leap out of the passenger seat of the Audi. He positioned himself behind a traffic control box in front of the cowboy-themed cafeteria Westward Ho and raised a 9mm pistol to exchange fire with the Grand Prix as it returned to creep past him.

The chase only ended because a new one began. Officers in a passing patrol car spotted the three remaining armed men in the Audi. Flipping their lights and sirens on, they began a second high-speed pursuit on crowded US 1. The astonished policemen watched a man lean out of the rear of the Audi and spray their patrol car with machine-gun fire. Two miles later, the Audi pulled over close to a wooded area and the three men sprinted into the trees, untouched by police gunfire.

Panting and covered in scratches, one of the fugitives was soon captured wearing only a snug yellow bathing suit. Talking to the police in Spanish, he claimed he'd been jogging, become disorientated, and somehow lost his shoes. He was driven back to the Audi just in time to watch a crime-scene technician pop the trunk. Inside lay a corpse outfitted in brown, from socks to shoes, shirt to trousers. In contrasting stark white were the adhesive tape that covered his mouth and the 45 pounds of white powder pressed against his body in an open duffel bag. Moments later, the gunman who'd hidden himself behind the traffic control box was also found, nonchalantly browsing car parts in an automotive center while bleeding from a shoulder wound. He'd been watching through the window as police interviewed witnesses less than a hundred meters away.

It would be the first large investigation for the brand-new captain of the county homicide bureau, Marshall Frank. Previously, he had worked as a detective sergeant in homicide for seven years before leading the crime-scene section. A heavy smoker, Frank dressed in J. C. Penney suits and aviator sunglasses and carried a small bottle of Old Spice in his pocket alongside a handkerchief to mask the heavy stench of Florida decompositions.

A week into the investigation, Frank received a kind note from State Attorney Janet Reno, congratulating him on his department's performance. Seven days later brought a swing in mood. A grand jury had refused to indict either of Frank's suspects on murder, citing a lack of prosecutorial evidence. "It has come to my attention that the Department now considers this to be a case of second order priority," Reno wrote, reminding Frank that if the murder case wasn't brought to trial within one hundred and eighty days of the arrest, both men would automatically receive immunity. Frank, she chided, needed to force his detectives to develop the evidence and tie the suspects directly to the body.

The investigative files doubled in thickness and doubled again. Eighty-one leads were pursued that led Frank's men to stolen cars, a murdered maid, abduction, aggravated assaults, immigration offenses, organized crime, and concealed firearms. Yet despite the combined efforts of Reno and Frank, the grand jury still refused to indict the suspects on anything other than weapons violations and assault charges.

Within a month on the job, Marshall Frank began to understand how difficult a post he had been handed. It came with pressure from the state attorney and from Miami's news media. The body in the trunk wasn't a simple murder. It involved a fledgling cocaine industry, illegal immigration, and violent acts executed in public. What Frank couldn't yet understand was that the case also concerned corruption. The Federal Bureau of Investigation was involved. The Bureau had opened a secret investigation before Frank had even arrived. While Marshall Frank joined Reno in worrying about the rising number of fatalities in the county, the FBI worried that the 45 pounds of milk sugar found in the back of the trunk had been placed there by Frank's detectives to conceal their theft of an equal amount of cocaine.

Was the homicide bureau itself corrupt? Miami would have little else to lean on if Janet Reno was correct in her belief that the county's murder rate was beginning an unusual acceleration. Still, in the middle of 1979, it was very hard to guess at the extent of Miami's looming crisis.

From Capt. Marshall Frank's point of view, the highway shootout was a presumed anomaly. Miami had seen nothing like it before. The idea that criminals would take such extraordinary risks in public again was nonsensical. Not even the finest homicide detective can determine a pattern from a single instance, but in retrospect, Miami was about to pose new problems and new questions for the rest of America to consider.

Within the year, drugs would become a part of the national conversation. Immigration would evolve into a virulent topic in South Florida as race was redefined in Miami. Dade County not only witnessed what the *New York Times* called the worst racial disturbances of the century but would behold something entirely new: enough Latin Americans suddenly spilling into a city to turn both black and white citizens into minorities.

These fluid American issues of race, immigration, and drugs would mainly be seen as South Florida's problems. In the coming hinge year, few thought of a future for Miami as bright as today's twenty-three million visitors, thriving service industries, vast port, and iridescent sky-line. Miami's suffering was to become so obvious in 1980 that its own leaders questioned its survival.

Most presume that the city's embrace of Latin American culture was a strength embedded in Miami's DNA, a natural consequence of history, geography, and planning. It's far from the truth. Today's city acceler-ated into being out of a traumatic 1980. There was little planning, little history, to build on. Geography seemed to be conspiring against the city, not working for it. The more closely you look at 1980, the more remark-able Miami's transformation into an aspiring international metropolis becomes.

PART 1

PART 1

CHAPTER 1

DECEMBER 1979

By 1979, there were several Miamis that barely lapped against one another, let alone integrated. The county itself was a strange beast, twenty-seven different municipalities with their own mayor, many with their own police departments. But Miami wasn't divided by municipalities; it was separated into tribes.

There was Anglo Miami, which the city's boosters were still hawking to white America: beaches, real estate, hotels, and entertainment. Tourists dominated the region. Dade had 1.6 million residents but 2.1 million international visitors a year. Anglo Miami was far from monolithic. There were southerners, migrants, and a large Jewish population that ran some of the most important businesses and institutions in Miami Beach.

Across the causeway in Little Havana and up the coast in Hialeah sat Latin Miami, created by the Cubans who'd fled Fidel Castro's revolution twenty years before. Whenever there was violence south of the border, Latin America coughed up a new pocket of immigrants. Most recently that meant that the Cuban population in Dade was being watered down by Nicaraguans, Salvadorans, and Colombians.

Then there was black Miami. It, too, had more divisions than cohesion. There was a strong Bahamian presence, plenty of Jamaicans. Both felt distinct from the African Americans who had moved south from Georgia, and those who were born and bred in Miami. The latest immigrants were only beginning to spill in: a large number of unwelcome Haitians. Arriving on rickety boats, fleeing both political persecution and economic despair, they were docking at a time when not one of Miami's communities was in the mood to reach out and welcome them.

For all the nuances, if you were black, white, or Latin, you tended to know so little about the other tribes that you regarded them as rigid blocs. Who knew a Jamaican turned his nose up at a Georgia-born black, or that a Puerto Rican couldn't stand another word from a Cuban, or that a Jew couldn't walk through the door at the all-white country club at La Gorce? There was enough inequality to go around, but in this one thing, the black community got the most generous helping.

In 1979, if you were black in Dade County, you most likely lived in one of three neighborhoods: Overtown, the Black Grove, or Liberty City. Liberty City was the youngest of the three, dating back to 1937, when President Franklin Roosevelt authorized the first large public housing project in the South. It was Roosevelt's response to local campaigns for better sanitation. In the '30s, Liberty City had what most houses in Overtown and the Black Grove did not: running water, modern kitchens, electricity. Overtown remained the center of black life in Miami until the arrival of I-95, the vast stretch of American highway that ran from Maine down the East Coast all the way to Miami. It stomped right through the middle of Miami's most prominent black neighborhood in 1965, a ravenous millipede with a thousand concrete legs.

Had the 3,000-kilometer highway been halted just 5 kilometers to the north, black Miami might have had a different history. Instead the highway, touted as "slum clearance," bulldozed through black Miami's main drags. Gone was much of Overtown's commercial heart, with its three movie theaters, its public pool, grocery store, and businesses. Goodbye to clubs that had hosted Ella Fitzgerald, to the Sir John Hotel, which had offered their finest suites to black entertainers banned from staying in whites-only Miami Beach. But more important, goodbye to a neighborhood where parents knew which house every child belonged to. Goodbye to the nighttime games of Moonlight Baby, where kids would use the bottle caps of Cola Nibs to mark the edge of their bodies on the pavement. Goodbye to unarmed black patrolmen walking black streets.

Overtown had its own all-black police station, with strict rules. Black officers couldn't carry a weapon home, since "no one wanted to see a black man with a gun." They could stop whites in Overtown but had no power of arrest over them. The closest affordable housing for Overtown's displaced was in and around the Liberty City projects. Block by block it began to turn from white to black, until neighboring white homeowners built a wall to separate themselves from ever-blacker Liberty City. White housewives in colorful plaids and horn-rimmed glasses carried protest signs: "We want this Nigger moved" and "Nigger go to Washington." Someone detonated a stick of dynamite in an empty apartment leased to blacks. Nothing worked, and by the end of the 1960s the first proud black owners inside Liberty City were joined by many of Overtown's twenty thousand displaced. As white flight accelerated, house prices declined, local businesses faltered, and unemployment and crime began to rise. By 1968, Liberty City had assumed a new reputation. The CND—the Central-North District—had earned the nickname "Central Negro District" from both the city and the county police departments.

There was still beauty in Liberty City, still sunrises where the light would smart off the sides of pastel-painted houses, and the dew on the grass would glisten, and churches would fill, and the jitney buses would chug patiently, waiting for the elderly to board. Still schoolchildren in white shirts tightening backpacks to their shoulders and catching as much shade as possible on the way to the school gates. There was still beauty, but you had to squint to see it.

Eighty percent of South Florida homes had air-conditioning in 1980, but in stifling hot Liberty City, only one in five homes could afford it. It was a neighborhood without a center, few jobs to offer, seventy-two churches but just six banks, not one of which was black-owned. There were plenty of places to pray for a positive future but few institutions willing to risk investment in one. The fact that a teenager called Arthur McDuffie got out at all was unusual. The fact that he came back, found a good job, earned steadily, and raised a family was rarer still.

Frederica Jones had been Arthur McDuffie's high school sweetheart at

Booker T. Washington, one of Miami's three segregated schools. They'd met while Frederica was walking home from the local store, where she'd bought a can of peas for her mother. She'd swung her groceries at her side, and McDuffie, who'd been watching her from across the street, fell into step beside her.

After a few moments of banter, McDuffie made a simple declaration. "I like you." Then he asked for Frederica's number. That night McDuffie called, and the two talked for an hour. At the end of the conversation McDuffie, two years Frederica's senior, asked, "Would you go with me?"

"Yes!" she said.

They became inseparable. They were in the Booker T. Washington band together. McDuffie was the baritone horn and Frederica a majorette. She watched McDuffie win the local swim meets. When McDuffie graduated, he joined the Marine Corps, and for the next three years, they communicated through letters. Then, within two months of his honorable discharge, they married. Two children quickly followed. After which came problems, separation, and, in 1978, divorce. McDuffie had always had a reputation as a ladies' man, and now he had a child with another woman to prove it.

Yet toward the end of 1979, the thirty-three-year-old McDuffie was back visiting the house he'd once shared with Frederica. He mowed the lawn, fixed the air conditioners, and trimmed the hedges of their neighbor, the last white family on the block. The warmth in the failed marriage seemed to be returning. The two spent the night of December 15, 1979, together, and McDuffie asked Frederica to join him on a trip to Hawaii—a vacation he'd just won at the office for his performance as the assistant manager at Coastal States Life Insurance.

The following day, Sunday, under bright 80-degree skies, Frederica, a nurse at Jackson Memorial Hospital, drove McDuffie back to his home. She parked the car feeling like there was positive momentum. They'd talked of remarriage in front of their families. The deal was that if McDuffie could make "certain changes" in his life, then they could go ahead and make it official. As they sat in the car, McDuffie kissed his ex-wife goodbye and promised to be back at her place that evening to take care of their children before her shift. Normally, Frederica worked only afternoons, but the hospital was short-staffed over the Christmas period and she'd agreed to work that night at 11:00.

Shortly after 2:00 p.m., McDuffie walked into 1157 NW 111th Street, the home he now shared with his younger sister, Dorothy, a legal clerk. It was a modest building, painted green. Inside there was a record collection and books of music. McDuffie played five instruments, all horns. There was an entire white wall "covered with plaques and certificates of achievement," including his "Most Outstanding" award from his Marine Corps platoon. He wasn't a war hero, hadn't fought in Vietnam, but McDuffie had been faithful to the corps, a military policeman who had done his job impeccably.

A dutiful father, McDuffie had already wrapped Christmas presents for his two daughters and hidden them in a closet in his bedroom. His nine-year-old would get a wagon, a jack-in-the-box, and clothes. His oldest would get a watch, a tape recorder, a radio, and a pair of roller skates.

He'd saved for months, but it hadn't been an easy year to make money. Under President Jimmy Carter, the country, most especially the South, had been battered. Unemployment was stubbornly high, and it looked like the president was being swept downstream by the economy. For all Carter's preaching of forbearance, the reality was that interest rates were up to 17 percent. In thirty years, inflation had never run higher. Gas prices had doubled in two years. Even hamburger meat was two dollars a pound.

Despite all this, Carter was about to enter an election year in comparatively good standing. Whatever America thought of his ability to steer the country, he retained the people's sympathy, with an approval rating of 61 percent. Six weeks before, the Iranian revolution had become very real to the distant United States. The sixty-two hostages captured in the American embassy in Tehran had helped generate a sudden sense of solidarity in the United States. Between that and the following month's Soviet invasion of Afghanistan, there was an understanding that Carter had a tricky hand to play. He would promise a strong and quick response to both situations. By the end of the year Carter led his presumptive challenger, Ronald Reagan, by an enormous 24-point margin.

Still, the mood was summed up best by the *Miami Herald* in 1979. It was a year the average American wallet had "barely survived." The unseen benefit, according to the paper, was that Miamians like McDuffie lived in Florida. They weren't being hammered on heating oil like the rest of the country.

By Miami standards, the evening of December 16 counted as cold, expected to dip below 70 degrees and then drop below 60 the following day. Miamians traditionally overreacted, digging out winter coats and scarves for a rare outing. McDuffie selected blue jeans, a navy shirt over a baby-blue undershirt, and a black motorcycle jacket. He searched his house for a hat to wear under his helmet. At 5:00 p.m., he closed the door behind him.

His own car, a 1969 green Grand Prix, wasn't parked in its usual spot in his driveway. A friend had borrowed it. So he climbed on an orange-and-black 1973 Kawasaki 2100, "a more or less permanent loan" from his cousin. McDuffie turned the key, revved the engine, and drove the motorcycle south to Fifty-Ninth Street, to his friend Lynwood Blackmon's house. He pulled up at the front door, feet still astride the bike, and talked to Blackmon's seven- and eight-year-old daughters. He explained to them that he couldn't help their father tune their car as he'd promised. His tools were in the back of the borrowed Grand Prix. Next he drove to his older brother's house, his most common stop, and found him washing his car in his driveway. McDuffie grinned, revved the engine, spat up dirt over the clean car, and sped away before his brother could grab him. He raced to the far end of the street, turned, and braked hard.

"You better slow that bike down," shouted his brother. McDuffie nodded, grinned, and pulled away.

Sometimes on weekends McDuffie moonlighted as a truck driver, making deliveries to Miami Beach. Sometimes he gave up his time to help jobless youngsters, teaching them how to paint houses. Just two years before, he'd painted the Range Funeral Home, where his body would arrive in exactly a week. On this particular Sunday evening, he was going to see Carolyn Battle, the twenty-six-year-old assistant that McDuffie had hired at Coastal Insurance. She was pretty, independent, and stylish, with a preference for dresses and wearing her hair in an Afro. He'd brought a helmet for her.

McDuffie shouldn't have been driving at all. His license had been suspended months before, and he'd paid his thirty-five-dollar traffic fine with a check that had bounced. He'd told a coworker that he was worried about getting stopped again, but there were no alternatives for driving back and forth to work. Public transport was pitiful in Miami, and Liberty City—barely serviced—was reliant on independent jitney operators who rarely worked weekends. Not having a car was a self-quarantine.

McDuffie collected Carolyn Battle. They drove fifteen minutes south, to the edge of Miami International Airport, where they watched planes arcing out over the ocean or dropping into landing patterns above the Everglades. Tiring of the airport, McDuffie drove Battle across MacArthur Causeway to Miami Beach. When McDuffie was a child, dusk would have found an exodus heading the other way: black Americans subject to a sunset curfew. But on December 16, on the three lanes that ran east over the bright blue shallows, McDuffie showed off, hitting eighty miles an hour. They walked in the sand, stopped for Pepsi, and then at 9:00 p.m. headed back to Battle's apartment at 3160 NW Forty-Sixth Street, just five blocks from the Airport Expressway.

At one in the morning, McDuffie slept in Battle's bed while she watched television on her couch. At 1:30 she woke him up. "Jesus," said McDuffie, reaching for his watch. He was far too late to show up at his ex-wife's house. Frederica would have taken the kids over to a babysitter two hours ago. How was he going to make that up to her? Had he blown it? McDuffie gathered his watch, his wedding ring, his medallion. Still dressed in his blue jeans, two blue shirts, and boots, he put on his knitted cap under his white helmet, tied his knapsack to the back of the Kawasaki, and headed north toward home.

Was it a wheelie, a rolled stop sign, a hand lifted from a handlebar to give the finger that caught the sergeant's attention? The officer would later offer all three explanations of why he'd first noticed the Kawasaki pass by him. It was 1:51 a.m. The sergeant got on the radio, described McDuffie's white helmet and the tag number of the motorbike, and flipped on his red light and siren. On a cool night, with the rider in jeans, jacket, and helmet, he couldn't have known if he was black, Latin, or white.

McDuffie appeared to glance in his mirror and then sped through a red light on NW Sixty-First Street. As the sergeant followed in his white-and-green county squad car, McDuffie blew through another red light and swept around corners, not even slowing for the stop signs. He'd picked a very quiet night for these traffic infractions. Within sixty seconds of the beginning of the chase, McDuffie was being followed by every available unit within Central District.

CHAPTER 2

As McDuffie began to weave and jig through the night, flipping off his lights and accelerating, he crossed from city line to county line and back again. Sirens wailed across the Central District. McDuffie was now followed by not one but two police departments. The city cops, in their dark blue uniforms, controlled a narrow but heavily populated area around Miami's downtown. The county cops, in brown-and-tan uniforms, covered the rest of unincorporated Dade's 2,400 square miles. The county cops were better known as the PSD, or Public Safety Department. In matters that seemed to land between their jurisdictions, the county force, with its greater numbers and larger budget, tended to take control.

For a moment, it seemed as if they'd all lost McDuffie between buildings. Then the sergeant who had first noted him saw the motorbike accelerate away, its lights still off. By now it seemed as if McDuffie were being followed by a freight train, eleven police cars long.

Even in the dead of night, city police chases are different from highway pursuits. "You go fast, you accelerate, brake. You take corners as you endeavor to stay on the radio, read street signs in the dark, keep an eye on the suspect." Officers were gripping their wheels, pushing the squad cars on corners. One county car spun out, hit a curb with a rim, bursting the tire. It limped on after McDuffie at walking speed.

The radio crackled with updates on the motorcyclist's position. They knew nothing about him. An orange-and-black bike, a tag number, a white helmet. Almost 2:00 a.m. Most had the same thought. This rider's fleeing a traffic violation at reckless speed. What had he done?

Was it the suspended license that spurred McDuffie's course of action? Did he think that the possibilities for 1980—a family reunification, his job, his freedom, bringing his ex-wife to Hawaii—were all at stake? Had he blown it all by oversleeping? A thirty-second high-speed chase along city streets can seem interminable, but McDuffie had now led the police for almost eight minutes. He took twenty-six turns, flipped his lights on and off, went at a deceptive crawl, feinted parking, and rode at over eighty miles an hour. There were now fourteen squad cars tracking him.

At 1:59, McDuffie finally made a sensible decision, pulling over by the on-ramp to I-395, the intersection by Decorator's Row, and put his kickstand down. From six in the morning until seven at night, this was a busy intersection, a familiar turn for any Miami Beach resident heading home from work in the city. But Miami was not a late-night town—not in these parts, anyway. Here it was just concrete and overpasses, the occasional rumble of a truck rolling on the highway above, but no late-night businesses to bring anyone to the street, and certainly not on a night as cold as this. Two green-and-white squad cars pulled in immediately behind him, each containing a single officer drawn from the county's force of 1,450. Moments later the blue-and-white cars of the city police joined them. In the faint light, the officers were easier to distinguish than their cars. County officers wore brown and tan, city officers a dark blue almost indistinguishable from the night.

Less than four minutes later, the sirens of Fire Rescue could be heard from several blocks away. As the ambulance slowed, its sirens were silenced, leaving just the flashing red light to illuminate the scene; enough for the attending medics to see that McDuffie's face was entirely covered in blood. Unit Five Fire Rescue wasn't sure what to make of McDuffie. He was now sitting up in the middle of the street. His eyes were swollen shut. Pulse and breathing were normal. A paramedic asked the police to remove his handcuffs.

As soon as they were removed, McDuffie's arms began to flail. The head of the Fire Rescue unit calmed McDuffie down, then bandaged his head, wiping clean an inch-long gash. He inserted a needle into the inside of McDuffie's right elbow. As McDuffie absorbed Ringer's lactate, a solution used to replace lost blood, the medic tried to shine a light in his eyes, but they were so swollen he couldn't force them open.

The police explained there'd been an accident. The John Doe had fallen from the bike at high speed. He'd hit his head. His helmet had spun off. Then he'd come up fighting and had to be subdued. No identification had been found. For a motorcyclist in Miami, the John Doe had been well protected—leather jacket, boots, jeans. The medic made a mental note that the man surprisingly had seemed to have escaped road rash, the usual abrasions and bruises associated with a high-speed accident.

Still conscious, McDuffie moved. He climbed onto the stretcher himself. The doors to the ambulance closed at 2:23 a.m. The vehicle sped to Jackson Memorial Hospital, where Frederica McDuffie was halfway through her night shift. Stationed in the ward above the Emergency Room, she watched the ambulance pull up and had the fleeting thought that it was a late admission for a Sunday night. By the time the ambulance unloaded, at 2:25, Arthur McDuffie was comatose. His blood loss was extreme. He received a transfusion of eleven pints, "his entire body capacity and then some." McDuffie was carried into the hospital, registered as a John Doe, and taken to D Ward, where hospitalized prisoners were often kept. The medic paused, then wrote on the Fire Rescue report that the injuries were sustained in a motorcycle accident.

Frederica McDuffie left her shift at 7:30 a.m., and her first call was to her ex-husband's house. His sister picked up. McDuffie couldn't come to the phone. His bedroom door was closed, she said, and she guessed that he must still be asleep. Later that day, Frederica would learn from McDuffie's oldest brother that her ex-husband had lost control of his motorbike and driven straight into a wall at over sixty miles an hour. He had been the 2:25 a.m. arrival at Jackson.

As soon as the hospital staff identified McDuffie, they moved him over to the main building. The morning of December 17, surgeons began to drill into his skull searching for a clot in hopes of removing it to relieve the growing pressure inside his skull. They found that "the entire brain was swelling uncontrollably." There was no remedy. The body was alive, but the brain was dying.

Frederica spent most of the next four days at McDuffie's bedside, inside her own place of work. The first time she saw him in the hospital, she doubted it was the man she'd married. His head was "so swollen there [were] no features in his face at all." His sister Dorothy thought his head resembled a basketball. She said his name, and he raised an arm, the only time he'd show any sign of comprehension. Frederica looked over her ex-husband's body, noted bruises and scratches on his arms and legs, and came to a professional conclusion she didn't share. "No accident could look like this."

On December 21, three days after his brain had ceased to function, the last of McDuffie's sisters drove up to Jackson. She'd had to fly in from Germany, where her husband was based with the US Army. At 2:00 p.m., shortly after her arrival, McDuffie's life support was unplugged. His mother, sisters, ex-wife, and brothers were allowed to sit with the body until they were ready for it be wheeled out.

Two hours later, the phone on Edna Buchanan's desk rang.

CHAPTER 3

Hearing the phone was easy, finding the phone was slightly more difficult. Edna Buchanan's desk at the *Miami Herald* was covered in competing stacks of paper, directories, and photographs.

When Buchanan finally picked up, the voice on the other end of the phone was familiar, reliable. It was the source's story that seemed extraordinary. A black motorcyclist in a coma in Jackson Memorial was dying or dead. He had been brought in by Fire Rescue from a traffic accident in the early morning of December 17. But there hadn't been an accident. He'd been beaten by a group of PSD officers. The multiple police reports had been written, then rewritten. If she dug, she could find the inconsistencies.

Crime reporters like Edna Buchanan walked a tricky path. Their access was dependent on the generosity of sources within police departments. Reporters suspected of having little understanding of the pressures of police work would find themselves on the outside of every crime scene, dealing with public information officers rather than detectives. Instead of sifting through scraps of truth, they'd be left standing beside every other reporter listening to standard lines and standard vocabulary, slapped with a grab bag of clichés and a press release to quote back to their readers.

Buchanan, known simply by her first name across every police department in the twenty-seven municipalities of Dade, didn't have that problem. She'd already married and divorced one cop; had attended the Police Benevolent Association Fourth of July picnics and bonded with officers' wives under a table while their husbands shot at the fireworks. Buchanan knew the stresses of the job. Her reputation among cops varied. Some considered her presumptuous and aggressive, but even her detractors understood that she was also hardworking, efficient, and fair. A policeman had once threatened her with arrest at a crime scene and had thrown her in the back of his patrol car; another officer let her out the other side. Buchanan never filed complaints with her editors, never sought to alert Internal Review. It was a small price for the stories obtained.

Buchanan's style of doing business was as incongruous as her physical appearance at a crime scene. Police reporters tended to be white males, in their thirties or forties. Miami's own archetype had been Henry Reno, Janet Reno's father, a tall, taciturn Dane who'd held Buchanan's job at the *Herald* for forty-three years. Back then, reporters covering the cops had desks inside the police stations. They didn't need advice from a detective about what to keep in or out of an article. In their own minds, they were "more or less a member of the department."

Instead of the besuited, mustachioed Reno, officers now faced forty-year-old Buchanan, whose slightness was emphasized by a blond bouffant that wasn't so much ahead of the 1980s as a nod to the 1950s. She had big blue eyes, always hidden behind sunglasses in the Miami sun, and one of the rarest physical attributes: no looping ridges on the tips of her fingers. Had Buchanan been on the other side of the law, she could have had a gloveless career in crime. In the early days, she attended crime scenes in high heels and silk scarves, carrying a handbag. She kept a gun in her glove compartment. By 1980 she favored flats, usually accompanied by one of two jumpsuits she kept by her front door, one beige, the other purple. Whenever her phone rang, which tended to be nightly since "if you called someone else she'd be pissed off," Buchanan was ready.

Her articles carried a jolt, almost always within her lead. "Gary Robinson died hungry," began one article. Robinson had pushed to the front of the line of a fast-food chicken restaurant. He tried to order fried chicken, was sent to the back of the line by the counterwoman, returned to the front, where they were now out of fried chicken, then swatted the server in the head. Robinson—drunk, rambunctious, aggressive, and still unfed—was shot in the head by a security guard. A senseless murder turned into a seven-paragraph meditation on how circumstances could quickly accelerate to death.

Buchanan's deadpan style seemed birthed in the staccato noir of the 1930s—a little Chandler, a dash of Hammett—and there were few reporters who had such a thirst for details. She revealed the bright colors that differentiated one South Florida life from another, and planted the macabre of Miami in the moment. What record was still spinning on the hi-fi by the body? What was in the oven? What book had been found in the corpse's hand? Cases that would have otherwise been ignored came to life, and for a local reporter at a premier newspaper in the South, Buchanan found that a surprising number of her stories migrated to the front page.

By the time Buchanan and her source ended their call on the morning of Friday, December 21, she'd made her decision: she would chase this story to its conclusion. Buchanan had her own formula for sorting the city's truths from its lies. If a story seemed particularly unbelievable, it usually turned out to be true.

———

In an open-plan office like the *Herald*'s, there was a football field of reporters lurking behind their Rolodex wheel of sources, telephone receivers pressed to their ears. Skinny notebook at the ready, Buchanan got a fresh dial tone and placed a call to the medical examiner's office.

"Have you had a black motorcyclist come in the last day or two?" she asked, preparing to jot a response in her invented shorthand.

"No," said the operator. Buchanan relaxed. *Thank God my source is wrong*, she thought. "But we've got one on the way," said the operator. "He just died."

Buchanan asked to be put through to Ronald Wright, the assistant medical examiner scheduled to conduct the autopsy. The two spoke, and she repeated her source's story. Buchanan hung up the phone only to place another call immediately. This time she went straight to the PSD's department of Internal Review, the division that policed the police. The man who answered the phone was cordial with Buchanan and assured her that "nothing was amiss. The motorcyclist simply had an accident trying to outrun the police." That was Buchanan's last phone call of the morning. She grabbed her car keys and headed to the gray bank of elevators. She needed to speak with the officers, despite what promised to be a chilly reception.

The relationship between the press and the PSD had reached a new low. The previous summer, the *Miami Herald* had published a three-part series on police brutality after the police raided the wrong house in the Central District and attacked an innocent black schoolteacher. Six months later, the *Herald* was still involved in a Freedom of Information suit against the police department. But the biggest blow to the PSD was that the exposé revealed a complicated and unhealthy truth: officers who were seen as aggressive, or who were being punished internally for infractions, were more likely to be posted to the predominantly black Central District. The more troubled an officer's situation, the more likely it was that he would be given the midnight shift. It was, according to Edna Buchanan, where "they sent the screw-ups that the brass didn't want to see in the daytime."

Central—which included Liberty City, where working-class black residents now made up over 90 percent of the population—was also the area with the highest crime rates. The area of Liberty City patrolled by county officers contained less than 5 percent of the county's population, but 23 percent of its robberies and 40 percent of its stabbings. The combination of unruly officers and high-pressure situations was volatile.

In a divided city like Miami, white policemen had little interaction with the black community. It hadn't always been that way. When Buchanan had first started reporting, police often covered medical emergencies. Officers who'd delivered babies wore a tiny stork on their lapels. They were just as likely to have aided your asthmatic child as they were to have arrested your troubled uncle. When the work was passed over to Fire Rescue, it had seemed entirely logical—except now the black community and white policemen most often crossed paths in reaction to moments of extreme stress, when crimes had just been committed or were in progress. Two decades before, James Baldwin had written that any white policeman in Harlem could "retreat from his uneasiness in only one direction: into a callousness which very shortly becomes second nature. He becomes more callous, the population becomes more hostile, the situation grows more tense, and the police force is increased." In Miami's case, Baldwin had his last assumption wrong.

With inflation moving fast in 1979, instead of augmenting the police force, cuts had been made across the PSD. That left the county police understaffed, which meant that the toughest and most troubled police officers were working overtime in the toughest and most troubled neighborhoods. One out of every five officers had been beaten in the course of making an arrest. Miami was a tinderbox, and as Baldwin had predicted, "One day to everyone's astonishment, someone drops a match in the powder keg and everything blows up."

Edna Buchanan slept with a portable scanner on all night by her bed, having trained herself to wake only when it squawked the high-pitched "three signal" of an emergency. Every morning she'd head first to the Miami Beach Police, close to her home on the Venetian Islands. The Beach was the municipality with the oldest voters in America, average age sixty-eight, aging folks in aging hotels, an army of bright clothes and deep wrinkles, dragging their chairs around the terraces seeking or hiding from the sun. Their numbers included the densest population of Holocaust survivors outside of Israel. Buchanan would drive south past the oval of the Kennel Club's dog-racing track on the southern edge of Ocean Drive, maybe stop at the bakery staffed by sixty-year-old women, concentration camp tattoos peeking from their sleeves.

From the beach, Buchanan would drive across the causeway to the city police, and finally to the county. She knew the names of all the sergeants who rode the desks, as well as their shifts. She stood in the lobbies, leafing through the police reports from the night before, sniffing out the oddities from the logs, sensing stories, preparing to follow leads.

Buchanan exited the *Herald* building from the rear, the only reporter with a key to the back door and a parking spot in the lot below. She always filled up at the end of the day in the *Herald*'s own gas station, just a block away. It would only take a reporter one lost story to understand the benefits of a full tank.

———

On the morning of December 22, when Buchanan strolled through the doors of the PSD building, it was hardly an unusual sight. Some of the officers bristled at her presence, but she had enough attitude, knew enough friendly faces in senior positions, that she was tolerated when she was not welcomed. At headquarters, she was allowed to listen to the eight-minute-long tape of the police chase. She noted that the pursuit ended at 1:59 a.m. "We have him," said a sergeant's voice. At 2:01, that same voice came back on the police radio. Buchanan could hear how breathless he was as he requested the ambulance.

Next, Buchanan turned to the accident report. There were two thousand employees at the PSD, but a few names "sprang off the page." Of the names on the report, the most troubling to Buchanan was Michael Watts. Four year ago, Watts had been honored as Officer of the Month for arresting a serial child murderer as the man raped a woman by the side of a Dade County highway. It was a vital arrest that had saved lives. But Watts had also turned two traffic violations into hospital stays, fracturing the skull of a black man arrested for running a light, and then dragging a black woman out of her car by her feet, bouncing her head on the pavement. The infraction was an expired inspection sticker. These weren't exceptions to the rule. Buchanan had received a phone call months before from one of Watts's friends, a female officer in the PSD. Watts's supervisor had noted that he "had difficulty in dealing with blacks," and then he'd been promptly transferred *to* Central. Watts had been furious. He'd told his friend he'd either kill or be killed in his new assignment. Since the friend had refused to go on the record, there was little Buchanan could do.

As Buchanan finished reading the McDuffie accident report, she noted the name of the company that had recovered the Kawasaki motorcycle from under I-395. She got back into her car and headed over to Barbon Towing, an unremarkable lot among many unremarkable lots on the edge of Miami's Wynwood district. Half an acre of poured concrete baked by the sun, the lot was cracked by weeds and protected by a taut chain-link fence topped with barbed wire. Buchanan inquired about the Kawasaki, and the owner looked relieved that someone cared. He'd found the bike in the middle of the street next to a pool of blood. "We were wondering when somebody was going to pick it up." This was an oddity. If there'd been any type of internal investigation underway, the motorbike should have already been seized as evidence; it shouldn't be sitting in the lot, untouched.

Buchanan asked if she could take a look. She stood with her pad and pen, noting that "every piece of glass and plastic on the machine was shattered—the speedometer, all of the gauges, all of the lights." Buchanan had covered accidents before, and it seemed odd to her that the damage was so complete. The lot's owner asked if she wanted to take the bike with her. For a moment she contemplated trying to attach the Kawasaki to her Camaro. Without the motorbike, she headed over to the medical examiner's office.

After McDuffie's body had been wheeled out of his hospital room, it had been taken downstairs on a gurney and rattled through the off-white corridors to the back of Jackson Memorial. This was Dr. Joseph H. Davis's domain, the medical examiner's office. It was familiar to the PSD homicide department and to the *Herald*'s crime reporters, another part of Buchanan's daily routine. Davis also hosted what was considered the best Christmas party in the wider law enforcement community. Only two days before, on December 20, Buchanan, Davis, and the city and county homicide detectives had celebrated together during the day, just a couple of doors down from the morgue.

Davis was supposed to be in the Caribbean for his Christmas vacation. Buchanan's phone call from the previous morning had been significant enough for him to miss his plane. He didn't remove his top assistant, Ronald Wright, from the scheduled autopsy, but he chose to attend.

Davis was used to watching the Dade County dead roll in. He had worked for the county for twenty-four years, before there was even a medical examiner's office. At first, he operated out of an abandoned garage in a refrigerated truck; but things had changed. In 1961, he'd operated with a budget of $1,000 and had overseen a couple of assistants. By the end of 1980, the budget ran to $1.1 million and forty-five employees, though it was far from perfect. Buchanan was often in the morgue when the drains would block and parts of the dead would return carried in puddles of dark water.

The father of six daughters and a son, Davis was a gardener and a cook who had taken the time to train his dachshund to sneeze on command. He was a genial eccentric, superb at his job. He'd served on the investigation committees into the deaths of President Kennedy and Martin Luther King Jr. and had once headed the National Association of Medical Examiners. For a man who worked only on the dead, he was a committed advocate for the living, pushing for legislation when he saw patterns, helping to improve Florida laws on traffic safety, electrical wiring, and pool installation. In his opinion, the fewer clients he had, the better.

It was just after eleven when Buchanan walked past what Davis referred to as "brain buckets," motorcycle helmets from fatal accidents that led to the entrance of the medical examiner's office. On Davis's desk sat a small sign: "A Cluttered Desk Is the Mark of Genius." It was something Buchanan would have noted with sympathy. Scattered around were hundreds of colored slides, "pictures most people could not conjure up in their most horrific nightmares. Riot victims, accident cases, close-ups of curiously patterned gunshot wounds." Overlaying the slides were messages from police, doctors, lawyers, and funeral homes. Beneath the slides and messages, the lens of a microscope peeked out. Books lined the floor, rising almost to the ceiling, each germane to common causes of death in Dade County: diving, guns, medicine, and cars.

Behind Davis's desk hung an Asian sword, a British-made anti-tank rifle, and a model of the Eastern Air Lines L-1011 jet that had plummeted into the Everglades on Dec 29, 1972. Davis had worked sixty straight hours with little rest on that case, "scrambling in and out of the twisted wreckage" noting the precise positions of the dead. Despite rupturing a disc in his spine, he had still attended a meeting of county officials, which he eventually left in an ambulance. Buchanan had witnessed it all.

Now Buchanan waited with two officers from the PSD's Internal Review while Davis and Wright began their methodical work behind closed doors. McDuffie's helmet sat close to his body. It had arrived hours after its owner, carried in by two PSD patrolmen. Had Buchanan witnessed the helmet arriving separately, it would have deepened her suspicions.

As soon as the autopsy was over, Wright and Davis presented their findings to Buchanan and the officers. The examination confirmed that a devastating blow had shattered McDuffie's skull. "The fatal fracture, directly between the eyes, was typical of the type of injury suffered when a motorcycle rider hurtles over the handlebars head first, smashing into a solid object, such as a pole or a bridge abutment."

Wright kept talking. The blow that had caused McDuffie's death had been extraordinary. "The skull was cracked almost cleanly in half, starting at the point of impact between the eyes and extending down through the base of the skull and ending at a point high on the occipital bone at the back of the head." The major horizontal fracture ended at the point where it met the vertical fracture. That meant that the blow to the front of the head had come first. There was only one way the medical examiner could see a blow of this force being delivered—from the speed gathered on a motorcycle.

Buchanan took notes. Wright continued: there were other blunt-impact injuries that could not be explained by a crash. He hastened to add that it was common for mortally injured motorcyclists to react aggressively in their confusion, and that it made sense that the officers might have to physically restrain him.

Buchanan could sense Internal Review's relief. The examiner's findings were consistent with the police report, but Buchanan wasn't satisfied. She knew that medical examiners' natural inclination was to support the police. Daily they found themselves working alongside detectives with shared objectives. In this case, she didn't doubt Ronald Wright's integrity, only his conclusion. Besides, Wright, ever cautious, had written "pending further investigation" on the death certificate.

From Jackson Memorial, Buchanan drove north to where McDuffie's motorcycle had come to a stop. It was a sunny, windy day. Buchanan parked on a side street and walked the scene. She immediately realized that there was a problem with the conclusion from the medical examiner's office. There was nothing that a motorcycle, or McDuffie, could have hit. "No pole, no bridge abutment, not even a curb." Wright's conclusion may have brought ease to Internal Review, but Buchanan now had evidence to back up her source.

———

That afternoon, Buchanan drove to Arthur McDuffie's house at 1157 NW 111th Street. Heading toward grief was, for most crime reporters, the worst part of the job. Buchanan felt differently. For her it was a chance to console and to connect. Over the years, she felt she'd witnessed every variety of reaction. She'd had men and women faint on her, she'd been screamed at, and she'd had doors slammed on her. She always went back knowing that grief could conjure extremes, but it often ended in the same place—with the acknowledgment that the victim deserved to be remembered, and that Buchanan could help ensure a voice was heard one last time.

Christmas was far from Buchanan's mind as she drove along Biscayne past the odd pockets of winter cheer that seemed forced in the sun. There were lights, puppet-populated villages, trains, and Santas sitting on top of houses against bright blue skies. There were kindly folks, wandering their blocks handing out candy canes to strangers. There was the sound of organ music rising up over the palm trees.

At McDuffie's house, she was welcomed into a roomful of grieving relatives. Buchanan quickly learned that she wasn't the only person who'd visited the I-395 underpass. McDuffie's mother, Eula Mae, a Miami Beach housekeeper, had already combed the area with help from her family. They showed Buchanan a broken frame from McDuffie's eyeglasses, the chin strap to his helmet, and part of a police sharpshooter's badge. There were no accusations openly voiced, but Buchanan sensed bewilderment. She borrowed a photograph of a smiling McDuffie wearing his Marine Corps uniform, held his mother's hand, and "promised to find out what really happened to her son." Driving back to the *Herald*, Buchanan immediately regretted the gesture. If the medical examiner's office, perhaps the most trusted institution in Dade County, had already concluded in opposition to her source's story, then what exactly could she promise a grieving mother?

Even Buchanan had her doubts. In ten years, she'd covered plenty of heroes and crooked cops, but on both ends of the spectrum, those officers usually worked alone or in small numbers. The thing that made her uncertain about this story was the math. If McDuffie had been beaten into a coma, then at least a dozen officers would have had to be involved in covering up the accident. Sure, there was the concept of the "thin blue line"—the idea that the police always stood together, united, impervious to leaks—but as a detective had once told Buchanan, that was just a concept. While there was a strong sense of brotherhood, the police still sought to be understood as individuals. "If the worst is true," thought Buchanan, "how can they be hanging in so tight? Wouldn't they all be sweating by now?"

Buchanan returned to her desk at the *Herald*. She went over every name on the accident report. One by one, she telephoned each officer at work and left a message. By the end of the day, not a single phone call had been returned.

By nightfall, a frustrated Buchanan had one last person to try: Charlie Black, the chief of detectives. Wide as a linebacker and grim in bearing, Black was an old-school investigator. "Always on the move like a locomotive, IQ must have been about 165, but loyal as loyal could be if you were there for him." But many weren't, offended by his bluntness. If he didn't think a detective was competent, he didn't just move him from homicide to another department, he suggested a new line of work. Buchanan knew Black's reputation and liked him for it.

"What do you have to say about Arthur McDuffie?" she began. There was a silence on the line. Charlie Black had never heard the name before. He asked if he could make a quick call of his own.

Within minutes, Buchanan's phone rang. It was Black and Marshall Frank, his captain of homicide, now six months into his job. Frank was already familiar with Buchanan, the daily visitor to the PSD. Dealing with her, he'd later write, was "like being plugged into an electrical socket." He'd seen her at crime scenes again and again and never met a reporter "who could ask more questions in less time."

Neither Black nor Frank had ever heard of McDuffie; and briefly, the roles were reversed. For the next ten minutes, two ranking detectives of Dade County asked the reporter to share her knowledge. Buchanan was stunned. "How come Homicide doesn't know about this?" A man died because of wounds sustained in front of their police officers. It should have been a homicide priority, and yet it hadn't even been brought to Marshall Frank's attention?

Black immediately made an unprecedented decision. He would put Marshall Frank on the McDuffie case; for the first time in county history, the Captain of Homicide would be the lead investigator. Black knew Buchanan too well to ask her to hold the story, but he also knew that appointing Frank would send a message. It was an admission that something was awry, the accusation was being taken seriously, and the truth was close at hand.

Buchanan hung up the phone. She appreciated Charlie Black's commitment to justice, but she couldn't concern herself with the speed or results of Frank's investigation. For the moment, she had information, but nothing in her own newspaper. As Buchanan got ready for bed, the rest of the city was still preparing for Christmas. Schoolchildren across the county had been asked to write letters of support to the hostages in Tehran. Kmart was reporting a sudden strong burst of last-minute sales despite the febrile inflation. At Kennedy Park, a snow machine sponsored by Burger King chugged to life, and the Miami moonlight was cut by white flurries as barefoot kids relished the novelty of frozen toes.

On Sunday, December 23, the *Herald* threw its annual Christmas party. By the time Buchanan got to a quiet newsroom, the celebrations had started elsewhere. Her fellow reporters would often head four blocks north to the 1800 Club, a "diminutive cave of a bar" tended by women in tight white tops and gold lamé pants. Buchanan, who wasn't social, preferred her desk.

As she wrote, skimpy crowds gathered a mile south to watch decorated boats splutter around Biscayne Bay in a Marine Parade. There were pirate girls in bikinis, hulls covered in flashing reindeer lights, and the occasional pop of a firework. Drunk buccaneers fell off their boats while firing fake cannons, and the head of a marching band sashayed along an almost empty Biscayne Boulevard.

By nightfall, the *Herald* emptied out. The more experienced employees leveraged their weight and took off for the holidays, which meant that Buchanan was left to deal with her biggest peeve: an inexperienced editor. Usually, she waited until a deadline to hand over copy to her editors "so that they don't have too much time to fiddle with it."

As soon as she handed in the draft, most of her article was questioned. The chin strap, the busted motorcycle, this analysis could be attributed to whom, exactly? Buchanan had seen them herself. What was the problem? She put Ronald Wright on the phone. He didn't have to come to the same conclusions, just confirm the details. Finally, the article was approved, barely scraping through for the Christmas Eve morning edition. Buchanan had her front page, but she seethed at the article. The editor had insisted she lead with the Internal Review's explanation of McDuffie's death. It was dulling a story that should have been sharp enough to cut through a reader's morning fog.

Outside the *Herald* building, the moon was peeking out, and a nearby candlelit vigil for the Iranian hostages was forming. The organizers had expected five thousand people, but only fifty had shown up, and the wind had risen and extinguished their candles. Only a rabbi drove up for the interfaith prayer service, and he turned around when he saw the depleted numbers.

The two policemen in the *Herald* parking lot weren't there to control the small crowd. They were there because they'd received telephone messages from Buchanan. Neither had responded. Now they were waiting to intercept an early copy of the newspaper from a delivery truck. They looked at it, studied the article closely, concluded that they were still safe, and went back to their homes to celebrate the holidays. The watered-down story hit the front lawns of Dade County that morning: "Cops' Role in Death Probed."

Buchanan's credo was simple: if in doubt, put it in the paper. She wasn't interested in sensationalism, but often the most sensational stories created the greatest change. Over the years, she'd inspired people to spontaneously raise money for an elderly rape victim. She'd received calls that led to the discovery of a missing child, and she'd fielded countless tips to help find suspects. Never had anything moved as quickly as this.

CHAPTER 4

The first violinist of the Broward Symphony Orchestra wore his pager on his belt and prayed that it wouldn't go off during the holiday concert. Capt. Marshall Frank, now the lead investigator on the McDuffie case, was already overworked. Home life was a present peace after a whirlwind of disorder. Divorced three times, father to four children, adopted father to three stepchildren, Frank was currently living at home with just one daughter. There was also a girlfriend to consider, a lawyer in the Felony Division. After the concert, Frank carefully closed the case on his instrument and drove home in his county-owned four-door Plymouth, painted a drab white with a radio antenna poking from the roof.

Frank had been promoted to captain of the PSD homicide unit the previous April. Shortly after dealing with the body in the trunk of the black Audi, he had been welcomed into his role with a call from the FBI's Miami office. The conversation was brief but clear: Frank had inherited a homicide bureau riddled with corruption. The FBI was weighing indictments. If that wasn't disturbing enough, the county murder rate was up 38 percent in 1979. If you'd asked Marshall Frank about priorities for 1980 over his 1979 Thanksgiving turkey, the answer would have been more detectives, clean detectives, people he could trust.

Florida's governor, Bob Graham, was aware of the McDuffie case. He was, after all, a Miami native, a practical, detail-driven man who preferred to fold his own laundry despite a retinue of staff in the governor's mansion. There had already been coverage in the *New York Times*. But it was still seen as a Miami problem, created by Dade, to be resolved in Dade and not, or at least not yet, of enough consequence to trouble a governor. The pressure would fall squarely on the county's PSD homicide bureau.

Frank sped down the six-lane freeway that cut through the middle of the city. Miami was concrete poured over swamp, a sprawling metropolis dependent on air-conditioning and the gods of the hurricane season. And while the nation as a whole was struggling to get construction projects off the ground because lending rates were still ballooning, that hadn't affected Miami. The proof lay along the coastal route, where a line of tall buildings now blocked off the ocean view.

This city was, in theory, directly connected to the rest of America. The highway Frank took that night from Broward to South Miami ran twenty feet above Overtown. If he'd headed north, he could have driven in a straight line all the way to his hometown of New York. Historically, Miami's troubles had come from the tristate area, home of organized crime and thousands looking for a cheap box in the sun.

Marshall Frank had arrived in Miami in 1947, before the first Cuban influx. Born to vaudeville parents, he was raised by his mother and his stepfather, a Jewish gangster with hands "soft as a baby's ass." When Frank was three, his older brother drowned in Flushing Bay. His mother's red hair turned white overnight. Between the family tragedy and Governor Dewey's push against organized crime, the family relocated to Florida, a state still considered "wide-open," as there seemed to be limitless possibilities for corruption.

Frank grew up in Miami watching his stepfather beaten by associates. When his stepfather drank, he would turn on Frank's mother and drag her across the apartment by her hair. By the time Frank graduated high school, his mother had been widowed and had remarried. His stepfather was a kinder lawbreaker, a bookie who ran a loan shark operation on the upper Beach. When his stepson wanted to enter the police force, all his stepfather had to do was make a call to smooth Frank's way. Marshall Frank's background interview with Internal Affairs lasted less than a minute. It involved a handshake and a wink, and there was Frank, a handsome, square-jawed young patrolman with a preference for aviator shades, a voice for radio, a shining badge, and a home life that was never mentioned.

Frank resisted the various temptations. Once, as a rookie, his sergeant had driven him down a street in upmarket Coral Gables and pointed to a house. The family's away, he said. It's full of furs, cash, coins. We could empty the place in twenty minutes. You in? No, Marshall Frank was not in. He'd spent his early life watching the intersection of crime and law enforcement, his stepfather's card games with cops and mobsters. He was definitely not in.

Frank joined homicide in 1968, and he worked his first murder case a full month later, a reflection of the sluggish pace of Miami life in the 1960s. His last murder case came in 1973, after which Frank passed his captain's exam and went on to head up the Crime Scene Section. Like every other captain across the PSD, he was now an administrator who wielded power. It left with him regrets, with a yearning to work cases again, and from time to time he wished he'd never taken the captain's exam. Now, unexpectedly, Marshall Frank had one more case to investigate.

The McDuffie investigation was, in many ways, no longer representative of modern Miami's homicides. That's not to say that confrontations between black residents and white officers had disappeared. The county police force, tilted heavily toward white officers recruited in the South, still wasn't a reflection of the people it represented. McDuffie was unrepresentative because there were suddenly entire *new* categories in homicide that hadn't earned any attention even a year before. If Marshall Frank had to have chosen a murder indicative of Miami at the very end of 1979, it would have been the body in the trunk of the Audi. The death of black males in police custody had a history in the American South. The body in the Audi was something entirely new; a murder of a Colombian, by Colombians, over a business dispute that originated in Colombia. Miami seemed to have provided only the location.

The challenge of imported murders had been increasingly obvious twelve weeks after Frank's promotion to captain of the homicide bureau.

In the middle of an afternoon in July 1979, three gunmen had walked into the upscale Dadeland Mall, murdered two Colombians in a liquor store with machine guns, shot and hit both store clerks, and then sprayed the entire parking lot with gunfire as they exited. There had been too many bullet holes in the dead men for the medical examiner to count, though as one Colombian had fallen, he'd managed to keep his bottle of Chivas intact.

The three gunmen had escaped, but what terrified Miami was what they chose to leave behind: a brand-new van with 108 miles on the odometer. Edna Buchanan dubbed it the "war wagon." Detective Al Singleton of Frank's homicide bureau had opened up the doors to show her the reinforced steel plates, the gun ports, the bulletproof vests, the black one-way glass, and the multitude of automatic weapons. Before going home that night, Singleton had bought himself a fourteen-shot Browning Hi-Power automatic and retired his six-shot Smith & Wesson. There was some small solace at the Dadeland scene. One of the murdered men's fingerprints matched prints taken from the steering wheel of the Audi used in the April shootout. Frank finally had his central suspect, albeit dead.

When he considered the growing list of unsolved murders of young Colombian men and women, Frank felt almost relieved to lead the McDuffie investigation. Of course, it would have been better if the incident had happened inside, where a scene might have been preserved days later, or if the area had been roped off for examination. But Frank was grateful for what remained. There was paperwork to pore over, a motorcycle to find and examine, and a detailed medical examiner's report, as well as potential witnesses. The only snag was that all the suspects and all the witnesses were his fellow officers. When cases began life as public knowledge with a political edge, the trouble flowed downhill to where Frank had now been placed.

When Frank asked detectives Al Singleton and Frank Wesolowski to join him in his office on Christmas Eve, Singleton's first thought was, *Oh, shit.* Homicide's offices were in the PSD building on Fourteenth Street. You got off the elevator on the second floor, walked down a hallway to the center of the building, took a left at a coffee shop called Finger

Charlie's. The detectives all worked at open-plan desks, but the major, shift commander, and Captain Frank all had their own offices. By the time Singleton and Wesolowski stepped in to meet with Frank, almost everyone in the building had read the article about McDuffie in that morning's *Herald*. Neither Singleton nor Wesolowski was eager to investigate their own, something Singleton considered "the least tasteful thing you can do as a police officer."

A wiry, no-nonsense New Yorker, Wesolowski, known simply as Ski, wore his top button open and his tie always loose. He specialized in working scenes and interrogating suspects. There were drinkers in the bureau, there were fishermen, but if you wanted to find Ski after work, you headed to the baseball and softball fields in South Miami. There, in the Florida sun, Ski still wore his Yankee pinstripes. Slight and extremely fit, he'd once coasted by Marshall Frank in a footrace at a barbeque while running backward. When Frank kept trying to get him to smoke on the way to a scene, Ski had taken his captain's pack of Benson & Hedges and tossed it out the window.

Wesolowski taught interrogation. New members of the squad were surprised by his choice of role model: Edna Buchanan. He described her as a digger. He found her frustrating to have at a scene, impossible to have in the office, but "God, she could keep them talking." "Keep them talking," he told his charges, "and you get your information." Buchanan had his respect, right down to the "Edna door" that would soon go up to prevent her casual strolls through the PSD's homicide bureau.

Wesolowski, like Marshall Frank, had finished his service in the marines before the escalation of Vietnam. Al Singleton, several years younger, had been a corporal in the marines, stationed in Da Nang and then Hue. A man so thin that he was known as Blade of Grass, or just Blade, he'd commanded a small unit through the jungles. One afternoon, while sitting next to the radioman and calling in coordinates for an ambush, he had an epiphany: *This is me at twenty years old*, he thought. *What am I going to do when I return home? If I return home, I'm not going to bag groceries.* The aim, he told himself, was to find a job with consequence.

He returned to his hometown of Cincinnati in 1973 with a plan. His father was a policeman. He would be a policeman, too. The only issue was that they didn't want him, striking him from the list for his less than perfect eyesight. Miami, on the other hand, was hiring. The physical wasn't as demanding, and so Singleton, with his trimmed mustache, became Ohio's loss and Florida's gain.

In his first year, Singleton made exactly $10,000. He rented a one-bedroom apartment and slept on the floor until he saved enough for a bed. In the summer of 1978, he was inducted into homicide, the holy grail of police work. Detectives had improvised their own uniform: a three-piece suit adorned with chains and fobs, and brand-new pagers attached to their belt. Almost all of them smoked cigars, considered a good way to mask the smell of decomposing bodies. Even inside Doc Davis's morgue, detectives would smoke in the corner as Davis took out his saws and went to work.

Homicide bureaus eased their rookies in with simple cases. Singleton's first murder wrapped before he even reached the station. A white teenage male confessed in the back of his car. He'd shot his twenty-four-year-old black victim through the head. The teenager sighed and added, "I'm tired of the black man fucking up the white man's world." The nonchalance of the phrase struck Singleton deeply. When he gave evidence in court, he waited to watch the judge react to those words. "He laid the hammer on him," said Singleton, and carried his first case to conviction.

———

Frank, Singleton, and Wesolowski put their holiday plans on hold and began to analyze the evidence in the McDuffie case. The tiny group was filled with mutual respect. Frank had once seen Wesolowski solve a murder in five minutes. Wesolowski had noticed a bloody footprint next to a body in a bathtub. It had four toes. Within minutes, Wesolowski had their suspect, a man who calmly opened a door in a condo unit a floor down, barefoot with a bandage on his little toe.

This would be different. Wesolowski had always followed cases with the idea that if he wasn't certain himself, he'd rather leave you on the street than waste the state's time. Looking at the McDuffie evidence, he imagined the temptations the officers felt after a long chase. You see a man resisting, maybe you get a kick in, maybe you got "to prove you're one of the boys." Wesolowski looked over the names of the officers, and Watts's name jumped out at him as quickly as it had at Buchanan.

The three detectives listened to the police tapes, and traced back the first inconsistency to a sergeant. "How did he get a fractured skull?" said an unknown voice on the recording. "Falling off the motor," said the sergeant. At 4:58 a.m. on December 17, the department put in a routine request to examine the accident scene. But when the investigators arrived, the scene had already been destroyed.

"Why'd they tidy the stuff so quick?" one officer asked another a little later over the radio.

"I have no idea."

Later, the same sergeant was recorded again. "He was hit with Kel-Lites," he said, referring to the metal flashlights encasing heavy batteries that officers often deployed like truncheons.

"Kel-Lites?" said a voice. "Oh, shit."

The detectives took note: this might contradict the sergeant's original statement, that McDuffie had broken his skull falling off the motorcycle. Then there was the Use of Force report that the first officer on the scene had submitted, signed by his sergeant. McDuffie had fallen from the bike while turning at high speed. His bike had skidded, his helmet had fallen off, and he'd hit his head. He'd then leapt to his feet and started to struggle with five county officers. The report stated that McDuffie had kicked an officer on the right leg and wounded another, until the next two officers to arrive had struck McDuffie between six and ten times because he had kicked at their knees. The report concluded that the officers used "only force necessary to subdue the subject."

Captain Frank interviewed the commander of the county's Central District. The commander confessed that he'd been "immediately suspicious" on the morning of the seventeenth. So why hadn't he, in the one week that had now passed, released the Use of Force report to Internal Review? Frank told the commander that officers from the city police department had already been talking. If the commander was trying to keep the case fenced within the county's PSD, then he hadn't accounted for the fact that he had no control over the city's police. The story would emerge, regardless.

Finally, there was the accident report from the PSD Internal Review. This was painful reading for Frank. The interviews had been conducted by Linda Saunders, a beautiful young detective in Internal Affairs. The only black investigator, she was regarded as a good prospect, but at the turn of 1980, she'd "never worked a major case in her life." Frank took one look at the transcripts and saw that Saunders had conducted only brief interviews with the officers concerned. Worse still, it was clear that the officers had railroaded her. She hadn't probed but "had let the officers say what they wanted."

Frank sat down with Saunders. When he asked her about the motorbike, she didn't know where it was. To Frank, who had learned how to read a scene under Doc Davis's tutelage, everything began with evidence. Frank was livid, but he didn't know where to direct his rage. Saunders's investigation should have never even begun. Any incident in which a suspect had received life-threatening injuries during an arrest should have landed immediately on Frank's own desk at homicide. Why hadn't the commander at Central or the chief of Internal Review handed the damned thing over?

After Frank dismissed Saunders, she stopped by Sergeant Lonnie Lawrence's office. The streets Lawrence helped safeguard were 17 percent black, but the PSD was 7 percent black, with no blacks represented "in the higher orders." The previous summer, three black officers—including Lawrence—had passed the sergeant's exam, but not one had received a promotion. In response Lawrence had helped found the Progressive Officer's Club and filed suit against the county. The extraordinary thing? The county listened. The county manager went on to fire the director of the PSD, Bud Purdy—a law and order man, a traditional sheriff who was well thought of by his own department, but a man who was highly resistant to change. Thanks to that suit, Lawrence received a sergeant's badge and a promotion. He was now the public information officer, the filter through which the police reached the media and the media reached the police.

"You know the incident that occurred the other night involving a motorcyclist?" asked Saunders.

Lawrence had missed the morning paper but knew the outlines of the case. Traffic violation. Motorcyclist flees. High-speed accident. Deep coma at Jackson Memorial. Pulled the plug days later.

"Yeah," said Lawrence.

"It's been determined that it wasn't an accident. That it was deliberate."

Lawrence looked up. "Okay," he said, and the "-kay" he left floating in the air like a contrail.

"We need to put something out."

Lawrence reached for his pen. "Who's the victim?"

"His name is McDuffie," Saunders said.

Lawrence paused, unsettled. "What's his first name?"

"Arthur McDuffie."

Lawrence didn't speak. He seemed to freeze in his chair, unreactive. Finally, he stood up and walked around the office. He took a breath and asked, "Tell me a little more about this Arthur McDuffie person . . . the victim." An insurance salesman. A father of three. An ex-marine. Lawrence nodded. No. It couldn't be. There must be more than one Duff. Lawrence asked, "What's his wife's name?"

"Frederica McDuffie," Saunders said.

Arthur McDuffie had been a high school classmate of Lawrence's at Booker T. Washington. They'd joined the marines the same year and even ended up stationed on the same aircraft carrier, the USS *Independence*. McDuffie and Lawrence had both been in the military police, and both had received honorable discharges before returning to Miami. Lawrence had headed straight to the police academy, while McDuffie—who'd briefly considered law enforcement—tried different jobs before settling as a salesman at Coastal Insurance. He'd married a friend of Lawrence's, Frederica Jones, and traveled around Florida, Georgia, and South Carolina selling policies. Lawrence knew that in the world of homicide, there were bodies and there were *victims*, the division between those who lived among criminals and innocents drawn from the majority of regular citizens. Arthur McDuffie, Lawrence knew, belonged to the latter category.

Lawrence heard the name again. *McDuffie*. A sense of shock overtook him, and then for the first time he could remember, Lawrence felt hatred. He listened as Saunders continued to talk. He knew the officers involved. But what now? He couldn't speak to them. These were his fellow officers. He didn't even want to leave his office. What, he thought, if I'm walking down the hallway and I bump into them? Someone's going to have to stop me. Otherwise, I'm going to pull my gun. I'm going to blow their damned brains out.

CHAPTER 5

After calling Barbon Towing to locate the motorbike, detective Al Singleton rang medical examiner Ronald Wright. Although Internal Review had yet to see the vehicle, Wright had examined it two days earlier. On the morning of December 22, after Wright delivered his conclusions to Buchanan and Internal Review, he'd decided to challenge his own analysis. He packed his brown, skull-shaped pipe with aromatic tobacco and drove over to Barbon Towing to locate the motorcycle. It took him only moments to see that at least some of the damage had been faked. Scratches on the left side of the tank should have been parallel to each other, but they weren't. There were inexplicable scratches on the other side as well. When bikes crash, they slide, scraping only one side of the gas tank, one peg stand, never both.

Now, on December 24, Wright told Singleton what he'd told Doc Davis earlier. The bike, he insisted, may have crashed, but it had also been "worked over either out of rage or an attempt to make it look like an accident . . . it's rotten, it smells, it's terrible."

After hanging up the phone, Wright and Davis took another look at their autopsy report on McDuffie. Meanwhile, Captain Frank sent a professional crash investigator to examine the bike. He concluded that Wright was only partially right. *All* the damage was faked; there had never been any collision at all.

Less than a day into his investigation, Frank was fairly "certain that McDuffie was murdered." That evening, Frank called four officers who had been involved in the McDuffie chase and told them that they were being relieved of duty. They would continue to receive their salaries pending the filing of criminal charges.

The next day, Singleton dug up the worksheets from December 17 that Internal Review still had. He studied the lists that each patrolman kept of every call he'd received while on duty and how much time he'd spent on each. No matter how an officer divided his or her shift, each of the worksheets should have added up to eight hours. Singleton found that several of the officers had edited themselves out of the accident report entirely. "Instead of taking the time to write out a new worksheet, they just Wited-Out that they were there." Some of the worksheets didn't even add up to eight hours anymore.

An awkward moment awaited. Singleton drove north to Central and served a superior who had once earmarked him for the homicide department with a warrant to search the police locker room. Singleton held the paper in his hand, embarrassed.

"Son," said the man, "do what you've got to do."

Singleton and Wesolowski went through the lockers of the suspected officers one by one, looking for Kel-Lites, nightsticks, evidence to use to gain leverage in the coming interviews. There were plenty of inconsistencies for the investigators to concentrate on. The police report stated that McDuffie had fallen at high speed and been separated from the Kawasaki. If he had been separated from the vehicle, then why was a pool of blood found right next to his motorbike? Where was his road rash? If his helmet had fallen off during the crash, why had the strap been neatly cut? And why did the helmet have dents in several places, yet the skull fracture indicated only one enormous blow? How could an accident account for the patterns of damage on the bike?

Then, on the same day, another painful moment for Singleton. He had to approach the McDuffie family's lawyer in the middle of her news conference. He had a subpoena for the clothes McDuffie had been wearing the night he'd been admitted to the hospital. Those blue shirts, cut away by ER doctors and once wet with blood, had hardened into a rust-colored ball.

It didn't look good grabbing the evidence in front of the press; it looked suspiciously like a cover-up of a cover-up. But Frank's team couldn't concern itself with bad PR. This was about closing the gap in time between when Frank should have been alerted to McDuffie's plight on December 17 and presenting the state attorney's office with a solid case as soon as possible.

They worked most of Christmas Day, putting up floodlights and flares under the expressway ramp as they removed parts of North Miami Avenue with a screeching saw, the bloodstained concrete gently placed in white boxes and entered into evidence.

———

On December 26, while everyone else was still digesting Christmas turkey, Marshall Frank sat down with Edna Buchanan. Over the years, Frank had seen the reporter frequently clicking around crime scenes in her heels, a regular, not always welcome, visitor to the PSD building. He'd fielded her calls and formed a friendly enough rapport, but he wasn't among those who were a more or less direct line for Buchanan. Before, the police had been incidental to the crime stories that Buchanan wrote, fellow observers of death. Now, they were the suspected criminals *and* the investigators.

"It's like a jigsaw puzzle," Frank told her, "one of the most intensive investigations I have ever been party to." The same was true for Buchanan. As a crime reporter, she usually wrote a single article on a murder, perhaps a follow-up if the case was noteworthy. McDuffie's beating seemed to be lending itself to multiple stories. It was about the police and the county, about race and conspiracy. Buchanan and the *Herald* were only getting started. And yet, while her first article on McDuffie may have been the catalyst for the entire investigation, there was an unpleasant side effect. Forewarned by the *Herald*, it seemed as if every patrolman near the scene of McDuffie's beating had already found a lawyer. Would even one officer turn against his own colleagues, and, if not, how could you prosecute a case without a single witness?

At the *Herald*, Mike Baxter, an assistant city editor, started pulling additional reporters to cover McDuffie. The paper had its own investigative teams—such as the one that had spent months working on the police brutality story the previous summer—but this would be a more ad hoc group, plucked from the city desk.

While the detectives were used to working in teams, reporters were different. In detective work, a three-man team would accompany every lead investigator: together they'd find evidence, walk the scene, canvass neighborhoods, interrogate suspects, and consult with the medical examiner. Every man or woman on the team would get to lead; it was just a matter of rotation. Once weaned on an easy case, even rookies were thrown into the rotation.

The *Herald* was more territorial. Buchanan had found the story alone. She'd investigated alone. She preferred it that way. When other reporters ventured onto her beat, she kicked them off. Besides, hers was the only byline on the original story, which had been syndicated and was now spreading across the United States.

Buchanan was notoriously independent, a trait she attributed to nurture rather than nature. She was born Edna Rydzik to a mother who had gotten pregnant at sixteen. Her father, a gambler, raised her on New York tabloids, which he bought for the race results. She devoured the crime section and fixated on bank robbers and mad bombers. When Buchanan was seven, her father abandoned the family. At age twelve, she started working summers in Paterson, New Jersey, alternating between a job at a candle factory and one plucking threads off finished coats. She wore hand-me-downs to school, was picked on, and despised class. Dropping out of high school in tenth grade, she found employment at the sock counter at a local Woolworth's and then at the wire switchboards at Westinghouse. At home, her relationship with her unstable mother was always uneasy. It was an exhausting life, and when her mother took her to South Florida for a brief holiday in 1961, the two looked at each other and finally agreed on something. They would never leave Miami.

The *Miami Beach Daily Sun* hired her—no experience necessary—

and she reluctantly covered the *Social Register*. It was the sort of tabloid where a rigorous work ethic was a necessity, especially during an eight-month period when she was their only reporter on staff. Any given day she might have half a dozen stories in the paper, as well as the greyhound picks and an anonymous letter to the editor.

———

In 1963, Edna Rydzik married journalist James Buchanan in Miami Beach. One day, while she was out doing errands, she popped the trunk of the family car for a bag-laden grocery clerk and then suddenly slammed it shut. It contained a dozen machine guns. She quickly found out that her husband, like many in Miami, was secretly employed by the CIA in their largest office outside of Langley. The guns were intended for anti-Castro forces in Cuba. Buchanan kept her mouth shut and found other stories to chase.

One rare day when her fellow journalists actually made it into the newsroom, an editor ordered a senior reporter to take a picture of a bloated corpse that had been discovered on the shore. The reporter wrinkled her nose and refused. Buchanan's voice came from the other end of the newsroom. "I'll do it, I'll do it." Death wasn't the end; it was the beginning. She'd made it out of the Northeast factories, out of Paterson, New Jersey; and as soon as she had the required five years of experience, she applied to the *Miami Herald* for a position, a leap from a circulation of ten thousand to five hundred thousand.

During her first interview, the city editor at the *Herald* told her they liked writers who had mastered the art of brevity. She followed up with a one-word letter: "Obits?" And the job was hers.

Within a year, she went from writing about houseboat bans and garbage strikes to the court beat. In no time, her sources expanded to include judges, bondsmen, and lawyers, the guilty and the innocent. Mostly she loved the drama of court, which made her an obvious choice when the *Herald* elected to restart their police beat.

Initially, she felt being a woman in the newsroom was a weight. Male editors would carp about running henhouses if women erred. The atmosphere changed after she formed a bond with Gene Miller, the dean of the *Miami Herald* newsroom. Miller was a flirt, a drinker, an adventurer, and a gentleman who bled ink. He had benefited from his friendship with Janet Reno's father. Whenever Henry Reno found himself unable to write about compromised police officers, he'd slide the story to Miller. Most important, Miller was the only person at the *Herald* with two Pulitzer Prizes. He had the leeway to pick whatever cases he wanted.

When Buchanan was still married, she had spent time with her husband's best friend, a man called Frank Sturgis, who'd once fought beside Castro but then switched sides and ran guns to Castro's enemies in Cuba. Sturgis wasn't a household name until 1972, when he was detained at the Watergate Hotel and put under indefinite house arrest. This was the beginning of the Watergate beat, which the *Washington Post* dominated. Even though the saga was filled with Miami angles, the *Herald* kept missing the scoops. Finally, the paper got its chance in early 1973, when Sturgis obtained permission to leave his house to attend his mother's funeral in Miami.

The morning before Sturgis's visit, Buchanan received a call from her then ex-husband. Sturgis was willing to talk to her when he was in Miami. No limits on questions. Would she sit down with him? No, she said. But she offered the interview to Gene Miller. The "skinny, bespectacled reporter with the penchant for bow ties" nodded and thanked the small blond court reporter with the big blue eyes. Then he ignored her tip completely.

When the *Washington Post* ran an article on Sturgis's Miami visit, the entire newsroom was berated for missing a Watergate story taking place right under their feet. Buchanan stared at Miller until their eyes met. He looked away but it was the birth of a friendship.

Miller was known as the man who recruited reporters, trained them, honed them, and unleashed them. A friendship with Miller was no small thing. He was also famous for the "Miller chop." Begin an article with two or three long sentences. Then change course with two words. Buchanan arrived at the *Herald* writing in a similar vein. One young editor came by waving her work, nodded, and said, "Ahh, the pyramid style." Buchanan hadn't been to journalism school or college; she hadn't even graduated from high school. She had no idea what the pyramid style was, nor the Miller chop. All she knew was that readers wouldn't follow the jump to the inner pages of a newspaper unless the lead was riveting. In a roomful of editors whom she often regarded as overeducated pedants, "Gene likes it" was Buchanan's pass to push her stories into print.

By the time she broke the story of Arthur McDuffie, Buchanan was possibly the paper's premier workaholic. She'd had five stories published in the *Herald* on a single day and fantasized about the masthead reading, "*The Miami Herald* by Edna Buchanan." A couple of her fellow reporters had pulled her aside and advised her to write just one story a day because she was making them look bad, but not Miller. He encouraged Buchanan to fill her notebooks with stories. She did, one of the few who used every corner of the pad, then worked her way back to the front on the reverse pages.

Everyone knew Buchanan was a workhorse, but because McDuffie was such a big story, one editor decided that there was enough material to keep at least four of his top journalists busy. He knew Buchanan's number by heart, and thought that the best part of the morning was when she arrived, clutching the strangest stories of the night. This time, he herded five city reporters into the *Herald*'s main conference room and began to break the story into pieces.

"Who wants the family?"

Buchanan raised her hand.

"Who wants the investigation?"

Buchanan raised her hand.

"Who wants state attorney?"

Buchanan.

"The hospital?" Buchanan. "Michael Watts?" Buchanan.

Buchanan left the meeting with the majority of the work. To other reporters, it seemed overly territorial. But at the same time, no one doubted

that she had the sources to take it on. She knew the tollbooth operators who kept up with her stories; she knew hospital administrators, the
mayor, the undertakers. She'd even leave handfuls of nickels and dimes to
get alerts from the retirees and the homeless who spent their days attending court cases. Buchanan had the city covered.

First, Buchanan dug into the police officers' past. She'd joked before
that the biggest red flag was an Officer of the Month award, and it proved
true. One of the officers present at McDuffie's arrest had won for arresting the rapist of a ninety-year-old woman. Another had saved the life
of a girl who had overdosed. Watts, she knew, had arrested a serial killer.
Yet these same cops had one more thing in common—an unusually high
number of complaints from the citizens of Central. Five cops, forty-seven
complaints. Watts had received a grade of 1.5 out of 10 for attitude in a
recent departmental evaluation.

For the police who had participated in, or witnessed, the McDuffie incident, the choice was stark. They could stay lawyered up, await charges,
and fight the machinery of the State of Florida that was rolling their
way; or they could try to cooperate with the investigation and turn state's
evidence. Forever, they would be seen as having ratted on their fellow officers, but at least they'd be spared the probable humiliation of serving a
lengthy prison sentence as an ex-cop.

The first to step forward and break the thin blue line was the first
believed to have laid his hands on McDuffie: twenty-four-year-old
Charles Veverka, the son of a high-ranking officer. When he walked into
Marshall Frank's office and agreed to talk, the relief on both sides was
palpable. He carried with him his first police report. It was the original, he said, written on the scene, before he had been told to begin the
rewrites. Veverka would escape jail, and Frank would have his evidence
corroborated, even if he wasn't entirely convinced by Veverka's version
of events. Why, Frank asked himself, would McDuffie pull over, put his
kickstand down, and *then* throw a punch at an armed officer as other cars
arrived, as Veverka said he had?

You could almost feel the entire PSD building wince when Buchanan and the rest of the team ran their article on December 30. It was headlined, "Is the Real Horror Story Still to Come?" For every careful step forward that Marshall Frank's team took with the state attorney's office, Buchanan's coverage increased the public interest. It was grist for citizens, and an increase in wattage for the lights shining on the investigation. There was bad news awaiting the accused officers. For the first time in Florida's history, the press would be allowed to attend the depositions. There would be an estimated ninety-five witnesses called concerning the suspected beating and the cover-up. That was enough to keep the *Herald*'s coverage flowing for weeks to come.

It was often said that Miami had no physical center, though many pointed to the location and importance of the *Miami Herald* on Bayshore Drive. Oddly, the newspaper seemed to dictate policy more accurately than any local politician. How the *Herald* covered the McDuffie case would be vital as the city began to shape its own expectations for justice. It had been a dozen years since race riots had swept the nation, but the hope was that Marshall Frank's investigation would be airtight.

As the PSD's Lonnie Lawrence knew, McDuffie was a veteran, a father, a friend, an ordinary citizen. Until he had evaded the police on December 17, the former MP had spent more time *as* the law than breaking it. And when he had broken it, the offenses of bouncing a check and driving with a suspended license were utterly commonplace. A photograph that Edna Buchanan had borrowed from Eula Mae McDuffie, of her son smiling broadly in his marine uniform, demanded consideration. A Miamian had served his country, taken care of his children, worked hard, made a foolish error, and been given a death sentence.

CHAPTER 6

Like the rest of Miami, Mayor Maurice Ferré was "patently aware of every gruesome detail" of the *Herald*'s coverage of the McDuffie investigation. Mayor Ferré was handsome and engaging and had been, until recently, extremely wealthy. Born in Puerto Rico into a family that dominated the construction trade, his father had provided much of the rock and concrete for South Florida's postwar boom. The family's concrete, poured into the pillars of I-95 and Launch Pad 39A at Cape Canaveral, was part of the story of American progress. The Ferrés had also become one of the largest landowners in Miami during the 1960s—of property including 1,500 acres close to the airport, 8,500 acres in Dade, and Dupont Plaza, one of the cornerstones of the city. Ferré's father had believed firmly in the county but thought the city's leaders "were a bunch of rich farmers . . . who don't realize you have to spend money to have a beautiful city." Thanks to his son, now in his fourth term as Miami's mayor, many of the family's real estate holdings had been retained, in the belief that downtown would thrive in the 1970s and beyond.

The Ferrés were the first major "Latin anchor" family in Miami. Maurice Ferré graduated from Lawrenceville, a WASPy New Jersey boarding school, and was easily accepted into Miami's most exclusive clubs when their doors were still barred to blacks, Latins, and Jews. When he was in his twenties, the *Herald* had referred to him as "the young aristocrat," though his father thought he knew better. Maurice, he said, "would have been much happier poor than rich." Either way, the *Herald* concluded, the

Ferrés were the Kennedys of the Caribbean. Maurice had that Kennedy vibe, easy in front of the cameras, with a wide-open smile, the perfect part in his hair, and a flower in his lapel. Such a man, claimed the *Herald*, could aim as high as the presidency of the United States.

In 1963, Ferré became Miami's first Latin commissioner. In early 1968, he received a call from a Cuban friend who had been hired away by Dow Chemical to their headquarters in Michigan. The company had come to the conclusion that they would benefit from decentralization, and they were looking for a Latin American hub. The finalists were Miami, Mexico City, and San Juan, Puerto Rico. Miami, said Ferré's contact, was in third place, but in order to make a thorough analysis, Dow was sending evaluators to all three cities. Would Ferré meet with them?

It strengthened an idea that had occasionally been posited in Miami but never built on. Miami should face south to flourish. Since its birth, Miami had mainly looked north for prosperity. What, imagined Ferré, if you didn't constrain yourself by only looking at a map of the continental United States? On that map, Miami was always an outcast, a blister on the Floridian toe. But if you expanded your view, and looked at a broader map of North and South America and the Caribbean, then Miami suddenly became the center of spokes that stretched across a vast region.

Ferré put together a team composed entirely of Spanish-speaking businessmen, and when the group from Dow Chemical arrived at the Miami airport to change planes on their way home from Puerto Rico, Ferré greeted them holding a flight map. Every flight from San Juan to Michigan had to connect through Miami; Mexico City flights had to connect through Panama. Only Miami had direct flights, including one that ran regularly from Miami to Midland, Michigan, the home of Dow. Miami also had an American court system, and because of recent Cuban emigration, it had become a truly if not officially bilingual city.

Ferré invited the visitors from Dow to talk to the bilingual team he'd assembled at the airport, "bank presidents, professors, automobile dealers, engineers and lawyers." Ferré was proving a point: Miami had all the right people. More important, of the three cities, it had geography on its side, to say nothing of the climate. Michigan was under snow; Miami was lounging in shorts in winter sun. Dow would be the first industry giant to commit to Miami. Others followed. Combining a pro-business attitude and the socially liberal stance of a reformer, Ferré became Miami's first Latin mayor in 1973. The part-time job paid a pitiful $5,000 a year, but as one of the richest men in the state, Ferré let the city keep the inconsequential salary.

In 1978 he had helped convince native Miamian and governor Bob Graham and his legislature to welcome foreign banks to town under the Edge Act (1919). By 1980 Miami had more Edge Act banks than New York. The banks got the benefits of an American hub, but they also got to keep their capital close to the action in Latin America, deploying money south when they wished. While the nation was struggling under Carter and runaway inflation, Miami, due to Ferré, now had the infrastructure to welcome money coming in from Venezuela, Colombia, Mexico, and Argentina, helping the city become a rare bright spot on a darkening national map.

But while the city had moved slowly forward under Ferré during the 1970s, the family fortunes had not. Ferré's father had raised money for both the real estate purchases and a huge expansion of their concrete business. It made sense at a time when Florida was booming. Ferré Sr. had borrowed his first million from David Rockefeller and soared to create a family fortune estimated at $400 million. In the summer of 1976, the South Florida building industry hit a sudden slump, and the Ferré family businesses failed to meet their tax bills on six separate properties. A cement plant in Puerto Rico was shuttered. Bank loans were suddenly in default. The extended family fractured in a series of lawsuits. According to the *Miami Herald*, the debt totaled $200 million. The family company, the feted Maule Industries, filed for bankruptcy.

Ferré's father had pressed him to leave the mayor's job and concentrate on salvaging the business, but Ferré knew who he was. "Some men drink," he told the newspaper. "Some men chase women. Some men like to drive fast sports cars. As for me, I like politics." Even after Maule Industries was forced into a sale, despite dozens of sleepless nights, Ferré presented himself as an optimist. There were Saturdays at home for the first time in years. He was photographed out jogging with his teenage daughter and sons.

If there was a winner from Maule's collapse, it was the city of Miami, which now occupied all of Ferré's time as he began to collect his salary of $180.68 every other week. When the *Herald* challenged him over his net worth, the mayor first said that it was "zero." Then he thought a moment and added, "No, not zero. It's minus $25 million in guarantees." There was still a glass factory in Venezuela, and there were investments in Puerto Rico. There was also the best home in Brickell, La Santa Maria. With its thirteen bathrooms and a library packed with Ferré's books on Roman and English history, it wasn't an ordinary home. It was one of the last original mansions now surrounded by growing glass towers in Miami's burgeoning financial heart. It was also a place of enormous sentimental value to Ferré. He had met his neighbor and future wife, Mercedes, in the garden under a banyan tree when they were both still teenagers. An early marriage had been followed by six children before either of them turned thirty. But now that there was no longer an empire behind Mayor Ferré, at the start of 1980 he began to consider the inevitable: selling the family home.

The Herald, a frequent critic of many of the mayor's initiatives, seemed to go easier on Ferré after the family's financial losses. They called him "honest, sincere, ambitious and expedient enough to succeed in politics." But the mayor still believed that the *Herald* was too eager with "snap judgments." He'd tell reporters that newspapers were a necessary evil, absolutely essential to democracy. However, as 1980 broke, the *Herald* was back to regularly attacking Ferré's proposals. Florida's premier newspaper had always been in favor of killing off Miami's city government, handing the whole damn thing over to county. In the ideal world of the *Miami Herald*, Maurice Ferré's job didn't even exist.

The pattern of growth in most major American cities had been entirely unlike Miami's. Elsewhere, power had consolidated as cities grew, and disparate parts had gathered under city management. That is what had happened in both Chicago and New York around the turn of the twentieth century. Dominant interests—finance in New York, agriculture in Chicago—embedded themselves in the power structure from the earliest days.

Instead of consolidating, Miami gave up control of its seaport, airport, water and sewer systems, and area hospitals; they were all handed over to Dade County in 1956, with the idea of creating a regional government. The city was never strong enough to reclaim what it had ceded, and it was never weak enough for its government to die a natural death. It was as if two ideas had been put forward and neither one chosen. Greater Miami became a city served by both a large county and a smaller city government, leaving it in the hands of not one but two mayors, two commissions, and two police forces. It was why Arthur McDuffie, weaving back and forth across city and county lines on the early morning of the seventeenth of December, had been chased by men dressed in two different uniforms.

If New York and Chicago were middle-aged, sure of their position and unafraid to use their power to influence America, Miami was still a teenager, unsure of what it might become, uncertain of how others regarded it. The scaffolding of its governmental system seemed to be created to keep it that way. Neither the county nor the city mayor had veto power. In a crisis, the system wasn't designed for a fast, decisive response. If anything, it was designed so that one arm of local government could always blame the other. Mayor Ferré saw the problems clearly. He said that Miami had a Rube Goldberg school of government.

To maintain forward movement in the city-county equilibrium, Ferré was in frequent contact not with the county mayor but with the county manager, Merrett Stierheim, the real source of power in county government. Together, the two men gave Miami a fairly liberal bent. They were aware of weaknesses in the system, but they had different ideas of how to strengthen the city. It almost seemed as if there were a split between domestic and foreign policy. Stierheim concentrated on the nuts and bolts of Dade County: public transportation, management of public service departments, driving the county commission. Ferré was more of an influential secretary of state, seeing a wider picture, knowing that Miami could play a pivotal role in Latin America's connection to the United States.

Miami's division between county and city wasn't well understood in Washington, DC, or outside American borders. Ferré took full advantage of that. People presumed that he was mayor of a large metropolitan area rather than the tight city limits of Miami. The presumptions fit well when Ferré was on the offensive, luring businesses to the city and trying to position Miami as an international hub. But with the death of Arthur McDuffie presenting the city in an unflattering light, it was also obvious that Ferré needed to be the public face of Miami. Miamians might understand the McDuffie probe as a county problem, but across the nation and beyond, the case was simply Miami's issue.

Ferré didn't shy away. As ever, he was remarkably outspoken. In the wake of the McDuffie investigation, he was asked if there was racism in Miami. "I wouldn't want to be black in America. Would you?" No, Mr. Mayor, I mean, is *Miami* really that bad? "Oh, I don't have any question that Miami's a racist city. It always has been. And Florida is a racist state." And what did he think of the Anglos who ran Miami's greatest businesses? "The truth of the matter is that the establishment in this community does not believe in the democratic process."

Ferré knew Miami's real webs of power very well. They lay in the *Herald*, the banks, the centers of tourism, such as the airlines and cruise industry, and with the "Non-Group," a discreet cadre of powerful businessmen who tried to set the agenda for the city's problems, nudging politicians into order. The Non-Group's existence wouldn't be acknowledged for years to come. Their meetings took place at private residences. No one kept records or minutes. It would have been ripe ground for the *Herald*, but for critics who already felt the newspaper wielded too much power, any exposé would have bolstered that opinion. The Non-Group was headed by Alvah Chapman Jr., CEO of Knight Ridder, a Fortune 500 company based in Miami, that happened to own the *Miami Herald* as well as many newspapers across the United States. In theory, the Non-Group could decide on a way forward for Miami, the *Herald* could promote the path with an editorial, and the group's members could seed any initiative without ever involving local government.

The people of Miami had no knowledge of the collective power and influence of these individuals, but Mayor Ferré did. He was a founding member of the Non-Group. Though he had retired from the group when he became mayor, he could still pick up the phone and have a direct line to the dozen most powerful men in South Florida.

———

In the 1970s, Ferré had been the right man in the right moment, but now, as 1980 loomed, there were several reasons for him to adjust his stance. First, as the Puerto Rican proxy voice for the Spanish speakers of Miami, he could feel a new undercurrent. If the Cuban population continued to grow in influence, soon they would turn to a mayoral candidate who shared their heritage. Why should Cuban Americans rely on a Puerto Rican to act on their needs? The worry was that if the Cubans ran candidates and demanded that Cubans vote only for Cubans, then Ferré would have to swing wildly in a different direction, dependent on the black and Anglo vote.

Second, as a personal friend of President Jimmy Carter, Ferré was tethered to the incumbent. Their friendship had been seen as positive for Ferré in 1976, but which way would the wind blow in 1980 as Carter ran for reelection?

And now there was the McDuffie investigation, which was falling to Ferré even though the county police weren't his to corral. Buchanan's article was like an astronomer's sighting of an incoming meteorite. Everyone knew the case was hurtling toward Miami, that it could cause damage, but such forewarning brought the presumption of containment. Marshall Frank was busy ensuring the best possible investigation, and Ferré was trying to stay out of the blast zone while maintaining positive relationships with the black community.

Ferré believed that politicians had no control over their ocean of potential voters. They could face that ocean, predict the gathering swells, and ride them. That did not mean that Ferré had flexible beliefs. His ideas were deeply held. First among them was that Miami's geography was Miami's fate. This was his city's primary advantage. Second, immigration was an asset. Had Cuban emigration not provided Spanish speakers and the infrastructure they created, he couldn't have promoted Miami as the center of the Americas. Third, he believed in the creation of a taxable business base for Miami. Money, immigration, and riding the waves of Miami's delicate balance of races lay at the center of his vision.

There had been many issues for black voters through 1979, but now they all seemed to condense into this single investigation—what would happen to the accused officers? County, not city, cops were the first to arrive the night he had been stopped, but no one outside Miami would note the distinction. Black voters wanted a mayor who could oversee justice. They wanted the trial kept to Miami. They wanted their vote to carry weight. And if it didn't, then Ferré needed to worry not only about his city but also about his seat at the table. His healthy coalition could dissolve overnight.

CHAPTER 7

On and off for three straight weeks in early 1980, Capt. Marshall Frank took Detective Singleton to meetings at State Attorney Janet Reno's office as they started to build their case. Reno—a South Floridian through and through—had gone from a surprising appointee to a popular incumbent. Raised on the edge of the Everglades, the lanky, square-jawed Reno was reared by a father who had once held Edna Buchanan's job at the *Miami Herald* and a mother who worked at the rival *Miami News*. Reno had wanted to be a marine biologist, a baseball player, or a chemist, but she'd settled on the law. By the time she'd been appointed the first-ever woman to hold a state attorney's office in Florida in 1978, she had plenty of experience in both public and private practice.

And yet, as 1979 came to a close, a series of missteps led the only black-owned newspaper in the city, the *Miami Times*, to spit venom at Reno. Those policemen who had raided the wrong house and beaten a black schoolteacher hadn't been prosecuted yet. An innocent black man had been shot and killed by an officer for pulling over to urinate against a building, and Reno had waited four months to send that case before a grand jury. Was she really what she proclaimed to be, a Floridian concerned for *all* Floridians? Joe Oglesby, a black *Herald* reporter, once a fan of Reno when he'd covered the courts, now called her a "dawdling . . . disappointment."

It was supposed to be a time of transition for black Miami. The old guard who'd led the community through the civil rights era were going to step to one side. The next generation was led by the first black superintendent of the fifth-biggest school district in America, a man who was rapidly becoming a player on the national stage. Or at least he *had* been on the rise, until Janet Reno's office leveled charges against him for using school funds to buy gold-plated plumbing for a private residence. Signs were he would be rushed to trial. To the black community, the issue wasn't the superintendent's guilt but the speed at which the indictments moved. Six black leaders in a row had found themselves swept to trial. To the *Miami Times*, there seemed to be no such thing as a black victim important enough to get a fair trial. Black defendants were continually rushed into the judicial machinery.

A curious concoction of shy and blunt, Reno was not faring well under the media onslaught of 1980. Already she was under pressure from the black community, which meant that Marshall Frank was under pressure. This was the way of political relationships, as well as police departments. You had friends in high places, and when they moved up, you moved up. If you lost your protector, you'd probably roll downhill. Within the PSD, everyone knew how to take the departmental temperature. If the McDuffie case led to the resignation of chief of detectives Charlie Black, Marshall Frank knew he'd be next in line. Then again, between the McDuffie case and a spike in the county's murders, his wasn't the most attractive job. It would be like putting your head in a noose after you heard the creak of the trapdoor.

Frank held on to the hope that the McDuffie case was a chance to get things right, which meant he needed the assistant state attorneys to move carefully, in concert with the evidence he gathered. Reno selected her two top prosecutors and stayed close to the case. Her office had to accumulate physical evidence, select the right officers, and then level only the indictments that could stand up in a court of law.

Frank's case was moving toward its conclusion, but Reno's office had to decide what weight the evidence could bear. No one believed the McDuffie murder was premeditated, so first-degree murder wouldn't hold. The consideration of second-degree murder, an intentional killing that hadn't been preplanned, initiated hours of discussion between Frank, Detectives Singleton and Wesolowski, and Reno's assistant state attorneys. Murder two was common for crimes of passion, but Frank had two officers claiming that they'd seen McDuffie throw at least one punch. If the jury believed them, it meant the officers were justified in using force to subdue McDuffie. That left the assistant state attorneys with manslaughter, *if* they could prove individual officers had used excessive force.

Meanwhile, the series of articles that the *Herald* continued to unleash kept the pressure on the PSD. Buchanan, the lone *Herald* journalist at McDuffie's Liberty City funeral, reported on the marine honor guard, all white, standing outside the Jordan Grove Missionary Baptist Church. There was the flag-draped coffin open at the altar, half covered in yellow roses. Buchanan paid her respects. "He wore the Marine uniform he loved," she noted. "The brass buttons shone. His hands were folded peacefully."

Two church ladies hovered over the McDuffie family in their pew. They wore black dresses and long white gloves. Occasionally, as the family wept, they dipped down to wipe away tears with handkerchiefs. Eula McDuffie sobbed and rocked from side to side. McDuffie's oldest daughter, dressed in white ruffles, cried "Daddy!" as the coffin passed her by. Buchanan followed the procession to Evergreen Memorial Park to witness McDuffie being lowered into the ground. The marines fired their rifle volley into the air, and a trumpet played taps across the empty streets of Liberty City.

If there was any comfort for the black community, it was that their sense of outrage was spreading across Miami, breaking neighborhood and racial boundaries. Blacks and whites attended the next day's march outside the Metro Justice Building, all in agreement that the PSD cops had betrayed their city. A handful of officers who patrolled Liberty City held their own press conference without permission from their interim sheriff. "We want you to know that we're as outraged as you," the cops assured the black community.

When the indictments were handed down, the city discovered that

Reno's office had moved against five PSD officers. Two more had been immunized to testify against their colleagues. The state had a body, the medical examiner's evidence, the motorbike, depositions from Fire Rescue, and conclusions drawn by the doctors from Jackson. Reno appeared on the nightly news. "We reviewed all the evidence admissible in court and the charges are appropriate," she insisted. "We intend to get a conviction and if we get a conviction, we intend to ask for the maximum sentence. Thirty years for the four charged with manslaughter."

The lack of murder charges was a jolt to McDuffie's Liberty City neighborhood. "Evidence?" said local black leader Marvin Dunn in a televised response. "How about you take her to the cemetery? Is that enough evidence for you?" How, he asked, could the police not be charged with second-degree murder? Dunn stared into the camera and said, "I think the case will be tried in north Florida. Another community. They can be given a light sentence, get off with a couple of years on each count. They could be back in the streets in a year or two."

Perhaps Dunn took some comfort from Marshall Frank's words later that night. The homicide captain could not speak specifically about the investigation, but in a more general sense, he, too, let people know what was coming their way in the trial. "When all the facts are known," he told Edna Buchanan, "it will make your hair stand on end."

The McDuffie investigation was over. The charges had been brought and the trial was due to start in either March or April. That left Captain Frank, Edna Buchanan, and Dr. Joe Davis with several uninterrupted weeks to attend to their collective business of bodies. If any of them had been hoping for a little calm in the wake of the McDuffie investigation, it was not to be. Instead, independently, they were beginning to come to the same worrying conclusions. A doubling in the murder rate in under two years had caught everyone's attention, though to varying degrees. To the public it was a stat. For a crime reporter, a homicide captain, and the chief medical examiner—people who worked murders in man-hours—it was a doubling in the day-to-day labor of their departments.

There were plenty of cases for Dade law enforcement to pursue, but the county had already decided to pour its time and money into McDuffie. Race relations had a turbulent but familiar history. Reno's decision was sensible but reactive. Her suspicions about the trend heralded by the body in the back of the Audi from the spring of 1979 were being borne out in the first quarter of 1980 even as her own attention was diverted. There had already been thirty drug-related murders, and now the numbers were beginning to increase.

Murders connected to cocaine were even more insidious than the McDuffie case, because they threatened to undermine the entire justice system. The first place the corruption would appear was right in the middle of the PSD, in Marshall Frank's homicide squads. At exactly the same time the homicide bureau was gathering evidence to bring members of their own department to justice on behalf of Arthur McDuffie, federal agents were ending their examination of Marshall Frank's detectives. "Cops or Robbers?" asked the *Miami Herald*.

CHAPTER 8

As of 1980, billions of fresh dollars were starting to unsettle the state's foundation. The conservationist Marjory Stoneman Douglas had famously identified the Everglades as "a river of grass" that moved so slowly it had been long mistaken for a contained body of water. Drug money was similar: it never stopped moving, and yet, for the most part, it was hard to see the flow. The Everglades weren't just a metaphor. They were the favored dumping ground for the human discards of the drug trade, a frequent location for the deployment of Doc Davis's body bags. It was unsurprising that the homicide bureau was the first to be corrupted—it was among Miami's first institutions to have direct contact with the cocaine industry.

The FBI was now interviewing anyone who had picked up a phone in the homicide bureau, including Captain Frank himself. It was an extraordinary position for the PSD to be in. Just when their patrolmen were being picked apart in the *Miami Herald* ahead of the McDuffie trial, some of their most respected detectives were being accused of rot. The investigation centered around several of Marshall Frank's Spanish-speaking detectives. Frank stood to lose most of his bilingual squad members in a year just as crime spiked in the Latin-dominated cocaine industry.

Before Frank had taken over the homicide bureau, it had run a special investigations team, almost entirely dependent on Spanish speakers. Their fellow officers believed them to be excellent detectives but also began to notice strange behavior. One overheard them discussing buying a bar and had paused to wonder, *With what money?* Frank Wesolowski had been puzzled by an attempt to sell jewelry in the locker room at Christmastime. Al Singleton was walking a murder scene in south Dade when a detective looked him in the eye and swung a bathroom door shut, as if to hide something.

It bothered Singleton so much that he'd immediately sat down with his sergeant. "Listen," said Singleton, "if we get heavy-handed while we're doing our job, I can deal with that. But let me tell you something, I'm not a thief, and if someone steals in front of me, I'm going to fucking hand them up." Instead of reassuring Singleton, the sergeant had stared straight ahead.

Singleton's suspicions were correct. Months before, a drug dealer had walked into the FBI's Miami office to complain about the theft of 780 pounds of marijuana. He had been driving carefully in his van, his tag current, staying strictly at the speed limit, when two homicide detectives had pulled him over. While one detective questioned him, the other drove the van off. It was left in a Howard Johnson's parking lot for him, empty. The dealer was then kidnapped by his Colombian suppliers and beaten for three days. With a head covered in gashes, wearing a dark wig and fearing for his life, he'd sat down with the special agent in charge of the FBI's Miami office. The FBI operation began immediately. The *Herald* had first caught wind of the rot on December 27, 1979, the same day Buchanan published another front-page piece on Arthur McDuffie.

———

The target of the investigation was Mario Escandar. He was easy to find. Not because he had a Roman nose and an extensive array of floral shirts, but because he ran a clothing store near the FBI offices where agents had their suits altered. A Cuban who had once managed a Havana slot machine enterprise, Escandar had fled to Miami in 1959 and begun to deal cocaine. After ten years in America, he was convicted of selling narcotics, counterfeiting money, kidnapping, and escape from jail, which he accomplished using only a spoon.

If Miami had a Cold War specialty, it was in the complex world of double and triple agents that made it difficult for men like Mario Escandar to be brought to justice. It wasn't unusual for the PSD to find CIA-trained Cuban Americans among their criminal suspects. Often, they had run guns to Latin America and along the way worked for a foreign intelligence service. It was one of Marshall Frank's great frustrations. Murder investigations sometimes ran headlong into the wall of the most powerful American agency of all. In theory, the CIA's charter insisted that there was no intelligence collected inside the United States, but Miami seemed an obvious exception. If homicide detectives smelled a CIA connection, they could assume the case would remain unsolved. Escandar would be a rare instance in which a CIA-trained veteran would suffer in Miami's courts.

Back in the early 1970s, the largest drug sting the United States had ever run had netted Escandar. In 1972, unbeknownst to the PSD, he became an informant for the FBI. In 1977, he was arrested for kidnapping, a crime handled by homicide. Detectives helped him obtain a reduced sentence of just fifty-nine days. In theory, Escandar had been flipped by the PSD detectives in the aftermath. In reality, it was Escandar who did the flipping, happy to provide certain homicide detectives with cocaine, jewelry, and parties stocked with prostitutes.

Wiretaps went up in Escandar's house—and inside the homicide department, as fifty-two FBI agents gathered in Miami. Captain Frank knew nothing about the investigation, which lasted seven months. Twenty stenographers worked for eight weeks transcribing recordings.

The FBI estimated that Escandar had fifty to one hundred people working for him, including an ex-judge and at least six members of Frank's homicide squad. Frank had had no idea how vital his selection of Singleton and Wesolowski had been for the McDuffie case. Had they not been shiny and clean, the McDuffie investigation would have been destroyed long before the trial began. Their fellow detectives provided Escandar with the names of informants, intimidated his foes, stole cash, and confiscated drugs that he sold on their behalf. The transcripts made for uncomfortable reading.

On one of the "horrendous number of surreptitious tapes," Escandar referred to one of Frank's homicide squads as his "young men of iron." Conversations suddenly veered from planned violence to delaying a cocaine shipment because one man was worried about a conflict with the Jewish high holidays. Homicide detectives had been recorded recommending the murder of a trio of rival dealers with an outstanding $2.4 million debt. Later, one detective would confess to Singleton that he and his colleagues had even considered his execution.

Escandar was suspicious enough to fear his phone was tapped. He installed a second line. That was tapped as well. He stopped using the phone. Not to worry, the FBI had already planted microphones in his kitchen, his den, and his living room. They had hundreds of conversations taped and worked hard tying together oblique references with old, unsolved cases. At least three homicide victims were known to Mario Escandar. Each case involved police misconduct and the disappearance of money, drugs, and valuables. In one case, a small-time associate of Escandar's was shot through the head at such close range that "the victim wasn't in an easily recognizable state," yet a detective had surprised the medical examiner by identifying the body on the spot. Escandar had called in his condolences before the dead man's family had even been informed of his murder.

Even the property room at the PSD building had been infiltrated. More than $62,000 was released to an unknown man with a fictitious address, signed over by another compromised detective connected to Escandar.

————

It was hard to imagine that life could get more difficult for the homicide bureau. If there was hope for Frank, it was that the racial charge of the McDuffie trial could be assuaged by definitive proof of guilt. Cocaine was a problem whose extent was in no way understood either by the FBI or by the PSD homicide bureau—despite the fact that it had rotted Marshall Frank's department at exactly the moment when veteran bilingual detectives were essential. By the time his superiors were through reassigning or firing detectives, Frank would be left with exactly three men who had more than eighteen months' experience on homicide, including Singleton and Wesolowski.

The McDuffie case could be seen as a warning sign of rising tension, but the corrosion of cocaine within the homicide bureau was a red flag, drawing attention to the vulnerability of the city's institutions. The two were certainly regional stories poised to become national headlines. But the problems arising from an industry dominated by Colombians were both a criminal *and* an immigration issue. Most of the hundreds of Colombians living in the United States and involved in cocaine were there illegally. But unlike immigrants who entered the labor force on the first rung of the ladder, these men and women earned tens of thousands of dollars within months. Money gave them access to false identification, lawyers, and transportation. Local law enforcement barely registered their existence; there was no record of them in the first place. Those who found their way to the slabs of Doc Davis's morgue were almost always identified as "Juan Does." McDuffie was an innocent who had lain unrecognized for a single night, but the unclaimed corpses of the cocaine trade were rarely buried with a correct name.

On February 28, the defense attorneys of the accused officers in the McDuffie trial covered a judge's table with clippings from the *Herald* and other newspapers to prove it would be impossible to select jurors in Miami who wouldn't already have an opinion. As one *Herald* journalist said, "You'd have to be a gopher under a golf course not to know about it." The judge agreed that the "notoriety of the case permeates this community" and the trial would be better off if it were in Tampa— Hillsborough County.

If the trial turned out to be as divisive as many feared, Miami would be in the unfortunate position of having to leave a verdict to men and women who had no understanding of their city. What no one foresaw was that by the time the trial ended, Miami itself would have undergone a sudden and unforeseen upheaval. This would have nothing to do with the plethora of illegal Colombian immigrants living within Dade County and everything to do with Cuba, lying just ninety miles from Florida. Before the McDuffie trial could even begin, the city that Ferré was trying to direct slowly south was about to get such a violent tug in that direction that the entire United States would reconsider the benefits of immigration and recoil in fear.

PART 2

CHAPTER 9

Héctor Sanyustiz didn't want to start a revolution; he wasn't even aiming at Miami. He was the rare Cuban without a single relative living along the Eastern Seaboard of the United States. He'd been born in Oriente, the same province as the Castro brothers, as far from cosmopolitan Havana as possible. His earliest memories of the 1950s were of skipping school and running errands for prostitutes. Then came Castro's revolution. His friends, the hookers of San Miguel del Padrón, either stopped working or were rounded up for forced labor in camps.

He heard the cries of "Batista's gone!" during the days of jubilation. Two years later he sensed the worries during the Bay of Pigs. At sixteen, Sanyustiz was conscripted into the military and worked as a chauffeur until he fought with a group of officers and broke a first lieutenant's jaw. After a few months in jail, he was released with a dishonorable discharge and ended up driving an *aspirin*—the Cuban name for buses in Havana that only seemed to come once every four hours. Everything he saw, everything he did, was stifled and controlled by a watchful army, a police force, and the neighborhood defense committees (CDRs) that saw locals spying on behalf of their government on the comings and goings of every city block.

He lost his job in 1978. Braking hard to avoid hitting a dog, he was chastised by a young black passenger in a suit—the abrupt stop had caused coffee to spill down his shirt. Sanyustiz ignored him, and the man, identifying himself as a state prosecutor, grew angry. When the prosecutor reached his stop, Sanyustiz couldn't help himself; he needed to have the last word. "Get out of here, little lawyer!" he called out the window, within earshot of the other passengers.

At the end of Sanyustiz's shift, the prosecutor was waiting for him at the depot alongside two policemen. "You're never going to drive a bus again," he told him. Put on probation at work, Sanyustiz was soon caught smoking pot and immediately sentenced to nine months in prison. He was released on December 17, the same day Arthur McDuffie was beaten into a coma.

The government offered Sanyustiz two bottom-rung jobs: digging graves or hunting crocodiles in faraway swamps. He rejected both, and for the first time, asked himself if he should leave Cuba. He meandered through the streets on his motorbike, staring at embassies, trying to calculate the odds of bursting past guards and claiming asylum.

In March of 1980, after dropping his wife off at the pizzeria where she worked, he was hit by a bus, which propelled his moped into a truck. As bystanders screamed and a crowd gathered, Sanyustiz crawled out from beneath the semi. The vehicle had slammed into his motorcycle hard enough that a dozen bus passengers needed to be hospitalized, but Sanyustiz had barely a scratch. His photograph appeared in a Cuban tabloid: the luckiest man in Havana.

Sanyustiz knew that attention wasn't good. He'd just rejected two government jobs, and tabloid exposure could only antagonize the government. He worried he'd be labeled a malcontent or an enemy of the state. Jail was the most likely destination if he couldn't find a way out of Cuba at once.

Three weeks later, on April 1, 1980, Sanyustiz sat in bus 5054 with his foot hovering over the accelerator. He'd borrowed the vehicle from a friend at the depot who now sat beside him. There were five others in the back. Sanyustiz needed to get out of the country, but he was scared of the sea, unwilling to hijack a boat. Instead he put his faith in the government-owned bus.

It idled outside the Peruvian embassy, where four Cuban guards were standing watch at the gates. Sanyustiz put his foot down and accelerated.

He turned too soon, crashing into the fence fifty meters from the embassy entrance. He reversed, gathered speed, and swerved toward the guards, who were now prepared. The bus was peppered by gunfire: two shots struck Sanyustiz, one through the left leg, one in his right buttock. When the bus came to rest, it was halfway onto the embassy grounds. Sanyustiz opened the bus door and hobbled out, bleeding. In the crossfire, a guard had shot his own twenty-seven-year-old colleague. The Peruvian ambassador, still eating breakfast, rushed down the drive carrying a napkin. According to the Vienna Convention, the seven Cubans were now asylum seekers in Peru, and local authorities were prohibited from entering embassy grounds.

Castro immediately asked for the return of his citizens. The Peruvian ambassador refused. In response, Castro did something very strange: he removed all the Cuban guards from the embassy gates. If Peru was going to accept asylum seekers, said the Cuban state paper, *Granma*, let's see how they dealt without law and order.

The Peruvian embassy was left unguarded, gates gaping. By Saturday night, three hundred Havanans entered the grounds. The first to walk in were uncertain. Could this be true? They hesitated and looked around for hidden cameras, guards, Russians. No one stopped them. All Easter Sunday, people streamed through the gates, some with bags, others still wearing quinceañera dresses from the previous evening. By nightfall, the Interior Ministry set up barricades on the streets beyond the embassy and began to turn people back. To the Cuban government's embarrassment, over ten thousand jubilant asylum seekers had gathered on the embassy grounds. The message to the international community was clear: given the smallest window for action, a huge number of Cuban citizens would opt to leave their own country. Sanyustiz may have selected Peru, but the majority of those now crammed into Peruvian territory were thinking about a much closer objective.

———

Most Cuban immigrants were caught between two cities: Miami, Mayor Maurice Ferré's imagined center of the Americas, and Havana, the capital of a communist dictatorship. In the 1960s, tens of thousands of educated, productive citizens had emigrated from Cuba to the United States—not because they wanted to, but because Castro had driven them out. Those unbelievers had watched Castro embrace communism and feared what it would do to the country. Middle- and upper-class Cubans created an insular, homogeneous community in Miami, and their earliest successes came from Cubans providing services for other Cubans. Many had hoped that an aggressive American foreign policy would oust Castro and allow for their return. Which is why, even after two decades in the United States, entire communities had still avoided a full commitment to America in 1980. Miami's Little Havana was just that—a little Havana—and people could move cradle to grave within the limits of Ferré's city without speaking a word of English. The lingering hope of returning home bonded the community together, but time and again the dream was disappointed.

Twice in two years, President Kennedy had failed them. The first washout was at the Bay of Pigs in 1961. CIA agents based in Miami had trained 1,500 Cuban exiles to invade the island nation, and yet when they did, no US air cover had been granted to their forces. Nor had the Cuban people risen up alongside the invaders to topple Castro from within.

The second disappointment came a year later, during the Cuban missile crisis. The Cold War had climaxed in a nuclear showdown between the United States and the Soviet Union. The US had missile bases in Italy and Turkey, and the Soviets had a ballistic missile facility in Cuba, ninety miles from the coast of Florida. The countries threatened each other with mutual destruction, until Kennedy and Khrushchev came to an agreement: the Soviets would dismantle their weapons in Cuba, and the United States would agree never to invade Cuba preemptively again. The arrangement may have satisfied the rest of the world, but to Cuban Americans in Miami, the president had pulled a punch. He traveled to the Orange Bowl in Miami to assure the immigrant community otherwise. "This country will not rest content until Cuba is free of Russian influence," said Kennedy. Miami's Cubans, packed into the stadium, saw it differently. Kennedy may not have wanted a nuclear Cuba, but he had settled for a communist neighbor.

By the time Kennedy was assassinated in 1963, the US government had gradually accepted Castro's obduracy. Not so for Cubans in Miami. Anti-Castroism became the defining creed. Castro had divided families, annexed private property, and executed political opponents, and he ran a brutal prison system. To many Cuban exiles, anything other than active opposition was a dangerous path; and by the late 1960s, Miami was the only city in America where employees had to sign an oath, albeit unconstitutional, that they did not belong to the Communist Party.

The young immigrant community didn't have the resources to create television programming to spread their message, but radio was cheap, and Cuban stations appeared across the AM dial. They went from right-wing to extreme right-wing. The voices of a generation that had been driven from their country and failed to reclaim it were loud and angry, and the biggest insult to them was watching the American Left begin to warm to Castro.

By the mid-1970s, as a result of this rage, Miami became home to the greatest concentration of terrorist organizations in America, all of which targeted perceived Castro sympathizers. There were over thirty bombings in Miami in 1975 alone and more splinter groups than the FBI could count. People bought remote switches at hardware stores to turn on their car ignitions from across the street in case the vehicles were rigged with explosives. The ultimate goal for the anti-Castro factions was to force the dictator from power and wrest back control of Havana. In Miami, this led to plenty of jockeying for leadership positions, the idea being that whoever could represent Cubans in Miami would one day represent the Cuban people in Havana.

Until Cuban Americans had their own representatives in elected office, Puerto Rican–born mayor Maurice Ferré was their best chance at local, and national, representation. Despite the geographical proximity, Latin America was a low priority for the Carter administration. Iran, Afghanistan, and Russia dominated newsprint and foreign policy. Latin

America had become the poor cousin at the State Department. Even in Miami, in a county that had officially become bilingual in 1973, Anglos continued to look in one direction—north. The city's leadership wanted New Orleans's port, Atlanta's banks, New York's prominence. They wanted more than cruise ships and a growing population of retirees. But there was no cohesive plan for progress. Only a young Ferré had a vision: to make Miami the unofficial banker of Latin America and then its service center for commercial trade.

Henry Flagler, John D. Rockefeller's smarter half, had looked south as far back as the early 1900s. Creator of the Florida East Coast Railway, Flagler's dream wasn't to end his railroad in Miami; he wanted to drive it down all the way to Florida's prime port city of Key West and link it via seaplane to Cuba. His success made Miami the first city in the United States with international flights. The hurricane of 1935 had ended that dream, sweeping more than two hundred of Flagler's railroad workers off the Keys and destroying railroad bridges, as well as any further attempt to connect Havana and Miami. While the cities weren't linked together with steel rails, a bond had formed. And with little help or hindrance from the state or federal government, Miami was, by the late 1970s, the city in the United States with the highest proportion of Spanish speakers—Ferré's backroom infrastructure to turn the city south.

Ferré saw his city as the future epicenter of Latin America, but there was a flaw in his vision. Cuban exiles were the primary reason that Miami spoke Spanish, but Cuba was now the most atypical country in Latin America. It was part of the Caribbean rather than Central or South America. The United States had been its closest ally, and the United States was now its worst enemy. Cuba had produced America's most outspoken immigrant community, but as America had shifted center-left with Carter, Miami's Cubans defined themselves by degrees of anticommunism. Ferré was betting large on a community in constant conflict with itself.

By 1978, Cuba's own domestic tensions were laid bare. Castro's patron, communist Russia, was pouring its resources into missile programs and had little left with which to coddle Cuba. Cuba had also just suffered from a failed tobacco crop and a poor sugar harvest, increasing economic pressure. Castro was so desperate for other sources of income that he quietly reached out to the Cuban American community in Miami. In response, the Committee of 75 was formed in Little Havana, and a bizarre "amateur diplomacy" began between the seventy-five exiles and Castro's government. They negotiated a deal: in return for the release of over three thousand political prisoners inside Cuban jails, Castro would open Cuba for exiles to pay to visit their families for the first time since the revolution.

For Cubans in Miami, it was a stark choice. Did you want to reunite with relatives you hadn't seen in twenty years, or did you despise Castro so much that you wouldn't give him a nickel? Thousands decided to go, and in a single year, Cuban Americans poured $100 million into Havana as they rushed to visit their families. Relatives arrived carrying as much as they could: gifts of tape recorders, medicines, and cigarettes; photographs of swimming pools and men standing by their Firebirds. Teenage girls sashayed in Sasson jeans and suede boots, dabbed with Maybelline lipstick. It didn't matter if this was a true reflection of life in America or an exaggeration, the effect was the same. Cubans forgot Castro's twentieth annual request for belt tightening. They heard about Miami, where Cubans had built more businesses than existed in all of Havana before the revolution. They forgot about the ever more intrusive CDRs. The word was that in America people could do whatever they wanted and keep what they were worth. Which is why, despite the infusion of desperately needed cash, Castro soon put a stop to the flights.

Once the experiment ended, Cuban Americans turned not on those who'd gone but on those who'd negotiated the deal in the first place. Rumors abounded that Castro's agents had infiltrated the Committee of 75. Many believed the very idea of the committee had been planted by Cuban intelligence in the first place. To be one of the Committee of 75 was to check under your car for a bomb planted by an anti-Castro radical and change your daily route to work. In time, twenty out of the seventy-five would find explosives in their offices or residences. Two would die. In Miami a good rumor was as deadly as a fact.

A month into office, President Carter had ranked Cuba as the country with which he most wished to improve relations. He'd positioned himself as an ambassador of human rights throughout the world, but for the three thousand newly freed Cuban political prisoners—all promised visas to America if they so desired—the actual process of application, through the newly opened US Interests Section in Havana, seemed remarkably slow. Applications should have been processed at the rate of four hundred a month rather than the two per day that were actually completed. The streets of Havana were now pitted with released political prisoners suspended between two countries: unemployable outcasts in Cuba, and unprocessed asylum seekers to the United States. For a president so concerned with human rights, it seemed hypocritical of Carter. Men and women who had suffered for their political beliefs were in limbo. Miami wasn't the only simmering city in the hemisphere in the spring of 1980. Thanks to Héctor Sanyustiz, Havana would be brought to a boil first.

———

On the morning of April 4, a Monday, every member of the foreign press in Cuba either mingled with the vast crowd in the Peruvian embassy or clung to the gates for a good camera angle. In pictures shown around the world, not one patch of the spacious green lawns could be seen between the closely packed people. Young men were perched in the branches of the mango trees, all smiling. The only exception was a worried Héctor Sanyustiz, now hospitalized. Guarded by soldiers, he was attended by an aide to the Peruvian ambassador. The ambassador obstinately disregarded every attempt made by Cuban officials to get Sanyustiz to read and sign documents that would return him to Cuban custody.

The State Department in Washington, DC, was monitoring the embassy situation. The US government wanted to seem supportive of the asylum seekers, but they didn't want to corral themselves by announcing definitive commitments. The Carter administration set about harnessing allies in the region, getting as many nations as possible to commit to dividing up the potential refugees. Perhaps the United States would take one thousand, yet the US Interests Section in Havana had barely made a dent in processing the three thousand visas for the political prisoners who'd already been released over a year ago.

Washington was paying attention, but only in the way you look at a phone when you *don't* want it to ring. Miami, on the other hand, was riveted by the spectacle in the Peruvian embassy. What did it mean? Had Castro misplayed his hand again? He'd been trying to get a seat at the UN Security Council for a decade, but after he openly supported the recent Soviet invasion of Afghanistan, the seat had been torn from his grasp. Now he'd made a humiliating error in the middle of Havana. In front of the press. It seemed too good to be true. Had the death of his oldest lover the previous month unhinged him? Would Castro really let the discontented leave, even if they numbered in the tens of thousands?

The following Wednesday, the Cuban Miami community poured into the street in a show of support. A thousand, then five thousand, soon twenty thousand headed toward downtown Miami. Police sat by, reluctant to interfere; only a thunderous storm drove the crowds back home. The next day, it started all over again, convoys of trucks and cars blocking off traffic across Miami, men and women sitting on their car horns, waving Cuban and American flags out of their windows. At first, the rest of Miami waved back. They got it. This was spontaneous, a reaction to what might be a turning point in Cuban history. The *Herald* sent a reporter to the parades. "Nobody's in charge!" shouted a police officer into his walkie-talkie. "We have no control!"

Young men in combat fatigues led the marches. They banged on the doors of Little Havana's businesses, bullying the owners into shutting up shop in support of those in the Peruvian embassy. Others began a hunger strike near the José Martí Memorial. They swore they wouldn't eat until the asylum seekers were free. Less than a block away, activists set up a food donation center, where they collected box after box for the Peruvian embassy. Huge crowds gathered there every morning at dawn as protesters sat in the middle of the street.

Ferré instructed his police department to be tolerant, but the rest of the city's patience soon wore thin. Choruses of horns, shrill and discordant, blared day and night. A police officer glared at the Cubans and shook his head. "It's getting out of hand," he said. "We've got numerous complaints. People can't hear themselves. They can't sleep." The grievances of Cuban Americans didn't resonate for long with the rest of Miami. Many failed to grasp why this foreign policy concern—this strident denunciation of communism aimed at only one country—would be acted out on American streets.

Ferré did his best to calm Miami as the demonstrations continued unrelentingly and traffic suffocated the city. "You've got to realize that these people have pent-up emotion that probably goes back twenty years," he explained to a television news anchor. "Just think back when the US beat the Russian hockey team, how excited we all were. Well, how much more excited are the Cubans when they see a major break that might change the future of their country?"

The news anchor worried that the city would soon be awash in three or five thousand new immigrants, and that Jimmy Carter's efforts to spread the asylum seekers across Latin America were unlikely to succeed. "Miami's absorbed 600,000 Cubans," said Ferré. "They're a net benefit to our community. Cubans haven't taken from the public coffers but rendered taxes to us."

The anchor shifted back in his seat, still doubtful.

"We welcome people," insisted Ferré, "and that's an American tradition."

You could almost see Ferré attempting to position himself in front of the next demographic set of waves he so often measured. At the moment, it was an easy stance to take. If a few thousand Cuban immigrants made it to Miami, Ferré was certain they would be swallowed and aided by the entrepreneurial community. The resulting electoral support from Cuban Americans could only be a boon for the incumbent.

Word was leaking through to Little Havana that Castro wasn't even feeding the asylum seekers in the embassy, though he'd rejected the help of the Red Cross as well as the twenty tons of food already collected in Miami. The truth was more complicated. Castro *was* feeding people, just not all of them. He instructed troops to pass three thousand meals through the gate every day so people would fight for the food. By the third day, people were so hungry they were eating mango leaves and boiling fish bones. The ambassador's cat was strangled by a starving young man, roasted slowly over a small fire for ten hours, and shared with a dozen friends. Fights were breaking out at the gates as people grasped for boxes of rice and beans, and all of it was recorded for the evening broadcasts around Cuba. "Anti-social elements take the children's food," reported national television over the images.

For Anglo and black Miami, this was a side story, but to Cuban Miami, the daily marches were becoming a display of their own impotence. Castro was hanged in effigy, smoking a big cigar. On the morning of April 8, Maurice Ferré left for Washington, DC. He knew that many of the three thousand newly released Cuban political prisoners were still waiting for their visas to be processed, but now there were ten thousand asylum seekers to consider. There was no clear consensus on who should get preference: the people who'd been waiting for eighteen months, or the people suffering in the embassy. Ferré had decided to ask for blanket amnesty; the United States should process all who wanted to come. Do it in an orderly fashion, support them. This put him at odds with both Governor Graham and his president. "We better start talking about how we're going to handle this problem," Ferré told the press as he landed in Washington, and promised to pull his friend Jimmy Carter aside at a White House reception that very evening.

As Ferré met with White House officials, in Havana the power went out in the Peruvian embassy and the surrounding blocks. There was a hush, a worry that Cuban armed forces were lurking in the darkness. Instead, the Peruvian ambassador was surprised to see a single familiar figure at where the gates had stood. It was Fidel Castro. Moments later, the two men were sitting in the back of a government car, riding along Havana's seafront drive, the Malecón. As Castro asked the ambassador to turn over Héctor Sanyustiz and his fellow instigators, the ambassador looked down and noted the end of a rifle poking out from under the seat. As they neared the embassy once more, they passed armed special forces with bayonets attached to their rifles, hidden from the asylum seekers by a single row of buildings. The day before, a man had tried to crash his car through the gates to join the asylum seekers and had been shot dead alongside his wife. In the darkness, as they inched through partisan crowds close to the embassy, they chanted, "Worms! Worms!" at the asylum seekers. Neither the rifle, the darkness, the army, nor the noise swayed the ambassador. He held firm and calmly told Castro he would not be handing over Sanyustiz and his coconspirators.

When the car stopped outside the Peruvian embassy, Castro emerged and walked alone along the edge of the grounds—then entered. Ten thousand people fell silent. So did the crowd outside. Ten thousand people seemed to be holding their breath, waiting for Castro to speak. The whole embassy was in a state of emergency: three bathrooms, not a dozen beds, hundreds suffering from dysentery, all in darkness. Castro wandered among the asylum seekers, briefly walked the two square acres of misery, and marched back, past the ambassador, to his car. For once, the garrulous Castro had said nothing.

A day later, Ferré was back in Miami, tempering his message to match Carter's. "I think Washington wants everyone to be part of the solution," he said. This time, Governor Graham agreed. They would welcome any Cuban refugees who made it to Florida, as long as Carter helped. It was a census year. Every head would be counted, and monies distributed accordingly. If thousands of people suddenly arrived in Miami after the census, it would completely disrupt the school and housing budgets. Ferré and Governor Graham, along with Carter's White House representatives, all settled on the number ten thousand at a maximum, the worst-case scenario for the United States. It was a miserable underestimation.

CHAPTER 10

A week after the bus burst onto the grounds of the Peruvian embassy, Héctor Sanyustiz was still stuck in traction inside a military hospital in Havana, threatened with the amputation of a leg. Again and again, he was asked to sign papers transferring him from Peruvian custody back into Cuban hands. He never signed—not when thousands gathered in the courtyard below to bellow for his execution, not when a million Cubans marched past in support of Castro, calling for his death, not when Castro promised his people that the degenerate Héctor Sanyustiz would never leave the country.

Every march in Havana was mirrored in Miami. Cuban Americans arrived by the hundreds, eventually numbering twenty thousand strong. For Mayor Ferré, Bayfront Park was the only place to be on that April evening. The assembled throngs waved Cuban and American flags and wanted something to be done. Preferably today. This was Miami's problem. Seventy-five percent of the city was from one minority or another, and the Cubans were the largest minority of all. They had their own knowledge, their own expectations. And right now, the expectation was that the suffering families inside the Peruvian embassy in Havana should be allowed to come to the United States at once. It had happened before during the freedom flights of the 1960s when planeload after planeload of Cubans had landed in Miami. President Lyndon Johnson had stood in front of the Statue of Liberty and told Cubans they were welcome in the United States.

Ferré took the stage. "Let them come!" he said, and the crowd roared.

But Ferré was not representing the State Department, and therein lay the problem: Cuban Americans only had the numbers to influence one city. They had no way of exerting pressure all the way to Washington.

That's where Mayor Ferré excelled. He was a city mayor with a national voice and direct lines into both the State Department and the White House. After all, he could claim hand-signed notes from Jimmy Carter, an appointment to the Presidential Advisory Board on Ambassadorial Appointments, a prominent role in Carter's election campaign, and an open door to the White House through his bimonthly trips north. Ferré was the only politician in Miami who still stood to get an important audience at a national level.

He had a hundred Cuban friends, yet he'd won and run the city with only moderate Cuban support. In typical Ferré fashion, his bluntness hadn't aided his cause. Once, playing dominoes after dinner with three Cuban friends, he announced in front of a *Miami Herald* reporter that "the trouble with Cubans is they talk twice too much and think half enough." Even those sitting at his table had been outraged. And then he'd doubled down and blamed Castro's revolutionary victory on wealthy Cubans who had not taken responsibility for the country's poor.

If he had been a Cuban exile, his remarks would have attracted the attention of right-wing terror groups, but Ferré could get away with such comments because his actions had always been generous. When fourteen thousand unaccompanied minors had been sent from Cuba to escape Castro's communism in the early 1960s, the Ferré family had permitted the Catholic diocese to house the young in three family-owned properties. Back then, a twenty-six-year-old Maurice Ferré had sat in room after room full of cots and quietly consoled homesick children.

Now Ferré had the crowd rolling. Dressed in a white shirt, yellow tie, and beige jacket, he was in his element. Cuban refugees were still fleeing communism. "They're welcome in South Florida. Otherwise we'd have to tear down the Statue of Liberty!" A roar from the crowd. "Otherwise what we say is a hypocrisy to fact and the fact is that America has always been generous to people in need."

Later, on News 4, another Ferré kicked in, a man who knew the facts but wanted to remind you he knew the facts. He ran through a list of desperate refugees America had supported over the years, from Hungarian freedom fighters to Vietnamese boat people. Beside Ferré sat Ralph Renick, the most prominent television anchor in South Florida. He declared to the citizens of Miami, "Things are slipping from bad to worse under Fidel's dream. Even food is in short supply." This might not just be an exodus, he suggested, or a third wave of immigration. This could herald the end of Fidel Castro.

On April 16, after two weeks, it seemed as if there would be an orderly end to the ever more Dantesque scenes within the Peruvian embassy in Havana. By now five neighborhood cats had been captured, strangled, and slowly roasted, and hundreds of asylum seekers had slept in pools of urine and excrement. Finally Castro allowed the first plane to take off. It wasn't headed to Florida but to Costa Rica, more or less in accordance with Carter's wishes to share the burden of distributing refugees around the region. It landed at 8:25 a.m., watched by a handful of local journalists and Guillermo Martinez of the *Miami Herald*, the only reporter on the city desk whose own parents had once been imprisoned by Castro.

Martinez had been tipped off to the flight by the head of the State Department's Cuban Affairs office. Having secured permission and money from his editors to fly south, Martinez witnessed the arrival firsthand. Refugees wept, kissed the Costa Rican ground, and chanted for freedom. He listened to them talk about the beatings they'd received, the hunger they'd suffered, the illness, the fear that had circulated on the embassy grounds. "At least a dozen passengers had fresh cuts, like injured boxers, over their eyes." They moved around the airport in shoes made out of cardboard. As Martinez's sympathetic coverage hit the front page of the *Miami Herald*, Castro's reaction was immediate. All flights taking refugees out of Havana were halted.

Three days later, the exodus restarted, now entirely on Castro's terms. The Cuban government turned to a member of the Committee of 75 for advice. Miami's Cubans might have regarded the committee with suspicion, but that didn't stop the Cuban government from selecting Napoleón Vilaboa, a Miami car salesman, and persuading him to visit Havana to discuss how to defuse the embassy situation.

There was no press attendant at Vilaboa's meeting with the Cuban president, but Vilaboa later described "a violent, desperate" Castro seeking advice. Vilaboa said that an orderly exodus to South Florida should be arranged. He was thanked and sent back to Miami, and two days later his phone rang. The exodus would be permitted. Vilaboa would initiate it. All he had to do was come to a port by the name of Mariel, an unremarkable fishing village that was a forty-minute drive from Havana. Mariel was marked by a white colonial relic of a building set in the low hills above— the Cuban naval academy.

Vilaboa approached members of the exile community in Miami directly with extraordinary information. Not only did Castro intend to let all of the dissidents inside the Peruvian embassy go free, he was also willing to let Miami's Cubans pick up the relatives they had been trying to extract for two decades. No need to worry about American or Cuban airspace. Cuban Americans would be welcome in the fishing harbor of Mariel. They could come in whatever boats they chose. On a calm day, the trip from Key West could be made in six hours or less. So go now, collect your relatives, and if all goes well, you could be back in Miami within the day.

Though Vilaboa considered himself apolitical, it was not an available category in Miami. His own stated goals were simple enough: family reunification using his remaining friendships inside Cuba. From the beginning Vilaboa was suspect. Was he a hero, or was he being "used and mashed like a sweet potato on a dinner plate" by the Cuban leader? Inevitably, he'd soon be accused by the Cuban American community of being a patsy, a spy, a revolutionary, and an ignoramus.

Vilaboa drove to WQBA for the simple reason that the radio station "set the city's agenda regarding Cuba." He announced, in Spanish, that he was leaving for Mariel in his boat, the forty-one-foot fishing vessel *Ochun*. He didn't attempt to coordinate with either the governor or the mayor or anyone in Washington. The method was simple: ignore the Carter administration.

On the twenty-first of April, Napoleón Vilaboa's *Ochun* led a small flotilla of eight boats across the Straits of Florida. By evening, Vilaboa had achieved the unprecedented step of having six members of his own family ushered aboard. By midnight, they were in the Keys. The next morning, they had arrived in Miami. To WQBA, La Cubanísima, the message was clear. "Que vengan todos!" shouted the news director across the 2,400 square miles of Dade County. "Let them come! Let them all come!"

This landmark moment—the news of the outgoing boats—didn't even make the *Miami Herald*. The call to arms was in Spanish. Not until the boats arrived back in Key West did the *Herald* leap into action.

The immediate, most extraordinary realization was that Cuban Americans and the Castro government had the same goals and were telling the same story. "On the morning of April twenty-first, two Florida-based vessels left the port of Mariel with forty-eight antisocial elements aboard," stated Cuban radio. "Today, April twenty-second, a total of eleven vessels, also from Florida, will be taking more than three hundred of those elements to the United States. That's a good pace!"

Miami's WQBA agreed, but the Carter administration was caught off guard. Foreign policy was supposed to run through Secretary of State Cyrus Vance's department, not the streets of Little Havana. On the twenty-third of April, a news helicopter flying low over Key West spotted trailers and boats backed up along the single southern lane of US 1. By day's end, the docks of Key West were filled with captains of little to no experience. On brilliant turquoise waters and under bright Florida sunshine, they were undaunted by the 120-mile boat ride. From high above, the pilot was greeted by the beautiful sight of the white lines of boat wakes as dozens and dozens of small craft headed south in a motorized armada, countless arrows pointing to Castro's Cuba. Governor Graham happened to be in Miami at the Channel 10 studio, filming a public service announcement encouraging Floridians to use seat belts. Filming was interrupted as a reporter rushed past, hurrying to process the helicopter footage. Graham stayed to watch it. This is going to be big, thought the governor. Ferré had come to the same conclusion. Alongside the county manager, he'd quickly formed a crisis committee. The only remaining question was the *size* of the crisis coming Miami's way.

It was hard to tell if it was an opportunity, or a bind for Ferré. A Miami politician could embrace limited immigration and take only a limited risk. As the number of immigrants landing in Key West grew, then so would that risk. Cuban Americans might be the largest demographic in Miami, but Ferré knew they still hadn't registered in large enough numbers to win an election with only the Hispanic vote. There was vulnerability in the mayoral stance. A multitude of refugees could radicalize the black and Anglo communities, and Ferré could find himself jobless.

CHAPTER 11

An enterprising twenty-three-year-old Kansan, Janet Fix, was one of only two *Herald* reporters assigned to cover the Florida Keys. Acting on a Key West rumor, Fix had jumped a fence into a military base, flagged down a passing yacht, and made it to the naval dock in time to witness some of the very first refugees from Mariel arriving on a shrimp boat. While the few witnesses either aided the refugees or observed exiles kissing American soil, Fix was negotiating passage back to Mariel with the boat captain, still in search of his father. For the next eight days, she would report via radio, risking imprisonment, producing article after article as the *Herald*'s "Anonymous Crewman."

By April 26, just four days after Mariel was opened, Fix estimated that fifteen hundred American vessels were now anchored there, almost double the number of boats that had rescued the British army from Dunkirk. They were separated into groups according to their arrival date. Cuban authorities were telling crews that they faced a five-day wait, but many hadn't brought enough in the way of water, food, gas, or clothing. "Tourism skiffs" flitted between the boats, with patrol boats toting machine guns traveling in their wake. Tides rose and fell, but the prices only increased. A ham and cheese sandwich, five dollars instead of one. Seven bucks for a box of chicken and rice. Fix stuck to the shrimp and rum, the most reasonable fare. She reported on the "grim, businesslike" Cubans and the presence of Russian soldiers. All craft waited for the moment a small boat would pull alongside theirs with someone on board in a brown uniform announcing, "Your family is ready. Leave. Pronto." She watched as refugees boarded boats and sat in silence. When a boat pulled out of the harbor, the crews left behind could clearly hear the chorus of freedom from the departed when everyone "embraced, laughing and crying and speaking all at the same time."

In Havana, the Peruvian embassy still housed thousands seeking asylum. Those desperate enough to trust the state apparatus had accepted safe-conduct passes and were awaiting their opportunity to leave from home. Many had been beaten on their journey back to their houses, their own neighborhoods instructed by the government to welcome them with sticks and fists. Once inside their homes, the asylum seekers were monitored constantly. Their neighbors were ordered to pound on metal pots outside houses all night. Eggs, sticks, and rocks were thrown at or through windows. Graffiti was daubed on walls, pictures of worms crawling through dollar signs. The phone rang endlessly, all the calls obscene. "Get the fuck out of Cuba, scum." Their only hope was that a brother, father, sister, cousin had found enough money to head south to Mariel. Otherwise, asylum seekers would be caught in limbo.

The Cuban American community doubted patience as a strategy. Carter's State Department had proved sluggish processing actual political prisoners. It was more prudent to go with the smash-and-grab of Mariel. Had Carter moved to stop the boatlift within the opening forty-eight hours, Mariel's refugees might have measured in the hundreds, but by the time the first boats started arriving back in the Florida Keys, the president's awkward position had been spotlit by the American media. He was trapped between the moral high ground of accepting desperate refugees fleeing a communist dictatorship and the reality that Castro controlled the pace of the exodus.

Cuban Americans contemplating the trip south didn't call Mayor Ferré or Graham's office in Tallahassee. They rang the Coast Guard's Miami Operation Center by the hundreds. They were told to clear their departure with customs, not to exceed their limit on passengers, and to pack life jackets, file a float plan, and go straight to the Immigration and

Naturalization Service (INS) on their return. They were never advised that their actions were illegal. The Coast Guard, like every other institution, was awaiting clear signals from the White House.

Within three days, the Coast Guard began to realize that they were facing an unusual danger: total ignorance. Key West was swamped by Cuban Americans "attempting to buy a boat and hire a captain." In the controlled language of the Coast Guard, they were "totally inexperienced and had no appreciation of the risk they were taking." Dozens and dozens of boats continued to set out to sea amid a stretch of perfect weather. They herded together in groups of ten to twenty and motored toward a horizon so clear they could see Coast Guard cutters miles ahead, steel-gray markers that led straight to Mariel and reunions that had seemed impossible the week before.

Americans, like the *Herald*'s Fix, were thoroughly depressed by their first taste of Cuba. The port of Mariel "is grimy and industrial and the air is full of smoke and the buildings look like slums." Hundreds of South Florida boats creaked back and forth at anchor as their crews spotted snipers in trees and armed soldiers patrolling the banks. Fix reported that all visitors were banned from swimming; just as well, as the American craft were given no choice but to pump full septic tanks into the waters. The smaller boats, with barely any shade, had been hoping to get in and out of Cuba in a day. Weeks lay ahead for them. The tops of bald men's heads burned, peeled, and then burned again, wallets emptied, and water rations ran low.

Both Governor Graham and Mayor Ferré flew south to Key West as the refugees began to arrive. Carter stayed away. Responsibility for the situation got passed down, first from the president to Vice President Walter Mondale, then to Carter's chief of staff, who was too busy running the reelection campaign, then into State. Finally, it landed in one of the weakest agencies of the federal government: the Bureau of Refugee Programs, where it was handed to Ambassador at Large Victor Palmieri.

Three weeks before, Palmieri had been presented with Ted Kennedy's new Immigration and Nationality Act. Based on recent immigration of

Vietnamese boat people and Soviet Jews, the act was predicated on refugees being processed in countries with embassies or coming through countries with embassies on their way to the United States. But Cuba had no American embassy, and Castro had ensured that Florida was the only possible destination. It was impossible for Palmieri to know who, or how many, were coming.

The first few days, the arrivals were greeted in an almost casual manner on a broiling, overextended, and understaffed Key West. Cubans mingled with reporters around the Latin American Chamber of Commerce and hitched rides to Miami, where they were supposed to report for INS processing. A special agent in customs based in Miami at the time estimated that hundreds "just came in and melded into the community," never having reported. By the fourth day, the informality had disappeared. Boats could only unload at the Truman Annex, part of a naval installation. Refugees now began their lives in America inside a chain-link fence.

Once the bus route to Miami was formalized, it was clear that every refugee would soon become Mayor Ferré's problem. Carter's continued rhetoric of sharing the burden of Cuban refugees with all willing international partners sounded more and more like hollow electoral posturing. To any Cuba watcher, it was clear that Castro was aiming specifically at South Florida. Miami had selected itself as the beacon for Cuba's politically oppressed, and now Castro was planning to overload a city with political dissidents.

CHAPTER 12

Janet Fix's reports from inside Mariel showed that the giddy adventure had quickly dissipated into unnerved frustration. Russian surveillance helicopters now passed overhead all day. Spotlights skittered over the boats all night. Onshore, flares went off, but no one knew what they meant. Fix counted the boats as they arrived, dozens at a time, yet only thirty-five had left Mariel.

The most extraordinary entrance in Mariel was made by a red, white, and blue party boat called the *Calusa*. On April 26 at 10:00 p.m., it glided into the harbor in the darkness, missed the buoys, and wedged against a shoal in an ebbing tide. Captain Roy Jensen, always dressed in sneakers, jeans, and no shirt, already had plenty of friends in Mariel—half of South Florida's captains seemed to be there—but Cuban authorities stopped any American boats from approaching the distressed vessel. Finally, a small outboard approached, and two men explained that they represented a Cuban salvage company. They told Jensen that he had two options. He could pay them $10,000 now to be towed off, or $50,000 in the morning.

Jensen negotiated and settled on paying them $2,000 to do nothing at all. He jettisoned his fuel barrels and ran all of the *Calusa*'s fresh water into the harbor. But as the lightened boat eased off the shoal, it was caught in a current and headed toward a large rock. Desperate, Jensen threw the boat into gear and, escaping one rock, ran the *Calusa* aground on another.

The little outboard puttered back up to the *Calusa*'s side and the pilot told Jensen his time was up. The price was $10,000 for the tow. Once the boat was free and anchored, the salvage boat disappeared, only to return at midnight with five soldiers. They wanted the $10,000 in cash at once. A twenty-one-year-old passenger on the *Calusa* leapt into the filthy harbor waters with a plastic bag. For the next two hours, he swam slowly through the darkness among the American boats until he had begged a bagful of soggy five-, ten-, and twenty-dollar bills. Jensen received a receipt for $10,000 from the soldiers, and the *Calusa* was directed to its anchorage.

It was the talk of Mariel until, two days later, the first big storm of the season hit, creating chaos in the harbor. Boats broke free of their moorings; a shrimper smashed into its neighbors. Five boats were sunk, two legs broken, and one sailor suffered a heart attack. Between the cynical treatment of the *Calusa*, the waiting, and the knowledge that boats were vulnerable at Mariel, anxiety among the crews began to rise.

Those Cuban Americans yet to leave Key West suffered no such doubts. By April 24, there were no more marine charts for the region left in stores around Dade County. The Miami River had been emptied of speedboats in two days. People, panicked by the idea that the window of opportunity would close before their loved ones could be brought to Florida, overbid for boats, hitched them to trailers, and continued to head to the Keys. Soon, the waters would be filled with nautical virgins whose optimism disappeared in open water. The Coast Guard would begin to deal with strings of SOS calls, mostly unwarranted, as American boats continued to squeeze into moorages in Mariel without any permission at all from their own government.

South Florida prepared for their inevitable return. Ferré's office had already received a call from the INS asking if the city would let them use a building in Little Havana in case refugees came in numbers. The rules of the boatlift seemed to be inverted. Federal agencies were dependent on local government and a stream of volunteers. Ferré smelled a coming panic and tried to push the Carter administration for cruise ships to enter Havana so that potential refugees could be taken safely to Costa Rica, processed, and distributed among the willing countries of the world. The State Department disagreed, clinging to the hope that the flights to Costa

Rica could be resurrected. The only thing obvious was that, as the *Herald* pointed out, the US State Department "remained mired in confusion and indecision over what to do with the mass exodus from Cuba." The White House said that they might be willing to take more refugees than the original 3,500 they'd promised; at the same time, they were insisting that the flotilla should stop, and threatening to fine boat captains $1,000 per refugee. It was all talk. So far, there had been no enforcement at all.

Officially, the State Department announced that "the Cuban government is obviously not prepared to deal with this in a rational way." It wasn't rational if you were a refugee, or Jimmy Carter, but it was highly rational if you were Fidel Castro. He had taken a Cuban economy in tatters, combined with the public relations disaster of the Peruvian embassy, and turned them into a problem for an American president.

As the numbers of refugees began to increase, Ferré and the county manager coordinated to open up fairgrounds to use as a processing center. He and his Cuban American assistant city manager were stunned by the local support as the refugees arrived. Most of the early arrivals were families, the familiar continuation of two decades of Cuban emigration: children, doctors, political prisoners, the remnants of what had once been the middle class. There were opera singers and poets, and even Fidel Castro's official translator from the Cuban missile crisis. In the first days of the boatlift, few federal investigators were in attendance as people passed quickly onto the streets of Miami. It was a question of finding homes for families and then for individuals. Each refugee, once processed, got a "set of clean clothes, a $112 check from the federal government, a place to stay if needed and an appointment with a doctor." If there really were between three and ten thousand asylum seekers coming Miami's way, then the process of sponsorship would have to keep up with the rate of arrival.

Ferré had chips to cash in. From the moment when Carter had appointed him to the Presidential Advisory Board on Ambassadorial Appointments in 1977, Ferré had flown around Latin America, getting to know ambassadors and career diplomats. He'd visited the Dominican Republic, Colombia, Ecuador, Argentina, Brazil, Peru, and Chile, where he'd met with sixteen presidents, including Pinochet. It had led to friendships with undersecretaries and enough respect within the State Department to let him push the limits of his mayoral authority. How many other mayors had been invited four floors down in the Pentagon for a weeklong war game concerning Soviet troops in Cuba? For a midsize city with a part-time mayor, Ferré had gained extraordinary traction. Now he hoped to use it.

Again, he flew north to Washington on April 28, preoccupied with reports from Mariel that boat captains were proposing methods to avoid the threat of prospective fines the administration was now promising for bringing in refugees. The *Herald*'s Janet Fix had written that morning that captains were considering dropping refugees off on reefs in the Dry Tortugas.

Ferré's White House visit couldn't have come at a worse time. On April 24, in an unlikely gamble to end the Iranian hostage crisis, President Carter had green-lit a helicopter rescue sending ninety-three Delta Force commandos at high speed over the Iranian desert in a bid to free all fifty-two hostages remaining in Tehran. Instead of using the customary chain of command, the hostage plan was built around "an untried organization with a new command and control system." A national security team met in the Situation Room while Vance, Carter's secretary of state, was on vacation in Florida, effectively bypassing the State Department with the lives of Foreign Service officers on the line.

An error in refueling inside Iran had led to a massive explosion. A C-130 aircraft and a helicopter caught fire, burning eight airmen to death. The mission was aborted. The following day the *Miami News* called it "the most humiliating foul-up in American foreign policy since the Bay of Pigs." When Carter's chief of staff had learned of the failed mission, he'd rushed into the president's bathroom and vomited. The disastrous operation wasn't entirely unlike Carter's response to Mariel. Several different agencies, struggling to work together, suffered communication breakdowns in a highly stressful situation. On April 28, Vance resigned.

Ferré was accompanied through the White House down the red carpet of the West Wing, past the chief of staff's office, past the vice president's office, to the Roosevelt Room across the hall from the Oval

Office. So close to Carter, Ferré was told the president wouldn't see him and that the meeting concerning Mariel had been delegated to Vice President Mondale. Ferré would not be allowed into that meeting, either. He was stationed outside while Mondale was briefed.

Miami's mayor listened patiently to what he interpreted as muffled chaos. By the end of the meeting, Ferré guessed that the new secretary of state was unlikely to place the issue of Mariel any higher on his list of brushfires than Vance had. He waited over an hour until Mondale finally exited, saw Ferré, and did his best to walk past—a perfect metaphor for how the administration was attempting to deal with Mariel.

Ferré fell in step. "I've flown all the way up from Miami," he said. "You've got to listen to me."

"I don't have the time," said a hurried Mondale, explaining that it was now up to the Bureau of Refugee Programs.

"Give me thirty seconds," said Ferré. Mondale paused and nodded. "Don't stop these people in the middle of the ocean," pleaded Miami's mayor. "You're going to have people drowning. It's not the American tradition. We open the door."

"We've opened that door many times with Cuba," said Mondale. "We've been more than generous."

"One more time," said Ferré.

Mondale began to walk away, uncommitted. "It hasn't been determined," he said. As Ferré was escorted from the White House, he heard nothing but whispers of dissatisfaction.

Returning with no help imminent at a federal level, Ferré rang Governor Graham and asked him to declare Miami a disaster area. "When you have one thousand to two thousand people without food or clothes or homes, that's a disaster," Ferré said. As he spoke, the number of refugees grew to 3,252, with the arrival of 640, already nearing one of the president's initial limits. Carter called, once again, for a hemispheric effort to absorb the refugees and hinted that maybe, just maybe, the administration would receive more refugees. But in no way would the United States commit to handling all 10,000 then at the Peruvian embassy.

In the Florida Straits, the feeling was growing that some form of disaster was inevitable. One Coast Guard commander rescued twenty-four refugees from various ships in a single rainswept afternoon. In Key West, relatives wept in the rain, prayed, and sang the Cuban national anthem. The swells were bigger than the craft the Coast Guard was trying to rescue. "Not one of these boats was suitable," said a commander. "None had VHF radios. They didn't have any navigational charts, and if they did, they wouldn't know how to use them." Most worryingly of all, ships were being deliberately overloaded, with people "pressed knee to knee, shoulder to shoulder. There was barely room to breathe."

Some respite came at the beginning of May with the arrival of the Federal Emergency Management Agency (FEMA). Their man on the ground quickly alienated everyone involved in the relief effort by announcing that he'd come to South Florida to "straighten out the mess created by the state and local governments" when it was the state government, local governments, and countless unpaid volunteers who had bought time while the Carter administration dithered.

But Castro wasn't just sending the politically oppressed. By the end of the first week, when many new arrivals were already on the streets of Miami, an entirely new type of immigrant was recognized, pushed to America alongside desperate families: the common prisoner.

CHAPTER 13

The *Herald*'s Guillermo Martinez was the first to take note. After a day of watching arrivals spill onto American soil, Martinez found himself alone at the dock as a lobster boat pulled up, brimming with young men. The Coast Guard was playing Tom Petty's "Refugee." Martinez studied the men, with similar haircuts and hands marked by tattoos. He called out over the music, "How many of you have come directly from jail?"

He counted dozens of raised arms. What was Castro up to? After the ship docked, Martinez walked beside the refugees on their way to being processed. He followed one man wearing pants and a shirt made out of burlap sacks. He held his trousers up. The captain had removed his belt as a precaution.

"Why did you decide to come?" Martinez asked. The refugee started laughing.

"Were you in jail?"

The man nodded.

"Why'd they put you in jail?"

"Because I had a gun."

"Why'd you have a gun?"

He looked up at Martinez as if he'd asked why the sky was blue. "To kill all the cockroaches." Castro had added not one but two new types of refugees to Mariel: the contents of his jails and the men and women held in Cuban mental institutions.

He was nothing if not deliberate in the timing of his torture of Jimmy

Carter. On Mother's Day, Castro released 420 convicts and mental patients jammed alongside ordinary family members on a hundred-foot-long red, white, and blue catamaran called *America*. The boat had been hired out of Chesapeake Bay by dozens of exiles, many of whom now idled in Key West awaiting three hundred relations. They had paid between $500 and $1,000 in advance for each relative and instead watched the catamaran disgorge prisoner after prisoner.

They were deliberately released on the busiest day the boatlift had seen so far. The *America*'s captain had tried to protest the passengers he was forced to take. "I said I didn't come down here to pick up these people. They said if I didn't take them, they would seize my boat, name it the *Fidel*, and put me before a firing squad." Before they'd sailed a mile, one man tried to strangle a fellow refugee and had been lashed to the boat's railings. Another boat traveling close by held only prostitutes. Another, only transvestites, who "combed their hair and primped so they would look their best as they took their first steps toward a free life."

The arrival was intended to be a positive photo op—immigrants arriving on the red, white, and blue craft. Instead, the families on board cowered, and when the *America* docked in front of the press, hundreds of tattooed young men found their way onto the nation's front pages. An anticipated boat, beacon to the press, symbol of everything going wrong in the boatlift.

Even though Guillermo Martinez had already raised the issue of criminals in the *Herald*, it was an article on the front page of the *New York Times* on May 10 that came to define the boatlift. The story told of both the *America* and the *Valley Chief*. For days, the *Times* reporter had been posing as a Cuban American in search of his family at Mariel. From the docks, he'd witnessed guards instructing young men from mental institutions to say they'd been in the embassy. Many suffered from schizophrenia or had developmental difficulties. Others were vagrants, thieves, or vandals, camouflaged by a few political prisoners. Not one had been inside the Peruvian embassy. The *New York Times*' journalist knew he had a good story, something "a bit scandalous." The actual article was nuanced, showing how easily in a country like Cuba, sodden with corruption, even small infractions could lead to lengthy jail sentences. The story appeared under a headline that would cement the reaction of the rest of the country. "Retarded People and Criminals Are Included in Cuban Exodus." Radio Havana had an equally blunt assessment: "The United States has always wanted to pick the best brains of our people—so they can pick up also the bums."

Cuban American volunteers in Key West found clusters of their fellow immigrants that Florida had never seen. Not only sullen, tattooed men who had never expressed any wish to see the United States, but now hundreds of prostitutes openly propositioning federal workers as dozens of Cuban transvestites picked through the women's clothing pile. The heaps of clothes were sorted through with particular glee since in Cuba it was almost impossible to find fashionable items and here, they seemed to be free.

In theory, refugees were under federal jurisdiction unless they committed a felony in the United States, but by mid-May, refugees had been detained for moral turpitude and drug trafficking. They were taken to the Federal Correctional Institution in south Dade on the word of their fellow refugees. And then entire boatloads began to arrive with "crowds dominated by young men who displayed none of the exuberance of most of the earlier refugees."

Soon the journalists' stories were corroborated. In Cuba, the police not only had taken men and women directly from jail but had rounded up recidivists and troublemakers who had already served time. Everyone was taken to pose for passport photos, await their documents, and then be shuttled to El Mosquito, described as a "tropical concentration camp." There they were searched, had any valuables confiscated, and were then mixed in with the Peruvian embassy refugees. One man walked the *Herald*'s Martinez around the hangar, pointing to men who had been in prison with him. That one had merely stolen an orange. Next to him were men who had done time for drugs, assault, and robbery. "I can tell you," said the former prisoner, "there are many convicts coming the same way."

Many openly admitted their prison backgrounds as they handed over their safe-conduct passes. Criminals may have represented no more than 4 percent of the boatlift, but only 3 percent of the population of an average American city served time for felonies. They were the ones who kept police busy, crime reporters at work. By adding an entire nation's hardened criminals to a small city's population, Castro was about to skew Miami's crime statistics. Although Edna Buchanan was already overworked by April, neither she nor Marshall Frank had conceived of the way an immigration burst could affect their respective beats.

At the beginning of May, Carter decided to prop up the Coast Guard by diverting thirty-four navy ships from war games at Guantánamo to help shepherd the growing flotilla of refugees. But the navy had no way of peering into a passing refugee vessel and assessing its threat. Soon it became apparent to Ferré that Castro had also unloaded the unwanted. Not just prostitutes and rapists, or murderers and child molesters, but also those considered drains on the economy. Old men with no family, gay men rejected first by the Cuban state and then by their extended families in Miami.

The changing demographics of the boatlift only deepened the divisions on Miami's airwaves. On WNWS, an AM station, three Anglo DJs talked as much about Mariel as did any Cuban. They called Cubans "spics," advocated sending the new arrivals directly to Alaska, and warned their listeners that they were "picking up the tab for our friend Mayor Ferré's incoming buddies from Cuba."

On WEDB, managed by black Miamians, there were constant updates on the McDuffie trial, which was underway, but also questions about whether newly arrived Cubans would be treated more favorably than newly arrived Haitians. In Little Havana, WQBA continued an all-news format. They created a miniature studio on the street with a live microphone. Whatever was needed for a refugee was relayed immediately. When the INS stopped transporting refugees into Miami from Key West, WQBA sponsored their own buses. "This," said the station's news director, "is radio at its best." In April alone, the radio station had raised half a million dollars to help the new arrivals. The *Times* article on Mariel's criminals had a profound effect. The *Herald* would later claim that the story transformed "what had been sympathetic and even admiring press coverage . . . into the media equivalent of a lynch mob."

That article had inadvertently realigned the opinions of the country. The same *New York Times* that had prodded Carter to accept the refugees now called for an immediate enforcement of immigration law. Castro, stated a *Times* editorial, "mocks the generosity of the United States by dumping criminals, even leprosy patients, into the boats." Refugees had suddenly been converted from those seeking freedom to those threatening a benevolent country. The national narrative and the local truth had been cleaved. Across America, the revelation that 4 percent of the refugees had a criminal past was reason enough to turn against *all* immigrants. Within Dade County, goodwill remained the predominant reaction, but there was no doubt it was wavering. From afar the problem seemed one-dimensional. Locals, however, realized that the Mariel boatlift was compounding an immigration problem that already existed; the handful of illegal Colombian immigrants working in the cocaine trade had already embittered many Miami residents against Spanish speakers.

In early May there was a demonstration outside Miami's Federal Building. "Give Miami Back to Americans," read one sign. "Charity Should Begin at Home." "Crime and Disease Will Increase." American flags were draped across cars. The march was sparsely attended, heavy on journalists, low on marchers, but WNWS's anti-immigration line had seen its audience rise by 150 percent. Polls had already shown that Anglos were the most upset at the wave of immigration. Sixty-eight percent believed that the immigrants of Mariel would have a negative impact on the community, alongside 57 percent of blacks and 14 percent of Latins. Perfectly timed to exacerbate the issues, Miami's only country music radio station was bought out by Cuban owners. Out went country's Willie Nelson, and in came the salsa star Willy Chirino.

The *Herald* addressed the subject by interviewing Mayor Ferré. "Is there a saturation point? Can this community come to grips with immigration?"

"Yes," said Ferré, "in the same way that Boston came to grips with the huge Irish influx of the 1870s."

And how was that?

"It doesn't," said the mayor; some influxes redefine cites.

An assistant county manager was chosen to help turn off the tap. He looked at a line of immigrants from Mariel waiting to collect their federal checks and pointed at a space between two men. The man ahead received federal assistance. The man behind did not. It was official. No further arrivals would be eligible for refugee status under the Refugee Act of 1980. According to the Carter administration, thousands of checks should never have been issued. Housing, medical treatment, and job assistance would now have to come from Ferré and the county manager, with help from Governor Graham, if he could bring Tallahassee to look favorably on Miami, the bastard child to the south.

With federal assistance still limited and sluggish, Mayor Ferré chose to move the growing stream of immigrants into a place accustomed to crowds. The Orange Bowl was home to the Miami Dolphins. It had parking, bathrooms, a section for catering, even a helicopter landing pad. Refugees nestled on green canvas cots near concession stands, or on blankets spread over dirt floors. Everywhere you looked, another line formed. Lines for clothing, lines for food, lines for pillows, and a vast congregation for Mass. Outside, the National Guard was confronted with a situation they'd never seen. Cuban Americans were attempting to scale the fence in order to volunteer. "It's the most unbelievable thing I've ever seen," said one National Guardsman, looking out over children playing with a soccer ball. "Talk about taking care of your own."

On May 3, when Carter slammed the door shut on Cuban immigration, there was a huge sigh of relief from local agencies and from the Coast Guard, the INS, customs, and the navy. It was definitive. The grateful FBI was now using dozens of agents "trained in questioning techniques," alert to speech patterns from Cuban prisons, to try to cull the criminals from the hangars full of the latest arrivals.

And yet on May 6, the president suddenly reversed course yet again.

"Ours is a country of refugees," said Carter, at a luncheon for the League of Women Voters. "Those of us who have been here for a generation, or six or eight generations, ought to have just as open a heart to receive the new refugees as our ancestors were received in the past." He offered refugees "an open heart and open arms," and the next day a record 4,500 landed from Mariel. For the first time, refugees were arriving in Key West at almost 300 an hour, approximately thirty times the rate during the last Cuban surge, of 1968's Freedom Flights. Over 23,000 Cuban immigrants had now reached America in under a month.

Agencies across the region were stunned by the president's speech. Cautious captains who had been holding back set to sea, and Mariel refilled with those eager to bring their relatives north. Later on the sixth, hours after Carter's luncheon speech, a State Department official said, "We didn't know what the policy was. Here we were insisting that we were going to enforce a law that we knew was unenforceable. It was ridiculous." Local customs agents joked that Carter had gone from policy of the week, to the day, to the hour.

The very Cuban community that Ferré used as a beacon to draw banks and businesses to Miami would be expanding either way. If Miami's economy was truly sound, perhaps it could absorb a huge influx of immigration. If it wasn't sound, the city might collapse. Ferré didn't alter his stance. Three thousand or twenty-three thousand, all were welcome.

CHAPTER 14

The implications were obvious if you were Miamian. Of course, the city would be the chosen destination of those now in the Peruvian embassy. However, another problem had already entered Miami, only now had it been measured. The extent of South Florida's contamination by cocaine was remarkable, because the contagion had been caused by so few people. Mariel's immigrants were measured in the tens of thousands. Illegal Colombians in the narcotics industry were never more than a few hundred, often arriving with impeccable fake passports, occasionally deported, often returning within days in unregistered boats or private aircraft. The Dade County state attorney's office intuited the effect. The limited number of Colombians hadn't annexed South Florida, but in under two years "they have made it a free zone" where they conducted their business, their travel, and their crimes as if American law didn't exist.

Had anyone in Miami been following portly Isaac Kassin Kattan in the red Chevy Citation that spring, they would have been amazed at his habits. The forty-six-year-old Colombian pulled a U-turn across Biscayne Boulevard, came to a stop where no stops were legal, in front of a bank, and waved the security guard over. Together, they lugged two heavy suitcases into the bank and over to a teller's cage. Each contained hundreds of thousands of dollars in fives, tens, and twenties. It was a familiar routine for Kattan, a trip he took every day the bank was open.

The cash that had buoyed Miami's economy during Carter's year of ever-rising interest rates wasn't simply from the trade with Latin America that Mayor Ferré had carefully nurtured; it was the creation of an entirely new line of business. Isaac Kattan, a money launderer, was the dark, inverted reflection of Ferré's dream. Cocaine was a Latin enterprise, vastly lucrative, relying on Spanish speakers who manned the necessary infrastructure, the Latin "companies" that used Miami as a perfect base for vertical integration. Down south they had the coca harvests, the maceration pits, the manufacture, and the means of concealment. South Florida was about transportation, distribution, and banking, just as Ferré had intended. Isaac Kattan was the final node in a network. The rapid rise of the cocaine business meant little without a financier knowledgeable enough to hide and then shift the narcotics profits.

In Washington, DC, the Treasury Department could look out across the United States and expect to find every one of its twelve federal banks running a surplus or deficit of approximately $100 million. That number would indicate how much money needed to be added or withdrawn from a particular region. But instead of a deficit of $100 million, Miami had suddenly run a surplus of $5.5 *billion* in 1979. The Treasury Department ran the numbers again, amazed. Then they projected the numbers for the coming year. Nineteen eighty would bring at least a $7 billion surplus.

There simply weren't any legitimate businesses that could contribute that much cash to a regional economy. Even established East Coast criminal operators like the Mafia had never operated on that scale. Tourism, Florida's most famous industry, netted only $5.2 billion a year. The only answer was drugs. It could now be added to race and immigration as one of three unavoidable crises buffeting Miami at exactly the same time.

During the late 1970s, due to all the aggressive and intelligent steps taken at the city level by Mayor Ferré and at the state level by Governor Bob Graham, South Florida had made extraordinary advances in establishing itself as a viable alternative to New York for international banking. It had been part of Ferré's strategy of turning the city to face south. The first way to do that was to make Miami a service center for Latin American banking, in the same way European money flowed through London and Frankfurt.

Ferré's plan had been highly successful. Forty-three banks from around the world now had offices in Miami. Thanks to Graham, as of June 1980, international banking transactions would be exempted from certain taxes, lowering the cost of conducting offshore financial operations for any company working through a Florida bank.

If drugs were now being directed at the United States, the corrupting influence of their early profits was already being felt to the south. As drug money undermined rickety institutions in countries such as Colombia and Bolivia, Miami benefited from legitimate capital flight of those South American citizens looking for a safe financial haven. That money headed to South Florida and was eagerly greeted by the area's banks. Many of those same banks had also welcomed drug dollars with few questions. The legitimate capital flight and illegitimate drug dollars mingled with local currency, emerging the same shade of green, making it all but impossible to separate good money from bad.

In the world of Washington bureaucracy, where initiatives were usually drowned quietly in internal committees, Operation Greenback moved forward with extraordinary speed. It was going to be a multi-agency affair, consisting of federal prosecutors, customs, the IRS, a group from the Drug Enforcement Administration (DEA), and one from the FBI. In theory, each agency would provide a minimum of seven men or women and cooperate in a regional investigation into the cocaine business. It would be based in Miami and led by Puerto Rican Jorge Rios-Torres, the only Spanish-speaking federal prosecutor in the Bureau of Narcotics and Dangerous Drugs. Indiana's Charlie Blau, a tall, bluff midwesterner who had grown up on the Missouri border, would now bolster his efforts. Rios-Torres and Blau were charged with identifying who was moving and laundering money and how they were doing it. Equally important, they were supposed to take note of whether they had the necessary legal tools to combat the laundering.

The question was easy to answer. In 1980, there was not a single anti–money laundering law in existence. Greenback was armed only with the Bank Secrecy Act, and the knowledge that anyone bringing $5,000 into or out of the country was supposed to fill out a form. Those who didn't fill out the form could be fined and jailed for up to five years. For the moment, that was all Greenback had.

Working with Rios-Torres was a customs attorney who had done some number crunching early in the year. Yes, 1980 was set to generate an extraordinary $7 billion surplus. But it was worse than that. The attorney confirmed the Treasury estimates that the drug-related underground economy in Dade County could create $411 billion a year. To him, it was a terrifying number. If withdrawn from the American economy, then "the vacuum that would be created would constitute a clear and present danger to the national security of the United States." Greenback was like a freshly appointed doctor asked to have a look at a virulent new disease. Having agreed that this could be the basis of a pandemic, Greenback was told to do the best it could with a bandage and a bottle of aspirin, much like the Coast Guard in response to Mariel.

———

Miami's $411 billion shadow economy was a double worry: the regional economy actually benefited from cocaine, while the national economy could be destroyed by its withdrawal. If cocaine had been legal, then the money launderer Isaac Kattan would have been considered one of the pioneers in a vibrant industry aimed at North America and beyond. Instead, Kattan carried with him a poison that could kill everything Ferré was working for. There they were, one man sitting astride a newfound empire, another who had lost one. For the moment, Kattan and Ferré shared Miami, living in neighboring buildings near the financial heart of the city—Ferré in the Santa Maria estate and Kattan in the up-start residential tower next door, Villa Regina. Work was no different. Kattan kept offices for his travel agency in the Dupont Plaza Hotel, next to one of the Ferré family's old holdings.

Kattan's family, Sephardic Jews, had fled to Syria from Germany in the early 1930s. Before the Second World War, Kattan's mother's family had established a successful textile business, manufacturing men's and women's underwear in western Colombia. By 1955, the family relocated to Cali, Colombia, where Kattan's father began working as an accountant for both emerald and coffee exporters.

Kattan now lived in an apartment on Brickell Avenue, just another Latin businessman who preferred to hover close to the center of Miami. Five foot nine, 195 pounds, thick around the middle, he was kind, polite, and fluent in English and Spanish. A local real estate specialist estimated that 40 percent of all sales of over $300,000 around Miami were paid for "with money that smells." Kattan was responsible for many of those purchases, buying and selling apartments to use as stash houses in a continuous attempt to limit the knowledge and movement of his own couriers. All the apartments were spartan. Only Kattan's home held the spoils of his money-laundering operation: a new Apple computer, five electronic counting machines, and a Western Union telex machine that he used to speculate on gold bullion and deutsche marks.

The family also ran a travel agency, Viaje Pacifico, and a currency exchange house. Both legitimate businesses had been established in the 1960s by Kattan's father. Currency control laws in Colombia were highly restrictive by the end of the 1970s. If you were Colombian, you couldn't hold, import, or export dollars. Travel agencies and currency exchange houses were the exceptions to the rule. That made Isaac Kattan an obvious source for legitimate Colombian businessmen. In Cali or Bogotá they could give him pesos. In the United States, he could credit their overseas accounts in dollars so they could buy merchandise for their businesses without paying the exorbitant government exchange rates.

Kattan did not have to create a new shop for this laundering operation, only expand the two arms of an established family business. In 1977, he formed a partnership with Jaime Escobar, the man responsible for the financial side of Medellín's fledgling cocaine industry. Cocaine bosses had a problem entirely unlike that of Colombia's businessmen. They had far too many dollars in the United States and needed pesos to buy chemicals and settle their accounts in Peru and Bolivia, where their coca was grown and converted into paste. Kattan was the matchmaker between pesos and dollars, between the legitimate and the illegitimate. The true beauty was that he was in a position to charge on both ends of the transaction.

Kattan's name had already been raised and dismissed by customs and by IRS agents unconnected to the new team at Greenback. Rather than trying to skirt American laws, Kattan complied with them. He dutifully filled out currency transaction reports, and it was a stack of those documents that had first drawn the attention of Operation Greenback. They already knew Kattan's name, but for the moment, there were so many potential suspects to concentrate on that they were in no way ready to follow, let alone arrest, him. To Kattan, 1980 was merely a continuation of the last two stunningly successful years. There was no reason to worry. While the men and women involved with cocaine distribution remained in the United States illegally, Kattan was simply a well-behaved Colombian citizen, signer of customs forms, dotter of i's, crosser of t's. He adhered to immigration rules. And in the spring of 1980, there were many more urgent ways for the United States to allocate resources than to start tracking the business dealings of the portly financier. He could legally fly into the country with dollars he had supposedly acquired from American tourists in Colombia, as long as he declared the amounts to customs. In 1979, he carried $90 million into or out of New York and Miami.

For the moment, Kattan could be forgiven for thinking that his 1980 was going to be as untroubled as the previous year, when he'd personally laundered over $300 million for cocaine traffickers. His own income in 1979, at a time when the CEO of Chevrolet made $1.6 million, was estimated at $28 million, making him perhaps the highest-paid middleman in the United States.

Miami faced an awaiting tide of immigrants, including hundreds who were likely to be drawn to the cocaine industry, a race-charged trial of a dead marine, and a wave of money never seen before in American history. Race was at least a familiar battleground. Immigration, even large-scale, was something Miami had seen before. But the cocaine-tinged $7 billion that floated around Miami carried a temptation that immediately corrupted everyone from real estate brokers and developers to lawyers, car dealers, and PSD detectives.

CHAPTER 15

Miami was not a city that needed any more criminals. On a foggy day in early May, the *Miami Herald* noted a new record in Dade County: four murders in four hours. Though she despised politics, Buchanan could still have given an accurate reading of Miami's current temperature. It was close to boiling. The murders were up yet again, but increasing at a bizarre rate, and this was *before* any of the newly arrived immigrants with criminal records had a chance to add to her or Capt. Marshall Frank's woes.

After the McDuffie investigation had settled, Buchanan had spent part of the early spring on Miami's strangest murder cases. Again and again, they began to include the word "cocaine." It was hard to remember that Buchanan was a crime reporter and not a homicide reporter. In early March, she'd attended a cocaine bust in Opa-locka, a city of fanciful minarets just north of Miami. She'd waited over three hours for a locksmith to open a warehouse safe, only to find the second-largest haul of cocaine yet recorded. She penned the rare Buchanan article without a body, but she had caught the importance of the connection. The safe, in effect, held $20 million. These were the stakes *behind* the bloodshed she covered.

To make matters worse for Miami, only seven of Marshall Frank's fifteen day-shift detectives were left to cover homicides, thanks to the ongoing cocaine corruption investigation. The FBI's public flaying of the PSD's homicide bureau over the Escandar case strengthened the distrust between federal and local agencies. Cooperation was unlikely, but without cooperation it was hard to see how the complicated riddles of cocaine-related violence would be unraveled. Publicly, Marshall Frank told Buchanan that Miami was becoming a "homicide factory." Privately, of all the incongruous thoughts, Frank kept returning to Lucille Ball's struggles on the assembly line in *I Love Lucy*, where willing hands and good intentions couldn't cope with an impossible pace.

There was a growing sense that Ferré's Miami, spotlit just months before as a city of great promise by the *Financial Times*, was now flailing. Black Miami was filled with talk about Tampa and the McDuffie trial. The hundreds of boats still in Mariel only pointed to the fact that there were still thousands and thousands of refugees heading toward Miami, while the money moving through the hands of money launderers like Isaac Kattan was slowly destroying every institution and individual it touched.

When Edna Buchanan looked closely at the four who had died in four hours, she found the oddities. "The corpse had a familiar face," one of her articles began. It was about a Colombian man murdered a month after his brother. Another of the day's victims was the wife of a bicyclist murdered a year before. As if rising in levels of difficulty, the final murder of the day was a public execution in the international arrivals hall of the Miami airport: another Colombian, another connection to cocaine. A murder designed to horrify the Chamber of Commerce, it would be Buchanan's last stop of a busy day.

The flight from Bogotá had landed at midnight on May 8. A young Colombian, Carlos Murcia Fajardo, walked in step with his pregnant wife. He was pushing a wheelchair containing a disfigured woman, swathed in bandages. At the end of February, his sister-in-law had been shot thirty times. Fajardo's brother had been assassinated beside her. She was coming to Miami for treatment. As they waited for their luggage, a blue Honda motorbike arrived on the lower concourse. The passenger, riding pillion in a baby-blue three-piece suit and a wraparound helmet, hopped off and walked calmly into the airport. He approached the couple, pushed the wheelchair backward, and fired five times at Fajardo, hitting him twice in the head.

If Mariel was about to graft one country's prison population onto an American city, Buchanan was realizing that another country's violence had already been exported. If you added Miami's homegrown criminals, it was obvious the city was about to face a crime wave from three different avenues at exactly the same time its police force had been hollowed out by the corruption of cocaine money.

When Buchanan dug into the airport murder, she found that Fajardo had emerald interests in Colombia. He'd declared $250,000 in emeralds at customs, but the killer hadn't paused to search the dead man's pockets. In a world of multimillion-dollar cocaine deals, $250,000 in emeralds was a secondary consideration.

The airport murder was the sort of case where detectives had plenty of suspicions and little in the way of facts. They had stopped a woman at the airport who was there to meet Fajardo and who admitted knowing him but hadn't seen the murder. There was no reason to arrest her. With such a thorough separation between local and federal agencies, how could Marshall Frank's detectives know that she had been followed all day by the DEA? Their surveillance team had only retired at midnight, when the flight was landing. Instead of following up with a promised visit to the homicide bureau, the woman fled to Bogotá. A week later, she was arrested with 137 kilograms of cocaine. She was tied directly to Carlos Jader Álvarez, one of a group of four men thought to control a third of the Colombian cocaine industry in 1980. With an estimated net worth of half a billion dollars, he had a favored money launderer in Miami: Isaac Kattan.

Frank's detectives had little to follow up on. The murder had become fodder for the dark humor of the bureau, detectives reenacting the moment the bandaged woman in the wheelchair was sent spinning across the lower concourse by the killer, but it only hid the helplessness beneath. It was just another addition to Frank's least favorite designation: "Offender: Unknown." You could chase the murderers, but they were faceless. Captain Marshall Frank didn't have a single lead on a Colombian killer in the summer of 1980, despite the cordwood stack of dead accumulating in Doc Davis's county morgue.

The presumed truth of the cocaine business was that the moneymen stayed away from the drugs and the blood, and the assassins stayed away from the money. In theory, the two never intersected. Isaac Kattan, for instance, never carried a weapon. He had four full-time couriers, always unarmed. Instead, he relied on a complex network of safe houses and multiple banks. Complexity and movement were the antidotes to risk, not stasis and weaponry.

Kattan was insulated from the murders, but there was always the threat of violence. He worked for traffickers from both Medellín and Cali. He traveled interminably between both Colombian cities, and to Bogotá, Miami, and New York. There was no shortage of hit men in any one of those cities. One gang, run by Miami-based Paco Sepulveda, kept approximately twenty-five men in Dade County and New York and another twenty in Colombia. Kattan was favored by all sides because he was cautious, professional, and extremely good at what he did. But there was a time in every transaction, between the money being dropped off in one of his apartments in Brickell and its passage into Miami's financial system, when he was entirely accountable for it. Roughly $1 million a day passed through his hands. Every afternoon, Isaac Kattan spent hours on the telephone, running over figures with his clients in Colombia. Discrepancies and dollar figures were relentlessly examined. If there were mistakes or errors, Edna Buchanan's stories in the *Miami Herald* were ample evidence that there was no safe place in the city of Miami. You could be gunned down in an airport at midnight or in a liquor store in the middle of the day.

There wasn't much remarkable about the assassins. They were mostly country boys from the coffee-growing hills around Medellín who now lurked on the fringes of Colombian cocaine society in Miami. They had as much in common with an urbane sophisticate like Kattan as a Mississippi farmhand does with a Wall Street banker. One, called Anibal Jaramillo, part of Sepulveda's twenty-five-strong team in Miami, was typical of the men Capt. Marshall Frank looked for but could not find. He had multiple names, birthdays, and addresses. He also had steady work. One by one, Sepulveda's men had disposed of a gang known as the Pajaritos. Made up of young men who were fond of sports cars, they ran a business locating and then robbing their fellow Colombians during cocaine transactions. By March 1980, they were all inside Davis's morgue, the last gunned down outside a strip mall at lunchtime. Buchanan had arrived in time to see the body lying next to a black-and-gold Trans Am.

Jaramillo was rare for only one reason. The police already had a set of his fingerprints, albeit under an alias on a fake driving license. The prints had been taken two years before, on Biscayne Boulevard, when he'd been arrested trying to buy a friend a little more time in the back of his car with a hooker. A policeman had arrived, and Jaramillo quickly found himself charged with obstruction of justice.

Men like Anibal Jaramillo didn't need to speak English. They just carried lawyers' business cards in their back pockets and handed them to arresting officers. On a relatively light charge like obstruction, they were usually back on the streets within the day. It was a close-knit world; it no longer surprised Frank's squad that the Pajaritos, before their deaths, were represented by the same lawyers representing the group suspected of having killed them.

Unlike the asylum seekers of Mariel, the Colombians under Sepulveda weren't concerned with their legality or political persecution. They were the by-products of an enormously lucrative business spun around a dozen Miami money launderers like Isaac Kattan. Without the flow of money back south, the whole cocaine industry would have ground to a halt. A few hundred Colombians making billions of dollars in the United States were much more inconspicuous than they should have been. And yet, as of May 1980, Marshall Frank's men hadn't arrested a single enforcer or found a way into Colombian circles. The threat from Mariel grew and grew alongside the Colombian cocaine industry. But it was the Coast Guard rather than PSD homicide that correctly envisaged the first wave of death from Mariel. It would come during the boatlift, not in its troubled wake.

CHAPTER 16

The *Olo Yumi*, a thirty-six-foot-long twin-screw vessel, had left Mariel before dawn, grossly overloaded for the 110-mile crossing. Even before Janet Fix had departed Mariel on May 1, it had been noted by the *Herald* that boats were being deliberately overloaded despite the fact that there were still hundreds of vessels in the Mariel harbor. On the morning of May 17, though many boats had been prevented from leaving by Cuban authorities due to the twenty-knot winds, the *Olo Yumi* and three others were led into the straits by a Cuban patrol boat, guided to the edge of their territorial waters, and abandoned.

The seas were running at a choppy five feet, far from their worst, far from their best. The *Olo Yumi* was captained by a twenty-six-year-old Miami tow truck driver named Salvador Ojeda. He had set out in his mother's boat to collect seven family members. Soldiers on the docks of Mariel had boarded an extra forty-four passengers. "We had to take them," said Ojeda, referring to the mixture of families and single men directed aboard the *Olo Yumi*. "I wanted to take fewer, but they would have not given me my family." He had brought approximately twenty-five extra life jackets. The winds continued to rise.

Only two days before, Carter had sat in the Oval Office making final edits to a statement on Mariel. He changed the phrase "our country has provided a safe haven for these people," to "our country has provided a safe haven for *many of* these people." He corrected the text from supporting all members of Cuban American families to "close family members."

Carter also read the increasing danger of the situation. The real threat, he concluded, was that Castro had "callously played on the emotions of the Cuban American community, luring small, unsafe boats to venture on dangerous and unlawful trips to Cuba." Finally, he ordered an immediate end to the boatlift, but neither the navy nor the Coast Guard had control of Cuban waters. Hours before the *Olo Yumi* departed, *Granma*, the Cuban state newspaper, blithely announced that the sealift would not be stopped. "Carter governs in Florida, but in Mariel, Cuba governs."

To his credit, the president had done his best to make the seas safer. Carter had ordered extra Coast Guard vessels south, and then diverted the thirty-four ships from the US Navy to assist. In clear weather, even a myopic boat captain could have ignored nautical charts and simply followed the gray, steel-plated hulls of Coast Guard and navy ships all the way from Cuban waters to the docks of Key West. Carter certainly had no control over *when* boats left Mariel. As he wrote of Castro's calculated callousness, there would be no better example than the *Olo Yumi*.

Before leaving, the *Olo Yumi*'s passengers had been assured by Cuban authorities that the seas would remain calm. Even as the boat pulled out of Mariel, trouble began. With an engine sputtering in waters twenty-eight miles north of the harbor, the waves grew high enough to break across the boat. The Coast Guard had feared this kind of incident from the start of the boatlift.

By 8:15 a.m., one of the boat's two engines had died, and Ojeda was struggling to steer in the rising seas. It drifted beam to the wind, the widest point of the boat facing directly into the waves. Refugees stumbled aft, trying to help with regaining control of the steering. But having the passengers crowded close to the motors only made the boat more vulnerable. The ocean suddenly swept directly into the *Olo Yumi*. It was a green water loading, wherein the deck is submerged by rolling waves. The ship tipped upward, then dragged to one side, and capsized within seconds. Few were wearing their life jackets. Passengers either tried to get a purchase, or leapt into the ocean. As the prow rose, those who'd tried to hold on now fell on top of one another as they crashed into the water.

Most of the children had been herded into a small cabin belowdecks. One of the adults in the cabin managed to break a window as the ship tilted and began to fill rapidly with water. A twenty-five-year-old English teacher crawled through the glass, slicing his finger, leaving it hanging by the skin. A man known only as Reinaldo, a prisoner forced aboard the boat, passed children through the broken window. After he had pushed a tenth child through the hole, the cabin was fully submerged. He was the first to drown. For all the worry in Miami, here was a prisoner who had died saving lives.

Flailing passengers swam around the upturned blue hull desperate to find something, anything to help keep them afloat. Some had suffered broken arms and collarbones. All bobbed helplessly in the mounting seas.

The two fifty-five gallon drums of gasoline Ojeda had kept on deck for the return journey now rocked on their side, spilling their contents and creating a slick around the boat. A retired physician hung on to an upturned table. One father, traveling with a ten-year-old son and five-year-old daughter, saw a life jacket floating fifty meters from the *Olo Yumi*. His son splashed through the salt and gasoline to recover the life jacket. Swallowing a mixture of the two, he vomited, turned, and splashed back toward his sister, pulling her arms through the life jacket. The English teacher floating nearby continued to worry, not about drowning but about the presence of sharks that might be drawn to the blood from his lacerated finger.

Fourteen-year-old Ibis Guerrero had been thrown into the sea alongside her two sisters, her grandmother, her father, and her mother. She was the only one of them wearing a life jacket. For an hour and a half, they clung in a circle to the upturned boat as it slowly sank. Only the top five feet of the *Olo Yumi* were visible above the waves by 10:45 a.m. The gasoline, which had tickled the skin the first hour, now seemed to be burning it. Guerrero watched as her grandmother sank under the waves. The family screamed for help, together at first, then in bursts, then not at all. In the six-foot chop, it was impossible for any of the swimmers to be spotted by sailors in another vessel.

A thirty-six-year-old steelworker choked with tears when he saw the father of a five-year-old boy swept away by the current. The boy's mother, paddling near him, handed the steelworker her child. "Take care of my baby for me," she said, and sank under the waters. An hour before, he'd pulled off his trousers in the water, knowing he had his life savings of $1,500 sewn into the seams, and let them sink—anything to stay afloat with his own child. With the help of a life jacket, he now struggled to keep both children alive.

Ibis Guerrero lost her father next. Then her mother. Finally, her two sisters disappeared under the waves. She had gone from the youngest in an exiled family of six to an orphan in under an hour. Another mother handed Guerrero her four-year-old son, then also sank under the water.

Five days before, the *Courageous*, a Coast Guard cutter, had been diverted to the Bahamas to assist in a search-and-rescue operation after Cuban MIGs had sunk a local fishing vessel they claimed had strayed into Cuban waters, killing four men. On the seventeenth, at 11:03 a.m., the only thing that caught the eye of the *Courageous*'s helicopter pilot on a routine surveillance patrol was the light shining off the last remaining piece of the *Olo Yumi*'s prow still above water.

As the helicopter passed over the bow of the sinking ship, its crew could see two or three people clinging to it. The water was dotted with people, some facedown, some waving upward, some wearing life jackets, some clinging to pieces of wood. One man had managed to lash himself to a butane tank and bobbed awkwardly in the waves. Immediately, they lowered the winch and began to hoist up the desperate refugees as the pilot radioed in their position to the *Courageous*.

As the distraught passengers were pulled aboard the chopper, the Coast Guard hoist man noticed that their skin sloughed off, burned by the acidic mixture of salt water and gasoline. Helicopter winches, in general, were fickle. This one proved no better. After the eleventh survivor was hauled aboard, the winch burned out. The helicopter pilot had no choice. It tilted and moved off.

The *Courageous*'s two twenty-six-foot motor surfboats were thumping through swells of up to eight feet, powering toward the survivors. The Coast Guard cutter *Vigorous*, a little farther away, also had surfboats heading toward the distressed vessel. As they approached, the prow of the *Olo Yumi* disappeared. The surfboats dropped rescue nets over the side and began recovering survivors. Swimmers jumped into the water to help push the refugees up into the craft. Three more helicopters arrived. Ibis Guerrero was pulled to safety, too stunned to speak. After twenty minutes spent recovering the passengers, the helicopters pulled up and away and the surfboats withdrew. "All that was left were some empty life jackets floating about, dotting the dark green water like oversized chunks of last night's confetti."

The survivors were taken from the *Courageous* to the *Saipan*, a vast amphibious assault ship with a crew of eight hundred, including three doctors. The ship had a full working hospital. One doctor tried to cut off the sodden clothing from the survivors, but they were all in the same condition; their skin so badly burned by the mixture of gasoline and salt water that it came away with the clothes. Children, their stomachs filled with salt water and gasoline, suffered from vomiting and diarrhea.

The dead were delivered directly to Key West by helicopter into the middle of a new form of chaos, stunning in color and variation, with the FEMA-coordinated mission now fully underway. In the skies above, military planes roared in with twenty-seven tons of C rations. There were shiny leather gun belts of the National Guard, Highway Patrol troopers, Marine Patrol officers, Border Patrol officers, local police, and six hundred more prostitutes, many of whom had set up shop at the back of the hangar, using cardboard boxes and blankets to hide their work.

The next day Ibis Guerrero, still in such shock that she had barely said a word since her rescue, was given a dose of Valium before she entered the Lopez Funeral Home. "I'm not going to cry," she said, "because so many people have died and I want to be strong." One by one, the caskets were opened for her to say goodbye to her family members. She stopped for the longest time in front of the body of her sister. "She looks older, she looks different," whispered Guerrero. "She doesn't look like my sister."

The *Olo Yumi* was definitive proof that Cuban authorities were deliberately overloading the departing boats, letting passengers and ex-prisoners travel without life jackets, and breaking international laws of the sea that they themselves were signatories to. Cuban authorities disagreed. They claimed that they were allowing fewer people on board than the American captains demanded, and that overcrowding "was the result of American greed." The first accusation was dubious. The second was a lie. No one paid American captains to bring strangers or prisoners to Key West.

In one of the strangest coincidences, the same morning the *Olo Yumi* had set sail, Héctor Sanyustiz, the man who had initiated the boatlift, was finally taken to Mariel. The previous day, May 16, his wife and young son had arrived at his bedside. Family reunification, the same ploy Castro had used to tempt Cuban Americans to Mariel, was now dangled in front of Sanyustiz. The man who had sworn he wouldn't leave Cuba without the other bus passengers now changed his mind. He was taken to Mariel and asked to pick a ship. Ignoring the smaller vessels like the *Olo Yumi*, Sanyustiz chose the largest ship in Mariel and arrived among eight hundred.

Docking before the sobering news of the *Olo Yumi* had spread, Héctor Sanyustiz was processed in a crowded hangar where he was recognized by a friend. In a sea of thousands of refugees, a voice came over the loudspeaker, asking for silence. "We're here thanks to one bus driver. And he's reached the same freedom you have! He's here with us!" Sanyustiz felt a deep satisfaction at the roar of approval. Like so many others from Mariel, he began life in America in a ramshackle hotel on Miami Beach. For a man who craved anonymity, his timing was perfect: he arrived on May 17, possibly the worst day in the history of Miami, ensuring that his story was ignored by the press. It would be eighteen years before a nephew of his rang the *Herald* and Miami remembered that the Father of Mariel had always been among them.

The *Olo Yumi* would prove to be the greatest loss of life in the Mariel boatlift. The near misses were numerous. The Coast Guard saved all 200 refugees whose ship ran aground on a reef; another 354 refugees were towed in on the day the *Olo Yumi* sank. In total, eighty-three boats were guided out of Mariel that day into seven-foot seas delivering the boatlift its 51,000th refugee. The *Miami Herald*'s worst-case scenario for the city had arrived in less than three weeks, a fact unnoted because it came on the very same morning as the verdict in the McDuffie trial.

PART 3

CHAPTER 17

A month before the sinking of the *Olo Yumi*, Assistant State Attorney George Yoss had risen in a Tampa courtroom to deliver the opening statement of the McDuffie trial. The *Miami News* had described him as short in stature, boyish, and fierce. Yoss, dressed in a beige suit and red tie, was primed for a trial conducted in front of television cameras, a packed courtroom, and nineteen print journalists. He showed quiet anger, calm, and resolve, and yet at the outset, it was hard to shake the sense that he was an actor reading a script. Speaking without pause for two hours, Yoss detailed the McDuffie chase as he stared down the five well-dressed defendants.

As Yoss described the final moments of McDuffie's beating by the county police, he found his rhythm, growing louder and louder. "The evidence is going to show," said Yoss, moving toward the jury, "that at this point Arthur McDuffie wasn't talking, he wasn't saying anything, he wasn't moving, he wasn't fighting, he wasn't doing anything. He especially wasn't reaching for anybody's gun."

Suddenly Yoss marched back across the courtroom toward one particular officer. In a furious gesture, he jabbed a finger at the defendant so fast that one of his co-defendants had to push himself back in his chair to avoid contact. "This man," said Yoss, full of anger, "Alex Marrero, declared a one-sided war against Arthur McDuffie." Marrero stared straight through Yoss, his thinning sandy hair swept across his forehead, dark brows arched over a pair of eyes that seemed to be far, far away.

Yoss paused and then reversed course, rushing back toward the jury, stopping a meter short. "And he stood there over him, with the man handcuffed and his hands behind his back . . . and picked up his Kel-Lite and struck him, right on the head, not once, not twice, but three times. That second time, he struck him so hard blood splattered in excess of four feet away." Eula Mae McDuffie sat quietly in a light blue dress listening to the step-by-step description of how her son was beaten and how over a dozen police officers then conspired to cover up his death.

"There's no tighter fraternity than a police fraternity," said Yoss, near the end of his statement. "They have a code . . . You don't turn in evidence against a fellow officer and you don't rat on a cop."

Yoss straightened up. He nodded at the jury. There was silence as he concluded. Eula McDuffie rose, holding her bag in one hand, and left the courtroom.

There was just one small chink in Yoss's statement. If the thin blue line was so revered and had led to such an elaborate cover-up after such a repellent crime, then who were the men that Yoss had built his case around? He and fellow assistant state attorney Hank Adorno had immunized three policemen. The third, granted immunity just before the trial began, went by the nickname "Mad Dog." He had been immunized against Marshall Frank's advice. "What if he turns out to be one of your worst beaters?" the homicide captain had asked the assistant state attorneys. All three men had crossed the thin blue line, but neither the defense nor the prosecution could foresee if the jury would view them as liars, traitors, or men finally driven by their conscience to do the right thing.

But there was a very different worry for the television audience that tuned in that night from the houses and apartments in Overtown and Liberty City. Every single one of the six jurors Yoss had been talking to were middle-aged white men. Five defendants meant five defense lawyers. With the uptick in Miami's crime rate, the city had become a nursery for deeply experienced defense lawyers. The five appearing at the McDuffie trial had recently all worked in the state attorney's office. One had been a favorite for the job that Janet Reno now held.

The battle for jury selection had begun back on March 31 and immediately turned into a siege. Any hope that Circuit Judge Lenore Nesbitt held out for a quick return to Miami disappeared in the first two weeks, when the prosecution and defense failed to seat a single juror. In theory, defendants were guaranteed a jury of their peers. In practice, in 1980 Florida, jury selection was manipulated through the use of "peremptory challenges" and "challenges for cause." A peremptory challenge didn't need any explanation; a lawyer could object to any juror for no reason at all. In the McDuffie case, the defense issued these objections like acts of legalistic lightning, striking every black body that took to the stand. The prosecution, no less conspicuously, picked off anyone with connections to law enforcement.

In the three weeks that passed between the beginning of the search for a jury and George Yoss's opening statement on behalf of the prosecution, there was a reminder of geography. The Mariel boatlift and the McDuffie trial could sometimes seem bizarrely synchronized. Not only had Héctor Sanyustiz been released from prison on the day of Arthur McDuffie's beating, but as George Yoss had shaken his finger at Alex Marrero, the first boat from Miami had reached Mariel.

Mariel was the most recent proof that Ferré was right; Miami belonged as much to the Caribbean and Latin America as to the United States. The McDuffie trial proved Tampa belonged to Florida. It was a city with a distinct Anglo majority that the United States Commission on Civil Rights believed dealt very leniently with white officers accused of killing black suspects. Had the trial been held in Miami six weeks later, a jury of six representing the new demographics of Miami would have had one black juror, three Cuban Americans, and two Anglos. The American idea of race, a matter of black and white, would have been filtered by first-generation immigrants operating in a second language.

Miami's sins would be measured by the citizens of Hillsborough County, three hundred miles away. For black Miami, the seating of an all-white jury brought a sudden change in mood. Only weeks earlier, after a march where a fake coffin was carried to the steps of the Dade County

Courthouse, the charges against Officer Alex Marrero had been upped from manslaughter to second-degree murder. There had been relief that the charges now reflected the crime.

That was not how the defense attorneys felt. Presenting their own opening statements, the five agreed that this wasn't a trial but a politicized show trial, with their clients being offered as scapegoats to Miami politics. They blazed into the courtroom describing the trial as a "witch hunt." One defendant hadn't even arrived until after the beating because of a damaged rim on his patrol car. What was he on trial for, asked his attorney, "the felonious changing of a tire?"

The defense attorneys came up with a different scenario that they would be laying out for the jury: not one of the five defendants was responsible for Arthur McDuffie's death. The culprits, they suggested, were the three immunized officers who would be taking the stand as state's witnesses. Any blows that were landed by the defendants were the result of the victim's having fought "like hell." Ed O'Donnell, Marrero's ursine lawyer, was the most aggressive. His client, the only man accused of murder, was being hung out to dry by his department, O'Donnell said. He had been designated the lead witch of the witch hunt, and O'Donnell believed he could prove that the opposite was true: Marrero was the only policeman who had committed an act of heroism. After three weeks of inaction as the jury was selected, O'Donnell's aggressive stance was electrifying.

The *Herald*'s most decorated reporter had selected himself to cover the trial. Gene Miller, awarded two Pulitzer Prizes, was "the God of criminal journalism," with the leeway in the newsroom to pick and choose his subjects. He was the one journalist his fellow reporters studied at the trial. They watched him greet all the defense attorneys, watched them acknowledge him with smiles or, like Ed O'Donnell, walk over to shake his hand. If South Florida was considered to have one voice at the trial, it was Miller's. How Miller saw the trial would shape the expectations of half a million *Miami Herald* readers and their families.

After the trial began you could pick up the Spanish-language press, the black newspaper, and the *Herald* in the same week and assume you were reading papers from three different cities. *El Miami Herald* focused on the Peruvian embassy. The *Miami Times* on McDuffie. The *Miami Herald* headlined the struggling economy, the primary season, and the slow-motion drama of the Iranian hostages. Miller's trial coverage and Mariel were moving toward the center of the paper.

There was a notable absence in the courtroom: Gene Miller's friend Edna Buchanan. The journalist who'd initiated the investigation hoped to avoid the McDuffie trial altogether. One of the defense attorneys wanted the name of her original source back on December 21, but that was a secret Buchanan hadn't even shared with Gene Miller. When a subpoena server appeared in the *Herald*'s corridors, Buchanan slipped down the stairs and avoided her own car in case the server had doubled back to the parking lot. She wandered a couple of blocks to the Omni Mall and bought herself a pair of yellow shorts. It was the first time in 1980 she'd had a chance to shop.

The executive editor of the *Herald* had hidden Buchanan's notes in his own safe and offered her a free trip to the Bahamas until the end of the trial. Buchanan turned it down. Who'd walk the dogs or feed the cats? Who'd cover the crime? Just before the trial, a process server found Buchanan reading on her porch, and the *Herald* was forced into legal action to keep her from the stand.

Buchanan had implied to everyone that her original source needed to remain anonymous, though the source had reached back out to her, offering to cede anonymity. Buchanan turned the offer down, and instead the *Herald*'s lawyers worked double time, delaying the defense probing long enough for the case to pass her by. She sat at her desk as Miller settled down in Tampa for the duration of the trial, wondering if there would be any benefits from its being tried so far from the scene of the crime. In Judge Nesbitt's words, the trial was a "time bomb," but relocating her court seemed to Buchanan to be more like lengthening a fuse than disarming the device.

As the five defense lawyers had been shaping the jury alongside the prosecutors, Buchanan received a strange phone call. It was from Charles Veverka, one of the three immunized officers, now slated to be the first witness up in Tampa. He wanted to make a confession. He told Buchanan that he'd been so tortured by his involvement in the McDuffie beating that he had been the one who'd tipped her off back on December 21. He was, he claimed, her anonymous source.

Buchanan was incredulous. "It wasn't you," she said flatly. Veverka insisted that his voice sounded different because he'd disguised it at the time. Buchanan hung up on him, amazed. She'd known her source, the wife of a decorated police officer, for sixteen years. It worried Buchanan. If Veverka could attempt such a flagrant lie, then how seriously would he be taken as an immunized witness?

On the first day of his testimony, Veverka wore a dark suit and a white shirt with a long pointed collar. Guided by Yoss, he stood in front of the jury with a pointer aimed at an easel holding an aerial photograph of NW Thirty-Eighth Street. He was the first to reach McDuffie and said that he'd attempted to pull him off the Kawasaki but that McDuffie had "tried to take a punch at him."

"What did you do?" asked Yoss.

"I came back and hit him."

"With your right or your left hand?"

"My right."

"Hard or soft?"

"Hard."

"How hard?"

"As hard as I could."

Veverka described how McDuffie was then gang-tackled by several officers at once and torn from his grip. While McDuffie was being pummeled, Veverka backed away from the group and heard Marrero say, "Easy, one at a time." Once McDuffie had slumped to the ground, Marrero had planted one foot on either side of his prone body, which lay facedown, and struck him on the head with a Kel-Lite.

"Did he move between the blows?" asked Yoss.

"No, sir."

"Was he wearing a helmet?"

"No, sir."

"Was he reaching for a gun? Moving in any way?"

Again, "No, sir."

The blows had hit McDuffie's head so hard that Veverka, standing four feet away, had his boots bloodied.

Despite the testimony, Yoss was worried. Veverka's words were adequate, but everything about his performance had seemed reluctant. The defense went after Veverka for the entire second day. McDuffie's motorbike was wheeled into the courtroom, and Veverka was forced to go over how he'd dragged McDuffie off the back of the bike, how he'd struck him, how McDuffie had been tackled. And how, in the aftermath, Veverka had produced one report, then rewritten it, then rewritten it again: three different versions of the truth. The insinuation from the defense was clear. Veverka couldn't be considered the most credible of witnesses.

O'Donnell suggested that McDuffie was playing possum, pretending to be hurt, lying motionless on the pavement. "Weren't you calling him a nigger that night?" O'Donnell asked accusingly. "I might very well have," replied Veverka. O'Donnell could seem as if he were leaping about during cross-examination, but he was following a strict arc. Wherever he went, it circled back to a central theme. His client, Marrero, wasn't all that different from an immunized officer like Veverka. They'd chased the same man, used the same racist language during the struggle, fought the same fight, both admitted to using their full force striking blows against Arthur McDuffie. So why was one up for thirty years and the other walking free?

It got worse. The second police witness, also immunized, agreed with much of what Veverka had said, including the description of Marrero's terrifying participation. But he raised two major discrepancies. First, he testified that he had clearly heard McDuffie say, after pulling over, "I give up!" Second, he swore that McDuffie had never tried to punch Veverka in the first place. It was a sobering thought. If McDuffie had never thrown a punch, then all four officers facing manslaughter should have been facing murder-two charges.

By the time the third immunized witness testified, Yoss felt queasy. When William F. "Mad Dog" Hanlon took the stand, he was chewing gum. In the pages of the *Miami Herald*, Gene Miller's dislike came across immediately. Miller described Hanlon as "a squat, mean, reluctant ex-cop." Judge Nesbitt had him spit his gum into the bailiff's Kleenex.

Sitting before prosecutor George Yoss, Hanlon explained that, when he had arrived at the scene, McDuffie was no longer wearing a helmet. Hanlon, using a sawed-off nightstick, jabbed McDuffie several times in the back, aiming at the kidneys. The blows didn't subdue McDuffie. Hanlon then put the nightstick around McDuffie's neck, one hand on each end, and yanked back, trying to choke McDuffie off his feet. Eventually, they toppled to the ground. Hanlon straddled McDuffie, grabbed his wrists, and handcuffed him. McDuffie never said a word.

Hanlon agreed with the other immunized witnesses that the hardest blows had been delivered by Marrero, and that all three blows came after Hanlon had finished handcuffing the suspect. He called the blows "very severe" and revealed that in the predominantly black Central District, the police had a rating for how hard they beat suspects who were resisting arrest. The scale went from 1 to 30. In the station later that morning, when McDuffie was still a John Doe in a coma, he had been awarded a 29.5.

Hanlon described how Marrero had only stopped the beating when they could hear the sirens from Fire Rescue. While McDuffie lay motionless on the ground and officers backed away, Hanlon had talked to Marrero about the best places to break a man's leg and then struck McDuffie about the knees. It was said almost casually in the courtroom, but it was a chilling concept—an officer paid to protect Miami's citizens might help beat a citizen unconscious and then try to break his legs.

Marrero, continued Hanlon, had grabbed his nightstick and struck two blows of his own against McDuffie's legs, "a little harder than I did." Then the cover-up had begun. Hanlon had kicked over the bike, riding a patrol car up over the front tire. He'd found a watch on the ground that he'd presumed was McDuffie's and pulled out his service revolver, aimed at the watch, shot, and missed.

"Why?" asked the prosecution, sounding genuinely perplexed.

"I don't know," Hanlon said, looking sheepish.

He smashed the watch and threw the pieces down a sewer grate. Later that day, when he'd gone with Marrero to the tow shop, he'd acted as a lookout while Marrero and another policeman had broken off the oil cover pan on McDuffie's Kawasaki, which usually came loose in motorcycle crashes. They'd thrown it in a Dumpster, returned to headquarters, and informed Internal Review about the motorcycle crash.

On cross-examination, Hanlon buckled. He was recalcitrant, petty, often monosyllabic, admitting he'd changed his story of McDuffie's beating. Back during his first statement in January, he had accused only city officers rather than his county brethren.

The defense attorneys went at Hanlon, digging into his past performance as a police officer, calling him "crazy, paranoid," "a man who believed his telephone was tapped, saw apparitions and suffered visions." Hadn't he run through a black man's house while trying to break up a party, and shattered every window on the first floor? Again and again, Hanlon couldn't explain his own behavior.

Yoss looked at the jury as Hanlon absorbed punishment during his cross-examination. He read disbelief that this man was even a police officer. Luckily, they still had Ronald Wright, the assistant medical examiner, to hear from, and the all-important testimony of Marrero himself would follow.

There was now a clear sign of danger for Miami. Ferré had his theory of politics as a wave the politician rode but could not affect. This was a trial that could change the form and speed of that wave. Ferré had done much for black Miami in his seven years as mayor. The largest-ever building project, valued at $50 million, was breaking ground in Overtown. He would appoint the first black city attorney and the first black city manager and had, in his first term, brought suit in Washington, DC, against his own white chief of police, demanding a change in how black neighborhoods were policed. But if the state attorneys were to obtain only slim sentences, then where would a community turn when it felt un-represented? Black Miami may have been the weakest of the city's three tribes economically, but unrest could unravel an *entire* city. You only had to go back a dozen years to see how Newark and Detroit had suffered from urban riots. They were hardly centers of investment a dozen years later. They were symbols of how cities could come apart and stay apart.

CHAPTER 18

George Yoss and Hank Adorno had their trickiest witnesses out of the way. Now came two long-serving, well-respected officers, a relief in a courtroom where little good had been said about a policeman since the start of the trial. These were Ferré's men from the City of Miami Police Department. One had been so repelled by what he saw when he'd reached the McDuffie scene that he'd quit the same day, after eighteen years of service. Shaking his head, he'd approached the inert McDuffie and squatted beside him just as McDuffie received his last punch in the face. The officer testified that he'd muttered aloud, "Either you're going to be a vegetable or you're going to die." Then he'd stepped back as Marrero had struck McDuffie's legs, calling him a motherfucker.

In the afternoon, the second City of Miami policeman testified he'd seen up to fifteen county cops swinging at McDuffie when he'd arrived and wondered what the man had done to deserve such a punishment. He'd watched McDuffie beaten to the ground and exhaled the words "Jesus Christ." Yoss could see the jury warming to the witness until, in a flash, the city cop "drove a king-sized hole through the prosecution case."

Asked to rise by the state attorneys, he was ordered to walk along the line of defendants and stop by the man he saw beat McDuffie on the ground. To Yoss and Adorno's shock, he walked past Marrero and stopped in front of Michael Watts, the officer Edna Buchanan had singled out as a problem cop. The witness knew Alex Marrero, had often seen him drinking coffee at the Ranch House Restaurant. He was certain that he never saw him strike a blow. Neither, it turned out, had the first city policeman who, pushed by O'Donnell, admitted that eight days after the beating he'd failed to pick Marrero out of a lineup.

"The McDuffie trial is growing more preposterous by the day," wrote the black-owned *Times*. "It has quickly reached the point where nothing at all is assured. These men should all be convicted and sent to prison, but that possibility impresses us as being remote." Black people, continued the article, "may just do themselves a favor by expecting the worst out of Tampa." In the *Herald*, Miller's reporting was nowhere near as pessimistic. Only rarely had he let opinion seep onto the page.

Attorneys from both sides had been confused by Miller's articles. Yoss worried that because of Miller's coverage, the citizens of Miami still presumed he and Hank Adorno had a great case. Yoss knew they didn't. O'Donnell was equally perplexed by Miller. He found himself puzzled when he spoke to his girlfriend back in Miami and she commiserated with him on a rough day in court. "Where'd you get that?" asked O'Donnell. The *Herald*, she'd say. If O'Donnell hadn't seen Miller there every day with his own eyes, he would have wagered that he hadn't stuck around for the cross-examinations. Both sets of attorneys understood the danger. Miller was the barometer of the city's expectations. If the state attorney failed to obtain convictions for the five defendants, Miami would be caught completely by surprise, and surprise could lead to outrage, and outrage could lead anywhere at all.

The prosecution was more optimistic and even cheered as the week moved forward. The physical evidence of Marshall Frank's investigation slowly began to emerge as more witnesses appeared on the stand. Again, McDuffie's motorbike was wheeled into the courtroom, with its broken oil cover pan and smashed gauges and mirrors. If the fact that McDuffie had fled suggested a deep wrongdoing to the officers in pursuit, the beaten motorcycle was now a stationary beacon raising the question of why policemen would have done such a thing if their own actions hadn't necessitated a cover-up. For the first time, the jury heard about how the policemen had raked tire irons across the road to imitate an accident and repeatedly beaten McDuffie's helmet on the ground, and they were told that the officers had written three reports, not one.

While Gene Miller remained discreet in his coverage of the McDuffie trial, allowing mainly for the wry delivery of facts, the *Miami News* was forthright with opinion. On May 7, the man Marshall Frank's homicide bureau called "Doctor Death" suddenly revived the prosecution. "Chief Prosecutor Hank Adorno has saved the outspoken Wright and his autopsy findings for the end, like the baseball coach who saves his best relief pitcher for game-winning situations." Wearing a three-piece suit, a white shirt, and a striped tie, Ronald Wright took the stand with a skull in his hand. "Not a real one," wrote the *News*, as if the assistant medical examiner were an adjunct to the Addams Family.

As the defendants sat solemnly at the two defense tables, Wright began relating how he'd first heard of the case from Edna Buchanan. Using a black crayon to draw McDuffie's fractures onto the skull, he then switched to a red pen to sketch out the brain trauma. "Practically all the area of the frontal lobes was destroyed," he said. "As much fracture as you can get in the skull."

Wright placed science and facts back at the forefront of the trial. For the first time, the jury heard McDuffie's height—just under five foot ten—and his weight, 147 pounds. That made O'Donnell's suggestion earlier in the trial that "McDuffie had been waging a one-man war" against fifteen county officers dubious. One officer alone was six foot three and weighed over 200 pounds.

Could Dr. Wright estimate the amount of force used to bludgeon the skull of Arthur McDuffie?

"Equivalent to falling four stories," said Wright. "And landing between your eyes."

"On what?" asked Adorno.

"Concrete," replied Wright.

Wright was excellent on the cross-examination. When he was challenged as to why he had originally thought the beating was a motorcycle accident, he simply admitted it was a mistake. But even Wright's error gave weight to the prosecution's case for manslaughter or murder two. When a defense attorney kept asking how an expert could have been deceived, Wright simply answered, "I had never previously seen anyone with a skull fracture like that."

Though Wright had privately admitted to *Herald* reporters that he had been disturbed by what he'd seen in the autopsy, his performance on the stand remained unemotional and precise. To readers of the *Herald*, the stark violence confirmed another of Buchanan's anonymous police sources who was not a witness at the trial. He'd watched the McDuffie beating and described his colleagues "as a bunch of animals fighting for meat." No one would admit to wanting to kill McDuffie, but Wright's testimony reminded Miami that the alternative was more frightening: a black man could be beaten to death *accidentally* by officers only meaning to teach a suspect a lesson. The prosecution was buoyed by Wright. Perhaps not all five would receive convictions, but there had been a form of crescendo and it was about to end with the man Yoss and Adorno believed was the worst offender on the night McDuffie had been beaten into a coma: Alex Marrero.

Dressed in a three-piece suit, Alex Marrero came to the stand full of contradictions. A Cuban American fully accepted into a predominantly Anglo police force. A blue-collar guy with a white-collar girlfriend. An officer capable of bravery, an officer capable of aggression. A charming, popular cop, recipient of 119 jail visits from family, friends, and police supporters. They'd printed and distributed 100,000 flyers calling Marrero a victim of discrimination, suggesting that he'd been singled out as a Cuban immigrant.

And after the tattooed prisoners of Mariel began to appear around Miami in early May, sympathy *had* gradually hardened. The dismissive word "Marielito" wasn't imposed from outside Miami on the new immigrants. It was given to the new generation of refugees by Cuban Americans who had yet to spend twenty years in the United States.

Marrero was hardly a new arrival. Havana-born, Miami-raised, Alex Marrero had been the star catcher at Miami Springs High; a St. Louis

Cardinals prospect, noted the *Herald*, before a compound shoulder fracture ended his career. A decade before, a Cuban American officer had befriended him at the scene of his older sister's murder. Her husband had killed her, as well as Marrero's two young cousins. Marrero took to policing, but three tours in the Central District had seen him hospitalized four times for physical injuries. Four times he'd requested and had been denied transfers. The last time had been after one of his codefendants had been knocked out in Liberty City by a six-foot-three, 220-pound man wielding a wooden statue. Marrero had subdued and arrested the assailant and won the county's Officer of the Month award.

That was the award that Buchanan would come to think of as cursed. She kept the Officer of the Month press releases on her disordered desk. More often than not, the same cops ended up in trouble. Situations that led to officers winning awards were the flip side of the same volatile opportunities where they could jeopardize their careers.

On the witness stand, when Marrero was asked to describe his arrival at the scene in December, he said, "The first thing I saw was a group of brown shirts congregating. I saw officers falling down." He claimed to see McDuffie launch a karate kick at Veverka and Veverka swing at McDuffie with a Kel-Lite. With his attorney, Ed O'Donnell, playing the part of McDuffie, Marrero removed his jacket and the two men acted out the struggle in front of the jury. Marrero said he used his nightstick to strike McDuffie in the head near the right temple, that McDuffie had punched him in the stomach, and that Marrero had hit him as hard as possible on the right shoulder, causing both men to fall to the ground. That's when McDuffie went for Marrero's gun.

"I tried to throw him to the ground, and he grabs my gun and I felt him pulling my gun away, and I said, 'Oh, shit,' and I struck him in the right temple." O'Donnell encouraged Marrero to continue. "As he went for the gun, I struck him as hard as I could in this area here," he said, indicating the center of McDuffie's face. After that blow, McDuffie stopped moving. "He wasn't resisting anymore," said Marrero.

O'Donnell had elicited a very different story than the one painted by the prosecution. Alex Marrero was the hero, not the villain. Just as he had done in Liberty City, Marrero had come to the rescue of his fellow policemen and saved them from a deranged opponent.

"Alex," said O'Donnell softly, "did you have any intent to kill this man?"

"No, sir," said Marrero. "I feel badly this man is dead."

As he'd finished with his witness, O'Donnell walked back to his chair and glanced at the jury and believed he *knew*. "You could see the jury think, 'Yes, I understand now.'" Was that correct, or was the jury remembering all three of the immunized witnesses who'd stated that they had clearly seen Marrero raise his Kel-Lite over McDuffie?

O'Donnell had another surprise for the prosecution. Marrero told the jury he had left his heavy flashlight behind that night because his four-year-old son was playing with it. Instead, he'd borrowed a cheap plastic version from a female colleague, there in court to corroborate his account.

On cross-examination, Adorno forced Marrero through that night once again, waded a few minutes into further testimony, then doubled back to trick Marrero. "All right, as you grabbed your Kel-Lite, jumped out of the car, and ran to the struggle, did you—?"

"Sir," said Marrero calmly, "I didn't have a Kel-Lite."

Finally, Adorno backed Marrero into a corner, forcing the officer to admit that he had changed his activity log on the night of the incident. He had written that he was on a "10," an area check, assigned to an unmarked car scouring warehouses for burglars, and had never been at the McDuffie scene. When handed a copy of his own log, Marrero hesitated, caught in his lie. There was an agonizing moment of silence in the courtroom, the accused off balance, quiet, and flustered flashing an Achilles' heel before the jury. But then in blustered O'Donnell with loud objections that the activity sheet had never been admitted as an exhibit.

"I'm not going to let him introduce freak rules of evidence," shouted O'Donnell at Adorno.

By the time Judge Nesbitt calmed O'Donnell down, Marrero had had time to think. He must have heard about the chase while he was still on the area check, he testified. But why, then, asked Adorno, had he used Wite-Out on his report? Did he know what he'd Wited-Out?

"No."

"Would it refresh your memory," asked Adorno, "if I told you it was Northwest Thirty-Eighth Street?" This was the corner where McDuffie had pulled over.

It was both a point scored for Adorno and a distraction. Marrero had tried to cover up his presence at the scene. Yet his presence was hardly a revelation. Nor did it automatically make him a murderer. Adorno pressed on, handing Marrero the color photographs of McDuffie's shaven head from Wright's autopsy and forcing him to agree that he could have struck the blow that had left the ten-inch fracture. Adorno ended by asking if he'd used his left hand, that same one he'd used when he was a "power hitter" in his professional baseball career. Marrero said he had.

The closing arguments were potent. The defense attorneys went after the three immunized officers. They were in turn called a liar, a weasel, and a dog. McDuffie, the "ex-marine and karate expert," was "a madman who wouldn't quit fighting." McDuffie might have been on drugs. "He attacked the peace and dignity of the community." McDuffie risked the lives of the defendants and "had created his own destiny." Use of force was entirely justified. One attorney wept openly at the damage to his client's reputation, pleading through tear-filled eyes and a cracking voice that the jury not offer up his client "for sacrificial slaughter."

Adorno would speak for five hours in his closing argument for the state. He called McDuffie a lawbreaker who should have been arrested and prosecuted, not meted out street justice. The defense had tried to portray McDuffie as the Incredible Hulk, but Adorno reminded the jury that the 147-pound McDuffie "was totally incapacitated, bleeding, hand-cuffed, defenseless" when he was beaten into a coma. "Somebody went too far. Somebody used unnecessary force." He saved his harshest words for Marrero. "His actions demonstrated he acted from ill-will, hatred, and spite. He was not concerned about subduing Arthur McDuffie. He was only concerned with inflicting anguish and pain on that man." No one really expected McDuffie to die following the fight, Adorno admitted. All they expected him to do was live and to file a complaint. "And it would have been fifteen [officers] to one. And who would have believed McDuffie? He would have walked into the state attorney's office and we would have laughed in his face."

It was Friday afternoon, the sixteenth of May. To everyone's surprise, after Adorno ended his closing argument, Judge Nesbitt gave the case to the jury immediately rather than waiting for Monday. It was a decision made based on the logic that this had been a long, pained, and complicated trial. A jury might need days just to sift through evidence. It also left open a window of discomfort. If a jury returned a rapid verdict, one that the streets of Overtown and Liberty City found unjust, then it would come on a weekend, when every teenager was out of school, every working adult at home, every stoop occupied, and every radio on.

Questions hung over the jury room and the defendants. Who was guiltiest? Was it Veverka, the first on the scene, who may or may not have been punched by McDuffie? If he had acted calmly, could the whole incident have been avoided? Or should the blame have been placed on the first sergeant on the scene, who could have de-escalated the violence? Was it Marrero's fault? He had tried to transfer out of Central three times. He was a tough cop on tough streets who had behaved as if he were a soldier on patrol in enemy territory. But was he guilty of murder? How to explain that the most trustworthy witness of all, who knew Marrero, was certain that the officer holding the Kel-Lite *wasn't* Marrero? The assistant medical examiner believed that the injuries had been sustained by a Kel-Lite or a nightstick, but O'Donnell had at least cast doubt that his client had even carried a Kel-Lite that night.

These questions clouded the larger truth. Arthur McDuffie had led over a dozen police cars on a chase. He had pulled over and surrendered. He had been beaten by up to fifteen officers and had died of his wounds. Was it possible for the state to have a limited list of suspects and not be able to convict a single man?

Yoss continued to believe that their best bet remained Marrero. He had three witnesses who identified Marrero as the man straddling the prone McDuffie. Even if Marrero wasn't convicted on murder two, he would go down for manslaughter and falsifying reports.

On Saturday morning, Yoss waited in the house he had rented with Adorno, as his colleague went to pick up his girlfriend from Tampa Airport. Like the defense, O'Donnell was expecting they'd take the verdict on Monday, at the earliest. Certainly no one expected that the jury would reach a decision on all charges against the defendants before the day was out.

The jury took two hours and forty minutes to return their verdict, though in truth they came to their conclusion in a mere ninety minutes. The gap in time could be attributed to the judge and jury waiting for Adorno to rush back from the airport. News crews and journalists jammed the Hillsborough County courthouse. The *Herald*'s Gene Miller and his fellow journalists had unpublished opinions of their own. Just before the verdicts were read out, the journalists took a straw poll. Two officers would walk. One would most likely get jail time for tampering with evidence. Marrero would be spared the murder-two count but would be convicted of manslaughter.

Perhaps O'Donnell was the only person in the courthouse who professed not to be shocked by the jury's decision, read out in front of a silent courtroom. Every officer was declared innocent of every charge, including tampering with evidence. Marrero would walk on both murder two and manslaughter. Moments later, in the corridor outside the courtroom, Eula McDuffie raised her hands to the ceiling and screamed, "I want the world to know they're guilty!"

Alex Marrero's head sank to the table. He wept as O'Donnell draped an arm over his shoulder. Marrero banged his hands on the table in relief as his mother kissed a small crucifix she was holding. In a brief news conference after the verdict, Marrero looked into the camera and expressed his gratitude to the jury of six men who had set him free. "Thank God this country still has people who are honest and believe what's right."

CHAPTER 19

The two chiefs of police for the city and the county were in the same place at the same time in the early afternoon of May 17 as the verdict was announced. They stood side by side with State Attorney Janet Reno on a small stage at an anticrime rally in the middle of African Square Park—the heart of Liberty City, the heart of the Central District.

The rally had nothing to do with the Arthur McDuffie verdict. It had been previously planned by McDuffie's high school friend, the PSD's public information officer, Lonnie Lawrence, as a way to reestablish trust between the police and Liberty City's residents. African Square Park, built just two years before, was supposed to have been an oasis for residents, with its basketball court and concrete toys for toddlers, its benches, and plans for a straw market like you might see in Ghana or Nigeria. Instead it had become a home away from home for "muggers, burglars, rapists and drug dealers." Lonnie Lawrence was trying to reclaim the territory on behalf of Liberty City's citizens.

Since Lawrence's promotion the previous year, progress had been made. Not only had the county replaced their conservative sheriff with openly liberal Bobby Jones, they'd handed Jones half a million dollars to reform hiring practices in the department so that he could reach out to black and Latin neighborhoods. As the new sheriff in Dade, Bobby Jones was unusual. He was shiny and clean while several of his predecessors had been involved in corruption trials.

Everything was smooth until about 2:30 p.m., when Lonnie Lawrence's pager went off. Lawrence walked over to a pay phone and rang the PSD building. The McDuffie verdict, not expected until the following week, had just come through. Not guilty. *Not guilty? Already?* How could a jury conclude a six-week murder trial in the time it took to eat supper? "What extraordinarily talented jurors," wrote Joe Oglesby, the most prominent black reporter at the *Miami Herald*, "to be able to dig through a mountain of evidence so swiftly."

Lonnie Lawrence's colleague, Officer Marvin Wiley, standing on the other end of the platform next to Janet Reno, received the same news. Reno had just been alerted. The message from Yoss and Adorno was terse: "No dice. Sorry, boss." The officers scanned the crowd. Everyone at the rally was waiting for the verdict, but no one would have expected it this afternoon. Eyes met eyes, and Lawrence changed his mind. He felt bold emotion, anger. He couldn't *tell* the news had arrived in African Square Park, but he *sensed* it. It was as obvious to him as "the sweat on your back." Lawrence whispered to Bobby Jones while Wiley whispered to Reno: it was time to leave. "Not guilty. Let's move." In the car, on the way back to the PSD building, Lawrence told the interim sheriff, "I think we should mobilize."

"You think so?" asked Jones.

"I know so," said Lawrence.

As the Cuban station WQBA released the first news of the sinking of the *Olo Yumi*, over at WEDR the Ice Man, Clyde McDonald, came on air. He wasn't playing his usual mixture of Jermaine Jackson's "Let's Get Serious," the S.O.S. Band, and Shalamar. His line was clogged by furious callers. Radio personalities weren't journalists. Radio was the medium of *now*, and callers were reacting to the verdict with outrage. Despite the warnings of local leaders, the *Miami Times*, and the *Miami News*, no one had seriously considered that the cover-up of a murdered marine could lead to five acquittals. The *Miami Herald* had never even hinted at the possibility.

The Ice Man got Jerry Rushin, the general manager, on the line. He often mixed politics and current events into his hours on air, and on this day, after acknowledging the outrage, he advised folks to see what Reno would have to say on Monday. You couldn't *see* a man cry on the radio, but Rushin's own emotion crackled through black neighborhoods. Monday, it seemed, was two days too far away.

With both the city and county sheriffs back in their respective headquarters, decisions were taken to defuse the possibility of trouble that evening. The city police force was told to make no drug arrests or domestic arrests, and not to use their sirens in Liberty City, Overtown, or the Black Grove. They opted to increase their manpower in case of trouble by ordering a single extra patrol car out onto the streets. The black community would be left alone by city police to digest the verdict. County police, patrolling the other half of Liberty City, reacted almost identically. Squad leaders were told to remember their nightsticks and helmets. No other precautions were taken.

It was 80 degrees; the end of one of those soft Miami afternoons was fading out with impossible purples and blues. The royal poinciana trees were in bloom, shocks of bright red along city streets. The clocks would spring forward next week and Miami's summer would officially arrive. Once the heat falls on Miami, it's usually marked by regular thunderous afternoon downpours. But on May 17, it would stay dry, ideal conditions to hit the street.

Edna Buchanan was sitting at her desk in the *Herald* building that afternoon. At 3:00, when the news of the acquittals had been phoned in by Gene Miller, she'd called sheriff Bobby Jones just as he'd returned from African Square Park.

"What are we going to do about tonight?"

"What do you mean?" he'd said.

"Don't you think there'll be problems?"

"Our Safe Streets officers are out there," he'd said, referring to a tiny cohort of policemen dedicated to the neighborhood. "They'll keep things under control." "Jeez," thought Buchanan, as she put the receiver down, "this guy is so dense and he's in charge."

Within an hour, Buchanan managed to get Veverka on the phone in

Tampa. The state's first witness seemed stunned by the verdict, calling it "totally unbelievable." Not only was he dumbfounded by the speed of the jury's decision, he was amazed by the idea that the acquitted defendants could all become policemen again. But who would want *him*, someone who had crossed the thin blue line, on their force?

Before five o'clock, Buchanan was looking into the report of a Mariel refugee shot by a policeman when the two-way radio started squawking on a nearby desk. Three photographers, all *Herald* staff, were yelling for help. The photo desk editor, already on the phone, shouted for someone to turn the radio down. When no one reacted, he reached over and did it himself. Buchanan rushed over and turned it all the way up. "They're in trouble!" she shouted.

The photographers were trapped in their car, and their windows had been smashed. They were under fire. Buchanan ran back to her desk and rang city and county police. *Herald* staff awaited the photographers nervously downstairs. When the car finally rolled in, it had no windows left and was constellated with bullet holes and "battered by concrete blocks and rocks." The photographers had escaped with only cuts from flying glass. As they emerged bleeding from the car, you didn't have to be standing close by to see them shaking. There were hundreds of people on the street in Liberty City, they said, perhaps thousands, and exhibiting a fury no one had seen before.

Fearing a mob would come their way, security sealed the *Herald*'s building with the exception of the employee entrance, which led up a graded passageway to the elevator. The chief of security made a run to a suddenly deserted supermarket and bought a case of Wesson oil to pour down the gentle slope if rioters neared the building. Buchanan watched and wondered if that was the extent of their defenses.

Back at her desk, her phone rang again. Between her contacts and her reputation, the stories found her. The first to call was a police officer from an emergency room. He'd stopped and saved a young couple from being beaten by a mob, then been beaten bloody himself, only saved because he'd been off duty, without the giveaway brown shirt of the PSD.

Buchanan had attended crime scenes in the roughest part of Liberty City at night, been mugged, been accosted, always willing to cover a story, but even she saw the wisdom of a five-foot-five blonde working from her desk during what might be the start of a race riot.

Ten minutes north of the *Herald* building, a white Dodge Dart, driven by a teenager named Michael Kulp, turned down Sixty-Second Street. His brother Jeffrey, aged twenty-two, sat in the passenger seat. Asleep in the back was their friend Debra Getman, a twenty-three-year-old waitress. There was no radio in the car, no antenna to receive Tampa news, to hear the percolating anger. The Kulp brothers had moved south from Pennsylvania the year before. They had been up and down the East Coast working maintenance on a traveling carnival. Miami was a final stop. Now both worked in shipping at Burdines department store in downtown Miami, itinerant lives finally stabilizing.

Michael Kulp was hit by a piece of concrete that shattered his windscreen. The Dart swerved across the concrete divider at Sixty-Second Street and Twelfth Avenue, through two lanes of oncoming traffic, and bounced up onto the sidewalk. First it struck a seventy-five-year-old black man, breaking his ankle. Then it hit a ten-year-old black girl who had been running an errand with her aunt, slamming her into the side of a housing project. Her right leg was severed, her pelvis crushed, "smearing the wall with a wide swathe of blood." When Michael Kulp looked up, he saw a street filled with hundreds of furious faces.

Would the Kulp brothers have been treated any differently if they hadn't hit the child? Both were dragged from the car. One of the brothers started pleading with the men around him but was immediately hit by a hail of rocks from the crowd. "Get the crackers!" shouted a young man walking toward the car.

Debra Getman, roused in the back seat by the crash of the first rock through the windshield, now leapt out of the car. With the surrounding crowd concentrated on the two brothers, she ran through the projects to side streets. A black taxi driver stepped on his brakes, helped Getman into the back seat, and drove her out of the neighborhood.

Surrounded by the large crowd, the two men were punched and kicked "just like the cops did McDuffie," and then shot several times with a .25 automatic. They were both still alive, lying in the street. One man in the crowd carried over a slab of concrete and dropped it on Michael Kulp's head. Another man picked up a yellow *Miami Herald* newspaper dispenser and smashed it down on Jeffrey Kulp's head. The crowd watched as the Kulps suffered being "kicked, beaten and 'hit with an iron milk crate' and elbowed karate style in the throat." Though it was less than a five-minute drive from a temporary police command post, no help had arrived. The McDuffie beating had lasted three minutes. The Kulps were beaten for twenty minutes.

In the *Miami Herald* building, reporters were asked to head out into the riot. Crisis revealed a weakness. If the *Herald* had struggled to find Spanish-speaking reporters to cover the Mariel boatlift, now came the abrupt realization that they didn't have enough black reporters to cover a race riot. Apart from Joe Oglesby, there were no black reporters on the city desk. Oglesby had only just returned from Tampa, where he'd gone to hear the verdict alongside Gene Miller. Back in Miami, he was out on the street, and knew what his editors hadn't yet grasped. In a race riot, black reporters are targeted by both rioters *and* police. When Oglesby walked on a block with police present, he waved his pale notepad high above his head, evidence of membership in the fourth estate. When he walked on blocks dominated by rioters, he kept it tucked in his pants pocket.

Earni Young, a twenty-nine-year-old black woman, was a consumer reports columnist for the *Miami Herald*. While the Kulp brothers were being beaten, Young arrived in African Square Park, where, only four hours before, both police chiefs had been attending the community meeting. Now, she walked three blocks east, where she found the Kulp brothers still lying in the street.

Young watched as a green Cadillac turned onto the block. The car slowly drove over an unconscious Jeffrey Kulp, then stopped. The driver put the Cadillac in reverse, drove over Jeffrey Kulp again, ripping off an ear in the process. Then, even more slowly, he drove forward a third time.

"The crowd cheered and yelled," Young reported. "There were children no more than five or six years old standing in the doorways watching."

The driver then stopped the car, stepped out, walked over to the Kulp brothers, and stabbed them both with a screwdriver. A woman emerged from the crowd and placed towels over the brothers' heads.

When the Kulp brothers were no longer moving, the crowd pushed on. Approximately thirty minutes later, a black staff worker for the Dade Community Relations Board found the two men lying where they had fallen, one on the median strip, the other by a curb. He watched a black man walk toward the Kulps carrying a brick and bring it down on Jeffrey Kulp's head. It provoked others to begin another round of beating. While the staff worker ran to a telephone to call the police, an old homeless man approached Jeffrey Kulp and placed a red rose in his mouth.

Just before eight, Earni Young watched a police van and a squad car approach. What she presumed was a SWAT team leapt from the vehicles and ran toward the Kulp brothers. The crowd, hundreds strong again, pelted them with bricks and bottles. Gunfire erupted from the windows of nearby apartment buildings.

Young watched two officers gallop toward the Kulp brothers just as their vehicles came under fire. The van had been under fire all the way along the streets of Liberty City, but now that it was idling with the letters MPD on its side panel, it was a magnet for neighborhood lead. No citizen of Liberty City cared that only the county police had been on trial in Tampa. Any member of a police force had suddenly been transformed into a soldier from an unwelcome occupying army.

Bullets bounced off the sidewalk around the policemen. Muzzle flashes sparked from within apartment buildings as one of the officers tried to get a grip on the smaller brother, but Michael Kulp's body began to jump involuntarily. Kulp was so warm and wet with his own blood, the officer's hands kept slipping from his limbs. Only one of the officers seemed to be moving; the second stood there frozen, staring at the crowd hurling rocks toward him. Alone, the first officer managed to drag and then push Michael Kulp into the back of the police van. He returned for Jeffrey Kulp, the rose still in his torn mouth, but that body seemed heavier, harder to move. The second officer still stood there frozen, untouched by gunfire, an impervious uniformed statue.

Finally, the first officer, holding Jeffrey Kulp up by his waist, shifted his weight to one leg and kicked his colleague in the buttocks. The man suddenly came back to life and grabbed Kulp by the legs, and together they ran toward the police van amid gunfire. As they closed the door, the crowd watched in astonishment as this "dude from the projects came running out with a shotgun . . . and blew out the light" on the top of the police van.

The *Herald*'s Young saw the van race east on Sixty-Second Street. She waited for it to come back and disperse the crowd. No police returned, so Young walked away, looking for a quieter street. She made her way to NW Sixteenth and Sixty-First, where she came across "a group of missionaries playing hymns, with drums and cymbals and guitars. They were having their own private revival . . . just as if nothing was going on."

In the time during which the Kulp brothers were beaten, the sheer numbers of rock-throwing men on the street had driven county and city police to abandon many of their hastily constructed checkpoints they had belatedly set up in order to prevent more white motorists entering black neighborhoods. The further back they fell, the larger the perimeter became around the trouble zones. The larger it became, the more manpower was needed to secure it.

As the Kulp brothers were being rushed to Jackson Memorial Hospital, Sergeant Lonnie Lawrence listened to the sound of two thousand people repeating one word. "JUSTICE. JUSTICE. JUSTICE!" Two miles south of where the Kulp brothers had been beaten, Lawrence stood up and peered out of a third-floor window of the PSD building on Fourteenth Street, three long blocks from where the expressway crossed the Miami River. The crowd coming toward him was predominantly black, specked with a few white folks, marchers, reporters, cameramen, policemen. They were all moving together, a long, winding tail of people packed close. "Oh, shit," he thought.

There were men in suits, and women with their children, and people who had gathered soon after the McDuffie verdict was announced. Thank God this is an orderly crowd, thought Lawrence. These were professionals and activists gathered by the NAACP. It represented, according to George Knox, the black attorney for the City of Miami, the "orderly expression of hostility." This was the calm message, the black middle-class message.

Lawrence watched the crowd pulse and grow in front of his eyes. And then, suddenly, several things seemed to happen at once. A car turned onto the street and headed straight toward the marchers. The driver was a thirty-two-year-old nurse, a colleague of Frederica McDuffie's, late for her shift at Jackson Memorial. The crowd didn't want to part for her, because this was a show of solidarity, and you cannot be one if you part in two. But she kept her small green Chevrolet moving slowly forward, determined to get to work. And then everything started to change.

What sparked the violence? The gunshot that scared the nurse into pressing the accelerator? The people who leapt from the car's path, or the tire that rolled over the foot of a marcher too stubborn to move it? Was the gunshot aimed at the car, or at the building where Lonnie Lawrence was standing, looking down over the crowd? And how quickly was the police car parked in front of the PSD building overturned?

In moments, the white people who had dotted the streets disappeared, and all that was left was a crowd of black folk, numbering close to three thousand. Those black notables who'd gathered to talk—the president of Miami's Urban League, and the first black city commissioner, were shouting but couldn't be heard. Mama Range, who'd commanded respect for twenty years, who'd led the civil rights movement from the front lines in Miami, was holding a bullhorn, but no one could find batteries for it. And no one on the street except those immediately around her could see the five-foot-tall, 100-pound woman. She looked as slight as a sparrow in a storm.

Just eight weeks ago, Mama Range had said she saw this coming. She sat down with the *Miami Herald*'s Joe Oglesby and said, "Black Miami is bleeding to death." She worried about the popularity of Republican presidential candidate Ronald Reagan, and the rise of white conservatism. She worried that the McDuffie trial had been moved from Miami to Tampa "to gain acquittal verdicts for the police."

The crowd was moving beyond her. It wasn't time to listen; it was time to react. Anger had to be displayed—a belief that was shared by the black lawyers, black teachers, and ample ranks of the unemployed. Every black person in Dade County knew that the McDuffie trial was the time for justice, and that, once again, justice was not for them.

———

Lonnie Lawrence felt that he was no different from any other black man in Dade County. He could see a man in a suit snapping off police car aerials with one hand and slapping his chest with the other. He understood *him* because he was feeling an identical bottomless disappointment. An anger at the impossibility that this could happen, all those doubts that had plagued him since the beginning of the trial, an all-white jury sitting in front of a white judge.

This crowd was saying something. Lawrence could see the message taking shape in front of his eyes. He knew people down there. They were coming toward his building. And the police car that had been turned over was now on fire. The first rock came crashing through a window, and bullets snapped against the walls of the building. So what should he do? He's police. He's black. He's the public information officer. He was a friend of McDuffie's.

From up high, Lawrence watched as three or four shirtless young men broke away from the crowd and began to kick at the front door of the PSD building. There was a police car below. One that hadn't been overturned. The loudspeaker was on. Inside was George Knox, Ferré's hire as the first black city attorney, begging the people to pull back from the PSD building. Knox was everything you needed: tall, commanding, and well-known. But it didn't matter.

The crowd was closer now, and a squad car from nearby Sweetwater had its sirens screaming, its lights whipping across hundreds of faces. And because emotion was the only currency now, a rumor ran around that the car had rolled over a girl's foot. Another police car was vandalized. Armed men in the crowd pulled pistols from their waistbands and fired into the air, at the building, and Lawrence pulled away from the window, from the *ping* and *twang* of bullets.

PSD had plenty of veterans. Vietnam was a feeder school for the two dominant police departments that ran Miami, and those men, they all knew the difference between the high pop of a pistol and large-caliber booms. They knew that a rifle was now being aimed at the PSD building. And the vets, they took cover.

The riot was going to be big. Lawrence knew there were half a dozen areas across the county where something like this, some version of what was happening at the PSD, must also be taking place. It seemed like the police radios were competing in volume, one desperate to be heard over another.

Lawrence heard the emergency room at Jackson pleading for help. Every operating theater was already full, and the injured were being carried in. Two, three, five, twelve at a time. Housewives blinded by rocks through car windscreens, a cameraman knocked unconscious by a baseball bat to the back of the head, reporters beaten to the ground. They were all being carried into the same hospital where Frederica McDuffie was doing her shift the night her ex-husband was rushed in on a stretcher.

Bolting to the stairwell, Lawrence took the steps quickly. As he approached the ground floor, he heard what he feared: rioters had made it into the lobby. He had the absurd thought that there was still time to change his mind. He thought, I could just rip my shirt off my body and leap into the crowd as a civilian, not a policeman. I could be a half-naked black man. I could say, "Thank God you all got here, because they were beating my butt upstairs!"

Lawrence stood, in uniform, in front of a sea of faces. The noise outside was the roar of a vast crowd, but now it was splintered into a hundred subgroups with ideas of where to go and what to do, and also many men and women—though not the ones staring at Lawrence in the PSD lobby—who were just thinking, *HOME, HOME, HOME. Just let me get home.*

So Lawrence took a breath and said, "My brothers and my sisters, you do not want to come through this door. If you come into this building there are going to be a lot of you all dead. Because there are a lot of people in this building, around these corners, armed, and they're ready to take people out. They're *not* going to let you take this building."

There was a pause. A digestion. To Lawrence's relief, the men ducked back out into the night. Perhaps Lawrence could be forgiven for thinking that maybe that was how it was going to go, that the men and women who'd heard about Arthur McDuffie and knew for sure that there had been no justice for him were maybe going to take a deep breath and go home.

But the evening was only getting started. Lonnie Lawrence may have helped save one building but, hey, right around the corner, that's the Metro Justice Building, the office of Janet Reno, the state attorney. It's her office that had failed them. Not once, but half a dozen times this last year alone. Reno's on the sixth floor right now. So why not go burn her out?

Nearby, Capt. Marshall Frank was reversing desperately up an exit ramp to escape rioters, suddenly heading away from his own destination, the homicide bureau. Forget the human toll, the best crime lab in the whole Southeast of the United States was on the fifth floor of a building under attack. And in his own department, everything was hard copy, including the file folders trying to make sense of the spate of murders by Colombian suspects all over the county. Think of those investigations. Think of the criminal records. If the building burned, there goes the county, there goes the city. Cases would fall apart by the dozens. Events that haven't even happened yet, call them future crimes, what would be the chance of solving them if no one could match a photograph with a suspect, if no one could cross-check an alias, if the only copy of a fingerprint was just a wisp of smoke heading out over the Everglades?

As Frank reversed up the ramp, he caught sight of a baby-faced major marching seventy police officers in riot gear out from under the columns of I-95 directly toward the Justice Building, where a group of rioters were now stacking newspapers against the front door, trying to set a fire to smoke out the state attorney. The police inside the Justice Building were calling for help. With his three lines of officers armed with riot sticks, helmets, and face shields, he looked at the sky, grateful the light of the sunset was gone. Darkness would help cover the paucity of his force.

As soon as the police emerged from under the pillars of I-95, they were pelted with rocks from men standing on top of the overpass. The major could hear the sound of shattering glass, the low boom of a gas tank exploding from a patrol car, and the chant of "Pigs!" from all around. Supported by barking dogs, the major cut straight through the three-thousand-strong crowd. The arrest team grabbed a man who had tossed a Molotov cocktail at the column. He was handcuffed as he screamed, "Take me around the corner and whip me, too! Kill me, too!"

By the time the column reached the Justice Building, only the boldest rioters remained to watch the major wave in fire trucks. At that moment, a sniper opened fire from a parking garage a block away. A handful of officers sought cover behind a burning police car. Within seconds, it exploded and the major and his officers were hurled across the street. They stood up dazed and otherwise uninjured. A SWAT team arrived to scare off the sniper.

As Marshall Frank drove backward up the expressway ramp, his car was hit by gunfire. Absurdly, he realized it was the one day he'd managed to forget his police radio. Without the ability to communicate with his own men, he thought of Edna Buchanan and headed to the *Herald* offices. Buchanan came down to let him in the back door. Using her police radio, Frank began to check on his men and direct homicide operations from within the *Herald*. Two people whose professional lives centered around moving toward acts of violence were now penned inside the newsroom.

At 9:44, Sheriff Bobby Jones called Governor Graham. Send in the National Guard. It would take two hours and forty minutes, exactly the same time it had taken to reach the McDuffie verdict, for the first of the guards to appear on the streets of Miami.

Without enough policemen to man the perimeters of a vast area, drivers continued to enter neighborhoods still soaked with the blood of men and women attacked hours earlier. A fourteen-, fifteen-, and twenty-one-year-old were all pulled from their car and beaten to death with rocks and hammers, on the same street the Kulp brothers had been attacked. The number of rioters on the street made anything other than the rescue of bodies almost impossible.

The surprise wasn't that a riot had happened but that when it finally lulled, before dawn on Sunday, the National Guard and county and city police weren't in a position to retake the ground they'd ceded. Marshall Frank made it home before dawn, played Tchaikovsky to calm himself, and caught a few hours' sleep. When he woke, nothing had changed. Co-ordination between city, county, and federal agencies was still a problem for everything from locating barricades to finding parking spots for the police and the National Guard. A second day of rioting awaited. Some buildings were set on fire as many as five times before they burned to the ground as the riots provided Sunday headlines not just for the *Herald* but across the United States and beyond. Mayor Ferré's dynamic city on the rise was now a city on fire.

CHAPTER 20

By daybreak on Sunday, 213 fires had been started in Liberty City alone. When the county and city fire departments had answered calls the night before, they'd been shot at, then ordered to retreat. At Norton Tire, the largest employer in Liberty City, an estimated 100,000 tires were furiously blazing. As the sun rose, the thick black smoke would provide a backdrop to the riots, the central plume of an event in a city so divided it had more than one name. It was the McDuffie Riot, the Liberty City Riot, or the Miami Riot. In Liberty City itself, it was known as the Miami Rebellion.

Ferré had returned to the city at dusk on Saturday evening, touching down from a flight from New Jersey alongside the *Herald*'s executive editor. The morning of the riot, they had both been participating in a seminar, The Media and Terrorism, at Princeton University. At the conference, Ferré had been confronted with a question about a hypothetical town called Gentle Acres. A race riot had broken out, killing seven. How would he deal with it? When theory became a reality that afternoon, Ferré's first step was to rush back to Miami. It became very apparent that no one in Miami had been ready for such an event, certainly not the county or city mayors, their managers, or the sheriffs.

That Sunday, much of the violence was suddenly inverted. The previous night, the eight murders committed by black suspects had been committed up close, by groups, with enormous anger. Another 417 people were treated in area hospitals. The dead were, as McDuffie had been, almost unrecognizable. Eight black victims would be murdered on Sunday. The incidents were cold-blooded shootings, all committed from a distance with no logical selection of a victim other than that they had to be both black and inside the riot zone.

White men in a blue truck shot a fourteen-year-old boy in the head as he ran in a street alongside his sister. A forty-four-year-old cement finisher was sitting in his car outside a U-ToTe'm convenience store while his wife left the car to buy orange juice with their two daughters. He was killed behind the wheel. Another man, trying to stop a pair of teenagers from throwing rocks at cars, was shot in the back and killed by a white truck driver whose window had just been shattered.

The PSD would receive 22,000 calls from Dade residents in forty-eight hours as their officers filed 583 incident reports during the two days of rioting. The incidents ranged from a triple murder to a ketchup bottle thrown through a car window, from a Molotov cocktail hurtling into a principal's office to a PSD officer who had his helmet stolen from a checkpoint. Many incidents were downgraded purely because the department was overwhelmed. A group of men who'd shot at officers early on Sunday morning had only one of their number arrested. Thirty-one years old, he was charged with disorderly conduct. Forty-eight hours earlier, he might have faced an attempted murder charge.

The National Guard now defined the vast borders of an area both closed off and under curfew, its interior effectively lawless. It led to a schizophrenic day of continued looting, sometimes frenzied, sometimes almost casual. Convenience stores and meat markets were emptied, their glass fronts shattered before the buildings were set on fire. Churches rang their bells, people hurried to services, and barbeques of stolen meats were fired up across Liberty City.

At about twelve thirty, Mayor Ferré was driven south through the black smoke, along the empty expressway to Coral Gables for an emergency meeting of the Community Relations Board. Going from Liberty City to Coral Gables only underlined the stark differences in Dade County. The beautiful avenues were lined with barrel-trunked banyan trees. Their branches arced to meet over the streets, shady boulevards of tranquility. The houses with their orange tiled roofs happily hummed to the sound of air-conditioning and gurgling swimming-pool filters. Coral Gables belonged to an alternate world. Inside the boardroom, Ferré squeezed in between members of the press to join Janet Reno and a smattering of local leaders. Reno didn't mention that overnight she'd received so many death threats, she'd just moved her mother out of their house.

For Ferré, everything had been going well. Even as the family business suffered, the city thrived. Until April arrived, he'd had every reason to be proud of the rising commercial tax base. There were conferences; there was a trade fair that he had lobbied the Organization of American States to place in Miami, then turned into a huge success when eight thousand merchants appeared in 1978. Who else but Ferré could have persuaded the First Lady to do the ribbon cutting?

But in the month that had delivered both the trial and the boatlift, it suddenly seemed doubtful that such progress could be sustained. How could you attract money to a city where the Justice Building, a half mile from downtown, could come under attack? Liberty City's biggest employer, Norton Tire, was billowing black smoke high into the blue sky. There wasn't room in the schools for immigrant children or enough housing available. The Orange Bowl, sacred home of the undefeated Dolphins, brimmed with the stateless, the homeless, the jobless, while more boats were headed north from Mariel, crammed with refugees. Miami had become a very hard sell in a very short span of time.

Beside Ferré and Reno sat the local black leaders who had chosen to attend the board meeting. One absentee leader called the riots "a justified expression of black anger." He played a round of golf instead. The meeting ran for four hours. Ferré said, "I want you to know the eyes of the world are on Miami." Within the first hour, Janet Reno was blamed for the lack of convictions in the McDuffie case and was asked to resign, *now*, to save lives as the riot continued. It was four hours of talk with no action, and Ferré left disgusted at the finger-pointing and bickering. He stopped and talked to a *Herald* reporter on the way out. "In 1990 blacks will be living in the same rat-infested apartments they were living in 1960. And this community will say, 'Take two aspirins and go to bed.' They'll call another meeting, have the archbishop head it and say a prayer."

Inside the riot zone on Sunday, it was a netherworld of bizarre, often contrasting images. There was an untouched Harley store, with six armed white men standing outside, four with shotguns and two with assault rifles. Close by, at a Woolworth's, the shelves were empty, the walls on fire, the building smoldering and windowless, yet the store's Muzak system could be heard piping down empty streets. A parade of cars drove slowly down a block, each one with two men on its roof, holding down stolen refrigerators. Every now and then, you'd pass a pair of looters, zip-tied by police to a light pole, awaiting pickup by one of the few roving columns of police vehicles.

The looting wasn't all peaceful. As the mayor was speaking in Coral Gables, one of his assistant city attorneys was shot. Buchanan would find the story, driving around the edges of the riot on Sunday in her blue Camaro. The attorney had been riding with two officers. They'd pulled up in front of a looted Salvation Army shop, exited their car, and found themselves running beside cars loaded with furniture, trying to convince the drivers to stop. As the cars had pulled away and the three men turned around, all three were hit by gunfire.

"Arguably the worst race riot of the century" did not end with a roundup, or with arrests by the National Guard, now numbering 3,500. It squelched and slowed with typical violent Miami bursts of rain. Fires went from open flames to hissing embers. Synchronized to the weather, the mood of Liberty City turned from outrage, to casual looting, to a return to relative normalcy. From the Orange Bowl, the hopeful refugees of Mariel waited out the rains and climbed to the top of the bleachers for a better view of Miami's smoldering fires. So many had been lured by the photographs of the beautiful city their proud relatives had shared the year before. This was a very different America.

On Monday, schools were shut. Miami was ominous and quiet.

Downtown remained closed. With the National Guard still mobilized, city and county police moved slowly toward the centers of Overtown and Liberty City, shrinking the perimeters and reclaiming Miami block by block.

On Wednesday, the National Guard was sent home, schools were re-opened, and traffic restrictions lifted. A police officer on the corner of Twenty-Second Avenue and Eighty-Ninth Street cut down the effigy of a white woman hanged by the neck as the barricades at the perimeters were removed. There was the same eerie feeling in the wake of a hurricane. Miami looked familiar. But it felt different.

From a population standpoint, the city *was* different. Latins now comprised over 50 percent of Miami's population but only 17 percent of voters. Many still opted to keep hold of their Cuban citizenship. But what if that shifted? Or, rather, what would it take to accelerate the process of registration? If Mariel showed anything, it was that the hand on the scales had slipped. If Castro wasn't going to fall, then Miami was about to become a Latin city in every sense.

Black Miami had resorted to self-immolation just to be seen, still "a spectator in this sport of governing." Anglo Miami was liberal at the top of the food chain, by the end of the week bristling with ideas for how to reinvigorate Liberty City, how to help, how to fund initiatives, yet there was no talk of ceding or sharing power with either minority. The Non-Group still had no black members or women. But even its effect was limited, because true change could only come about through loosening state and federal purse strings, and neither Tallahassee nor Washington was looking favorably on the chaos in Miami during an election year.

The riot and Mariel had shown the fractures in the rickety contraption of Miami's city and county governance. White voters across the rest of Florida regarded the burst of immigration, the cocaine bloodshed, and the riots as problems created by forces beyond their own control—but somehow the fault of Floridians to the south. There were plenty of middle- and working-class Anglos in Miami who understood that the city's Latin "flavor" was fast becoming a majority of the ingredients.

Their resistance would become a central story in a poisonous election year. They would come to believe they had two choices: fight to preserve the old status quo or leave Miami altogether. Mayor Ferré's demographic wave that he'd always sought to interpret months in advance now seemed to be undergoing changes by the week.

CHAPTER 21

May had exhausted the city, but there was no doubt it had been an incredible month for the *Miami Herald*. One editor declared that "Miami was the center of the universe." Other news organizations certainly agreed. CBS had opened an office in February. By the time the riots hit, they had thirty-two employees covering Miami. Miami may have been losing respect, but it was gaining attention.

The *Herald*'s strength was blatant; excellent reporters covered a glut of national and international news. After a difficult beginning with the language issues, the paper would throw fifty-one journalists at covering either Mariel or the riot. Mariel was Miami's problem, but it shouldn't have been. It was an international incident in an election year, and the *Herald* was clearly leading the coverage.

No matter whether you turned to the *Miami Herald*, its Spanish-language counterpart, *El Miami Herald*, or the *News* or *Times*, you were now digesting news at an extraordinary rate, morning and afternoon editions in constant flux. Everyone looked for the professional readers of tea leaves to try to understand what would happen—what had *already* happened—to their city. The coverage from outside was either scathing or vague. Moscow covered Miami's problems by depicting the city as America's fetid nexus of what could go wrong when capitalism, race, and immigration were boiled together. Those had been the components for Mayor Ferré's creation of Miami as an unofficial regional capital; now they were being used against it.

The different tribes of Miami were digesting the bitterness of May and formulating responses, groping toward a consensus. Black Miami had nothing to build on. On the one hand, they had burned their largest neighborhood to the ground. On the other, they were asking for help to rebuild it, make it better, more robust than before, by addressing the underlying problems of poverty and unemployment. But there were ugly realities that impeded efforts at reconstruction. No insurer would secure a business when white ownership meant a guarantee of looting. Nor would a bank loan money. Governor Graham's proposal, to raise Dade's sales tax by 1 percent to fund $291 million to rebuild the riot-torn areas, was shot down in Tallahassee, where it was seen as a reward for civil disobedience. The counter was a measly $8 million in loan grants to burned-out businesses. Florida's politicians also refused to create a commission to investigate race relations in Dade County. After that vote, a *Herald* reporter followed the house members and their aides to their lounge, where they sang, "It's Hard to Be Humble" ("Lord, it's hard to be humble / When you're perfect in every way") and "Dixie."

———

Cuban Americans now had an entire new population to take care of. By June, between the Mariel boatlift and the steady stream of Haitians arriving in the Keys, Miami had received what equaled a third of its own population in six weeks. It was the rough equivalent of having Providence, Rhode Island, dropped into Dade County, only without any provisions for housing, schools, or jobs. Despite the uproar, it wasn't the city, the county, or federal agencies that spearheaded the absorption of Mariel's refugees. It was the Cuban community. Cuban businessmen reported to the Orange Bowl and gave hour-long seminars on the differences between Cuba and Miami. They found immigrants unsettled, scared of Miami's growing reputation for crime, desperate for jobs and housing, wanting to know what a parking ticket was and whether you had to pay it. Most often the questions were familiar. Where to find a job, a room, a way to move around the city, the same questions every generation of immigrants had always asked, with one advantage: they were hearing answers in their own language, in a town where the Cuban influence was already marked.

Miami's Anglos had been relatively passive spectators amid the unrest in May and continued to be divided in their response. While the wealthy stood firm in their support for Ferré's vision of tolerance, growth, and assistance, the middle class had had enough. They wanted a future without racial violence, without a surge of immigration. They wanted the past back tomorrow.

The talk in the *Herald* may have been of consensus, but it didn't exist outside of opinion columns. The opposite had happened. Differences and divisions were deepening, nowhere so starkly as in the civil issue of language. Back in 1973, in a gesture of goodwill, a county ordinance had been passed establishing Dade as bilingual. Now, in early July, as the boatlift continued, a forty-five-year-old housewife named Emmy Shafer was spurred to found Citizens of Dade United, with a goal to revoke that bilingual ordinance and return Miami, once and for all, to English.

Shafer was a Russian-born immigrant who had managed to survive eighteen months in a concentration camp at Dachau during the Second World War. She weighed only fifty pounds when American soldiers liberated her. Even in 1980, she still carried food in her purse. Shafer spoke six languages, none of them Spanish.

Before the end of July, Shafer had collected more than twice the number of signatures required to put an anti-bilingual ordinance on the November ballot. She received up to three hundred calls a day from people eager to sign on. "It was like giving gold away," she said. If the ordinance passed, it would "prevent Spanish from being used in public signs, emergency 911 calls, hurricane warnings and other public statements." If you were one of the tens of thousands of new immigrants from Cuba who hadn't yet had time to learn English, it was the equivalent of snuffing out the only candle in the room.

Shafer's campaign walked a thin line between calls for unification and outbursts of racism. At first, she had taken to radio stations, local papers, and television promoting the use of English as a way to unify the county.

"How can we have communication at home, on the street, in grocery stores, if we don't speak the same language?" It wasn't her only concern. When interviews ran longer, she'd talk about returning Miami to the way it used to be. "How come the Cubans get everything?" she asked. Her supporters were more direct. On a televised march in downtown Miami, one blond woman approached the camera. "I say put them on leaky boats." Moments later, another blond woman approached. "Make *me* a refugee," she said, "so I'll have some rights, okay?"

The odium also ricocheted. Within weeks of the start of her Citizens of Dade United campaign, Shafer found the first of many death threats in her mail, written in blue ink on white paper. "Will kill you soon—Omega 7." It wasn't an idle threat. In September, the same anti-Castro group would gun down an attaché to the Cuban mission in New York.

———

Luckily, Jimmy Carter was heading south to bring peace to Ferré's troubled city. Searching for that elusive consensus, Carter's White House had blamed the riots on Miami's "unique circumstances" and the pressure of the Mariel boatlift. It was a vastly inflated claim, backed up by the need to see the riot as a one-off in an election year, rather than representative of broader inner-city issues. A *Miami Herald* poll suggested that a mere 4 percent of blacks blamed incoming immigrants for the riots.

Carter would refer to the black vote as his "secret weapon" in the run-up to the presidential election. If Miami was anything to go by, that was a presumption. A pamphlet passed out in Liberty City and Overtown just before his arrival talked of the "lies and piss poor promises of reforms of these federal flunkies."

Six weeks after the start of Mariel and almost three weeks after the McDuffie riots, Carter landed in Miami. He would meet city leaders at the community center in the Scott Projects, the epicenter of the riots: 238 businesses had either been damaged or burned to the ground. The first to arrive at the meeting was Alvah Chapman, president of the Non-Group and CEO of the *Herald*'s parent company. Ferré may have been Miami's mayor, but he knew Chapman remained the true source of power across Dade County. The unofficial chairman of Miami was now sitting across from the president of the United States in Liberty City. Ferré sat between them, the mayor with muted power.

Chapman barely spoke. Ferré stared at the president, the friend who had let him use his position on the ambassadorial committee to travel throughout the Americas. Ferré prayed for boldness, but Jimmy Carter wasn't taking any position at all. Instead, he was rewarding Ferré's advocacy in an election year with silence. Finally, Carter simply said that he didn't want to impose anything on Miami from Washington. He asked for local solutions, which seemed to unnerve local leaders.

A crowd of black Miamians had assembled outside the meeting. News of what was going on inside, and what *wasn't* going on inside, began to leak. Lonnie Lawrence, the PSD's public information officer, was the local liaison for the Secret Service. He could feel the agitation building. "Down with Carter!" the crowd began to yell. The call-and-response went from one side of the street to the other.

"Who can we trust now?" asked the west.

"We can't trust nobody," returned the east.

"We want justice," shouted everyone together. "We can't get justice here!"

Lawrence understood. He'd sipped from "Colored Only" fountains in the Dade County Courthouse when he was a kid. He'd unpacked boxes of newly arrived books at Booker T. Washington with his friends, only to realize that the school board had only sent old, tattered volumes from high schools in white neighborhoods. No individual exerted those humiliations. They came from the county, the city, the federal government. "Promises, promises, promises," thought Lawrence, "are broken, broken, broken."

Lawrence moved back into the community center and approached his Secret Service counterpart to whisper a message intended for delivery to the president of the United States: "He needs to leave." Three weeks ago, he'd told a superior the same thing in the moments before the McDuffie riots started. Lawrence watched Carter come out, flanked by Ferré, and "just as [the president] ducked into the limo, a bottle hit the top." It was followed by a barrage of soda cans. "We need help!" shouted a bystander in the crowd.

Hustling over to the crowd, Lawrence pointed at the Secret Service and shouted into the crowd, "You know these guys have machine guns, right? You think for a minute they won't blow you away if you try to hurt the president?" He shook his head as the limousine pulled out. Only here, thought Lawrence, would Carter get bottles tossed his way. He felt he knew what was going to happen next. Whatever the deep-rooted issues of Overtown and Liberty City, Carter had other priorities. Mariel was the new problem. The issues stemming from the boatlift were, by definition, easier to fix than the old problems. Refugee agencies had sought Carter's attention that same morning, looking for an expansion in funding. The only people truly grateful to the president in Miami that day were the refugees. They had made it either thanks to Carter or thanks to his constant indecision. Yet the pelting of his car with cans and a bottle would mean that the president's memory of Miami was not one of gratitude.

Inside the limousine, Ferré attempted to talk, but Carter didn't say a word during the fifteen-minute drive between Liberty City and the airport. Ferré saw a man "not at peace with himself" and didn't know if the president held something against him personally, or was distracted or overwhelmed. Before, he had seen warmth in Carter. Now he was aloof and unengaged.

There was no immediate commitment from Carter, only a rumor that an aid package of $100 million was being prepared. That package, it turned out, would be shared by Liberty City, relief agencies that were over budget because of the boatlift, and the victims of the other explosion that weekend when Washington State's Mount St. Helens had erupted, killing fifty-seven.

It was hard not to feel despair at the vagueness. The bill had also come before Congress at a time when the administration was under pressure to restrain spending. Ferré, low on energy, sat down with the *Miami Herald*.

"We need to be honest with ourselves," he said. "We can't be scared of it and we can't hide from it . . . to try and hide the fact that one of our weaknesses is that we're racist is to deny the reality of where we are."

Carter remained more eager to measure the grayness of clouds than to paint silver linings. The city would have to move forward with limited federal help. Miami had so often been claimed by men who had nothing in common but corruption. But Governor Graham, Mayor Ferré, and Dade's county manager were all honest men and had all placed minorities in vital positions early in their tenures. They were equals in mastery of city, county, state, and federal codes and could have debated such arcana until dawn. Anywhere else, that might have counted as faint praise, but in the turbulent Miami of 1980, when Washington could seem like the capital of a different country, it was essential as the city floundered.

Even Carter's visit was a reason to act together, not remain divided. A generous response from the federal government might have acted as a trough for infighting and greed. As it was, the answer was clear. Miami had to find its own way out of problems created in part by its history, by its geography, and by the Carter administration, because no one was coming to help.

Ferré was left wondering what was a strength and what was a weakness. To make itself truly stable, the city had to rely on a variety of businesses, not just tourism, still the industry with the most gravitational force. Ferré couldn't afford to lose it, even if his desire was to lighten his city's dependence on South Florida's $5.2 billion tourist industry. Thanks to the Federal Reserve, Ferré now also knew that one of the main reasons the city had avoided the worst of the economic malaise under Carter was because it had been buoyed by $7 billion in cocaine cash. That summer, the issue was obvious to Miami's close observers. The riots and boatlift would surely ravage tourism. An anticorruption operation like Greenback could succeed in driving out the cocaine dollars, but if it happened quickly, there was a chance it could endanger a vulnerable regional economy.

Miami needed time to put forward a rebuilding program. Time to find a new consensus, time to absorb tens of thousands of refugees who spoke no English, time to send their children to school and find space to house them. Miami needed to build bridges between its myriad tribes and to stanch the blood pouring onto its streets. Instead, the murder rate ticked further upward.

CHAPTER 22

In the middle of June, Edna Buchanan finally put together the story she had been working on when the photographers' plea had come over the radio, signaling the start of the McDuffie riot. On the very day that Arthur McDuffie's death at the hands of police officers sparked the unrest, another man was killed by a police officer. If McDuffie was representative of Miami's past, the death of Juan Jose Toledo suggested the course of its immediate future.

Toledo's odyssey began with his arrest in Havana in April when he'd tried to sneak into the Peruvian embassy. Five foot seven and 140 pounds, Toledo was a handsome man with a prominent nose. Along with hundreds of others, he'd been thrown into the Combinado del Este prison following his arrest. There, he'd most likely been singled out because of his history of mental illness. Instead of help or medication, he was quickly passed through El Mosquito to Mariel and hurried to Florida. Toledo arrived on May 12 and tasted little of freedom. In four days, he was moved between Key West, the Orange Bowl, Opa-locka, and Little Havana.

At midnight on the sixteenth of May, he called his wife from the Orange Bowl. She had arrived in Miami almost eight and a half years before, pregnant with his child. Toledo had stayed in Cuba to fulfill his military service. He had never met his daughter. For all the strong political opinions in Little Havana, the raw hatred for Castro was reserved as much for his separation of families as for his politics. Finally, the Toledos were united.

Mother and daughter drove quickly over to the Orange Bowl. The guards listened to her story and slipped the girl inside to meet her father while her mother had to stay outside, linking fingers with her husband through the chain-link fence. Father and daughter hugged and shared cookies and milk, and the family talked until 3:00 a.m. Later the following day, on May 17, when the *Olo Yumi* was foundering in the Florida Straits and the McDuffie verdict was being delivered in Tampa, Juan Jose Toledo had a small, crooked sign hung around his neck: "Paranoid Schizophrenic." Without a word of English, he didn't object. A University of Miami student was hired by FEMA to chauffeur him to the Miami Mental Health Center.

During the drive, Toledo became more and more agitated. His eyes glazed over. He confessed to the student that he'd murdered his daughter, then his wife. Then he told the student that someone else had killed them, and he began talking of a massacre. When they arrived at the clinic, the student reported the conversations to a doctor, who prescribed an injection. No one could get close enough to administer it. Toledo walked out of the clinic, came back in again, left, returned. His eyes were now bulging. The clinic was well aware of how dangerous paranoid schizophrenics could be. Police were called.

Later that afternoon, as the first reports of violent reactions to the McDuffie verdict began to saturate the city, Toledo was found outside the clinic, holding a box cutter. He menaced other patients and then threatened to harm himself. Police were called five times. With officers struggling to set up perimeters in Liberty City, Toledo's case was ignored until 7:35 p.m., when the call was upgraded to a code 32—assault. The first officer to arrive was Jose Angel Perdomo, thirty-five, himself a Cuban refugee who had arrived in the United States at seventeen, without his parents. In the last two hours, Perdomo had been shot at three times.

A doctor quickly explained to Perdomo that Toledo had been persuaded to take sedatives with orange juice. Perdomo found Toledo still outdoors, now banging his head against the door of the clinic. "What's wrong with you, buddy? Get up!" ordered Perdomo, holding a riot club. "What's your problem?"

Toledo didn't seem to be listening to the officer as he shouted orders in English. Still armed with his box cutter, he staggered down an alley and curled up in a ball against a wall. "I've been abandoned," he muttered. "They've abandoned me." Suddenly, he jumped back to his feet, put the box cutter up to his throat, and then took off running, at first farther down the alley, then back toward Perdomo. Perdomo dropped his riot club and unholstered his weapon. A worker emerged from a neighboring beauty salon, watched Toledo swaying back and forth, and shouted, "Don't shoot the man, don't kill him!"

Perdomo fired twice, hitting Toledo in the right armpit and the abdomen. He was rushed to Jackson Memorial, now overflowing with riot victims, spent the night between an operating room and the intensive care unit, and was accidentally listed as a riot casualty. His wife, who had driven through the riot to search the Orange Bowl for him, appeared at the hospital on Sunday, May 18. She didn't recognize her husband; his face was swollen, and he was attached to tubes and a breathing apparatus.

Ten days later, on May 28, detectives would pull up to her house to inform her of her husband's death. Their daughter still knew nothing. "My father's here," she told everyone. "My father came from Cuba. But he got lost . . ."

It was a bundling of errors. Errors by mental health professionals, by guards, and by police, driven by a policy that unloaded Cuba's most distressed citizens in great numbers with no documentation of their afflictions. It was also a flare, alerting authorities of a coming change in statistics. Yes, Mariel would provide criminals, but it would also provide a disproportionate number of victims, unbalanced and unaccustomed to a new world. Miami's black community would no longer furnish the majority of the city's victims and criminals. Latin Americans were the new leaders in almost every Dade County category, and for a simple reason: they were now the majority population.

In July, the city and the county had begun to realize that this immigration wave was not as cataclysmic as the *New York Times* and other outlets had believed. Of all the Cuban refugees who had now entered the United States, roughly 96 percent were confirmed to have no criminal record of any kind. The fear that hordes of arrivals were bringing in leprosy and new strains of tuberculosis was also unfounded. Together, they ran to twelve individuals.

Yet Miami's momentary panic in May had stained the new arrivals. They had suffered to risk emigration; they had suffered in the Peruvian embassy or in their own homes. Many had been beaten before departure, made dangerous journeys, been put in camps both before and upon arrival. *If* they were lucky, sponsors had taken them in. Most were now in cramped quarters, looking for work. And a growing division revealed itself: among the older generation of Cuban immigrants, no one wanted to be mistaken for a Marielito.

Behind the unforgiving misperceptions was a genuine problem. To say 96 percent of Mariel's refugees had no criminal record meant that there were about 5,000 now inside the United States who did. This did not go unnoticed by Marshall Frank's homicide bureau and the city desk at the *Miami Herald*. By the time Buchanan wrote about Juan Jose Toledo, the boatlift had passed 113,000 refugees. The worst of the flow was over. Half the marines stationed in Key West had been sent home. The INS removed 30 percent of its staff in Key West and planned to go from seventy-seven employees to five the following week. By June, no boats had headed south for two weeks, though small numbers of vessels still headed north. "It's a mess," said President Carter, "but we're doing the best we can."

A week before the riots, the FBI had identified at least twenty Cuban spies during processing. Some were aimed at infiltrating anti-Castro movements. Others were political intelligence officers. Eventually the government had responded with rigor to unsettling reports that as many as four hundred Castro agents had been included in the boatlift. The spies were for the FBI and the CIA to track, but the question of who would take responsibility for the mentally unsound and the criminals remained unanswered. With so much attention absorbed by new demands, it was unsurprising that the summer of 1980 proved to be a boom time for those involved in the cocaine industry.

CHAPTER 23

Summer was also the one time of year Mayor Ferré would gather his wife, Mercedes, and their six children and head north to Vermont to a house he had helped design. It sat just outside Stowe, on the side of a mountain, a place unlike Miami in every way, with high altitude, cool breezes, and fewer than three thousand inhabitants, with barely a Latin American among them. Finally, Ferré could shut out Miami and breathe fresher air.

He could rest easy that his position as mayor was safe for the moment, if only because a sudden move to oust him had been unsuccessful. The Miami Police Department had failed to forgive him for calling a handful of their officers "bums" in the wake of the riot when they'd spray-painted the word "looter" over cars carrying stolen goods. His own police had spent the early summer mounting a petition to recall the mayor, despite an apology. It had failed miserably, but it was still one more fracture for the mayor to consider from a distance.

There was a lot for Ferré to contemplate in Vermont. With his fortunes at an ebb, he had raised $4.4 million dollars at the start of the summer by selling the family home, La Santa Maria, to a Canadian developer. He was no longer Isaac Kattan's neighbor. In many ways, the sale was the result of his own mayoral agenda. Ferré could either try to hold on to a large private home as office towers rose around it, paying a spiraling tax bill imposed by his own city government, or he could sell well, and acknowledge what he knew: Miami was changing rapidly. That the changes were brought about by success in both legal and illegal businesses was becoming more and more obvious by the month.

If you were the money launderer Isaac Kattan, the summer of 1980 brought difficulties of its own. Kattan's work depended on the successful arrival of smuggled cocaine. The routes from Colombia to South Florida stayed open, but with the US Navy and Coast Guard such a massive presence in the Straits of Florida, there was concern. That concern quickly turned to extraordinary opportunity. The Coast Guard's drug enforcement patrols were reduced by 90 percent during the boatlift. Washington estimated an extra billion dollars of narcotics had slipped into South Florida.

Much of the unregistered air traffic was running into South Florida thanks to another of Isaac Kattan's clients, Colombia's Carlos Lehder, a onetime resident of Miami Beach. After betting heavily on bringing a single load of cocaine into the United States via private aircraft in August 1977, Lehder had driven his profits into purchasing an island in the Caribbean called Norman's Cay. He had extended its runway and used it as a transshipment point where up to twenty planes a day, northbound from Colombia, could refuel before heading into the United States. The business was similar to Kattan's, with much of the initial risk being taken by the manufacturers in South America. Lehder, like Kattan, was a very well-rewarded provider of services. For his innovations in transportation, he was estimated to have earned over $200 million a year for the last two years. Any business that Carlos Lehder found hard to handle was referred to his friend Carlos Jader Álvarez. It made no difference to Isaac Kattan, who laundered money for both men.

There was a kink in the system the Colombians had set up. They had perfected the production and transportation of cocaine and the way the money was laundered. The weakness existed between the point of sale and the money's entry into banks. For days, or weeks, depending on the size of the operation, that money remained in the form the cocaine dealer had accepted it: often five-, ten-, and twenty-dollar bills.

Kattan had two major worries. The first was robbery. While Kattan was known as reliable and honest by clients in both Medellín and Cali, not everyone on the Miami end of the business was entirely logical. Kattan also laundered money for the cocaine dealer Griselda Blanco. She killed for debts and occasionally killed to not have to pay off her own debts. Her brother-in-law, Paco Sepulveda, was the man who provided hit men like Anibal Jaramillo. A late payment, even a misunderstanding, could result in a man like Jaramillo driving down Biscayne Boulevard and pulling up beside Kattan as he walked.

Kattan's second worry was having accounts closed by nervous banks and being responsible for a bottleneck of money. A day's worth of ten-dollar bills weighed roughly 220 pounds. That might require only a single extra trip to a bank. But a month's backlog weighed 6,600 pounds, the equivalent of seven adult male alligators. It was conspicuous to move around Miami, though Kattan had once ended up at the same bank six times in a single day and no bank manager had ever raised a red flag.

The more bottlenecks, the more launderers like Kattan were forced to use alternative methods. They were risky and extreme and for the most part successful. Kattan had used airplanes and boats to ship millions of dollars of cash to the Caribbean and Colombia. But nothing was better than a local Miami financial institution that asked few questions, satisfied with charging heavy fees.

In August 1980, there was a bottleneck. The increase of cocaine arriving in Miami during Mariel had now metamorphosed into rooms full of bills in every denomination, and Kattan was frantically searching for accommodating banks. He went to meet with the vice president of the installment loan department at the Great American Bank. The man, who had worked at the bank for fourteen years, was already running similar laundering operations for other Colombians. Inside Great American, Kattan didn't have to be subtle. One August day, a teller passing by the office reported seeing a large stack of bills sitting openly on the desk between the two men.

The method at Great American was simple: convert the cash immediately to a cashier's check. Date, fake payee and remitters, all would be entered into the bank's books. Then the check would be removed from a vault. Cashier's checks were as fungible as cash. Kattan could walk in with $900,000 in small bills and walk out weighed down by no more than three or four checks.

He wouldn't put a name on the checks yet. The bank would keep a duplicate copy so that their books would balance, but they would then void that particular number, as if the check had never been sent out for collection. Yet when a bank examiner went over the books, they'd still balance. And if the examiner queried the missing checks, a crooked loan officer could simply explain that there had been voided misprints. Eventually Great American would have a ledger full of voided checks that they had provided to Kattan, not one of them bearing his name.

Carlos Jader Álvarez, one of the three great cocaine dealers of his country and one of Isaac Kattan's most important clients, couldn't wait for Kattan to find a new financial institution to accommodate his heavy money flow. At the end of August, the boyish Álvarez asked a favor of his ex-wife, mother to five of his children. He wanted the thirty-six-year-old Maria Rojas to fly from Bogotá to Miami for three days and return with $1.6 million in hundred-dollar bills.

For eight straight months, Operation Greenback's search for the cocaine industry's greatest money launderers relied solely on participation from customs and the IRS. The FBI had never shown up, and neither customs nor the IRS had the DEA's experience in following smugglers and mules. They'd found cocaine in bicycle tubes, the vagina of a racehorse, and hidden by models in their luggage under layers of silk underwear intended to deter inspection.

Most of all, the DEA simply had better intelligence. The tips kept coming from the same fertile source. Only four months before, in April, in the Miami International Airport, authorities had seized 137 kilograms of Álvarez's cocaine. It had a street value of $24 million. A month later, in Bogotá, the same source had led to the seizure of 200 kilograms, also destined for Miami. Again, the same source had led the focus on Álvarez's ex-wife and for the first time, the DEA had decided to share the information with Greenback. If the DEA was correct, and Maria Rojas really was carrying the money, then the next question for Greenback was, how on earth was she hiding it?

The first half of the year had seen Greenback caught up in internecine squabbling as they established their offices and tried to identify potential targets. As Greenback sniffed around Miami, its agents became almost dizzy at the numbers. When they'd started out, they had decided to pursue all cases involving over $1 million. By the summer, they had moved the entry point of interest to $100 million. Now they knew that Kattan was one of twelve moneymen laundering at least $250 million a year. In a year of struggle, with America's biggest carmaker, General Motors, posting a loss of $763 million, cocaine was simply the best growth business in the world. And Miami, thick with riot smoke and refugees, was the epicenter of its finances.

———

Amid the chaos, Operation Greenback was moving with cloistered caution. While dealers caught selling cocaine could face over twenty years of prison time, under the current statutes, it was hard to see how anyone involved in money laundering would spend more than five years behind bars. First Greenback needed to prove that currency transaction reports were either not filed or misfiled deliberately. To move beyond that, they needed to prove there was a conspiracy between money launderers and banks. Rojas was at least a simpler target; all they needed to apply pressure on her was to prove that she was deliberately leaving the country with undeclared monies. Therein lay the strength of Greenback. If Rojas claimed the money had been earned in the United States, then Greenback's IRS agents could seize it. If she insisted it had been earned outside American borders, then it would belong to customs.

Rojas was followed up to the second floor of the Braniff terminal to her gate past the lockers where customs had found ten assassination kits containing submachine guns two weeks before. There, at 6:00 p.m., a customs inspector recruited that afternoon by Greenback carefully made announcements in both English and Spanish reminding departing passengers that there were currency reporting requirements. Anyone carrying more than $5,000 who failed to fill out the form would be subject to prosecution by the federal government and would have to forfeit their money. The inspector, imposing at six foot three, went from passenger to passenger, repeating his announcement, until he stopped next to the petite Rojas and offered her a form.

Was she taking more than $5,000 out of the country? the Puerto Rican–born inspector asked in Spanish.

"No," said Rojas.

He repeated the question one more time.

"I wish I had five thousand," said Rojas, smiling. "I don't."

He returned the smile. "I'm just giving you another opportunity."

Greenback's attorneys had agonized about this moment. Technically, no crime was committed until a suspect left the country. But when do you leave a country? Customs had followed couriers up to planes before. They'd allowed jets to taxi and then ordered them to return to the gates. They had even had a commercial pilot fly twelve miles over international waters and then return so that they could search a suitcase. None of these methods was ideal.

What if a plane was ordered to turn around twelve miles out and the guilty party guessed the reason and attempted to hijack the airliner? There had been nineteen skyjackings in the United States in the 1970s, but suddenly Miami had seen six since June, all perpetrated by Mariel refugees who had been forced onto boats to Key West and were now redirecting commercial flights into Havana. Federal attorneys had analyzed the situation repeatedly, finally deciding that as soon as you walked down the ramp to board your plane you became fair game.

Once boarding began, Rojas showed the gate agent her ticket and walked down the ramp, where two Greenback agents stood side by side with the customs inspector. With the inspector translating, the agents asked Rojas to step aside a moment and explained that they wanted to check her bags. Did she object? No. They asked her one final time if she was carrying more than $5,000. Again, a breezy smile and another no. Would she mind coming to the customs interrogation room for further investigation?

"That's okay," said Rojas.

The Greenback agents rode alongside her down the escalator to the room on the first floor. There she was informed, in Spanish, of her constitutional rights, and willingly signed a Consent to Search form. A Greenback agent pushed the cart with her luggage into the room. From the other side of a four-foot-tall counter, Rojas stood on tiptoe and identified the black-and-brown Samsonite luggage as her own. Agents began to search through her bags. Women's clothes, an eggbeater, toiletries, and six shrink-wrapped Monopoly boxes, the Spanish-language version. In her purse, $12,500 held tight by a rubber band.

"I got the money! I got the money!" shouted an amused agent, waving white, yellow, and gold Monopoly currency over his head. Inside Rojas's purse were Monopoly tokens and more packets of Monopoly money. The same thought occurred to the rest of the agents at once. "If she's got her Monopoly money in her bags, then what's in the boxes?"

At 7:30, the agents carefully cut through the cellophane on the pristine Monopoly sets. A quick bundle count revealed that each box contained $250,000 in immaculately stacked and wrapped fifty- and hundred-dollar bills. The missing Monopoly boards were later found under blue-and-white-patterned sheets, slid between the mattress and box spring of the bed where she'd slept in an apartment in the very same building where Isaac Kattan lived. As the real money was examined, Rojas seemed to enter a trance. She rose from her seat and walked calmly out of the room toward the airport exit. An agent fell into step beside her and gently steered her back to the examination room, where, with the help of a female customs inspector, she was strip-searched.

Rojas struggled for excuses. She'd met a man on the street, maybe his name was Richard, who'd offered her two hundred dollars to bring the Monopoly boxes back to Bogotá for someone named Jose Antonio—she didn't remember his full name. She didn't remember the name of the woman she'd stayed with in Miami. She didn't remember the address. Placed under arrest, Rojas finally burst into tears as one of Greenback's group supervisors explained that she would be taken for fingerprinting and photographing.

"I'm innocent," she told the supervisor in Spanish. "How could I have known what was in the Monopoly boxes when they were sealed?"

The supervisor quietly pointed out that she'd had Monopoly pieces in her purse and in her luggage. She had, he said, "no answer whatsoever."

As the Greenback agents walked her out of the airport, Rojas was allowed an unexpectedly long last breath of freedom. The Greenback agents found that all their cars had been towed. When the cars were finally reclaimed, Rojas shared her ride with two other smugglers. Customs, like homicide, was a busy place to be.

At the Greenback office, the agents finally had a pleasant aggravation. Greenback's attorneys considered the money evidence, rather than fungible, and the agents, without a single counting machine, had to itemize every single dollar bill's serial number. Happily unhappy agents would work through the night.

Rojas was detained with a $1 million bond and described as an "extremely dangerous bail risk." Rojas was sent first to a grand jury and then to Dade Women's Detention, a place that the presiding judge ruefully described as "hell on earth." The money went into the general Treasury fund. Treasury couldn't help but notice that Greenback, after a slow eight months, had effectively earned back its budget in a single operation. Despite the success, Greenback remained a Treasury Department secret. To Mayor Ferré, returning from his vacation, Rojas's arrest went unnoticed. In Buchanan's relentless days, there was no room for a minor, frictionless arrest.

By pure chance, a female DEA agent had been on the flight to Bogotá that Maria Rojas had failed to join. Had the Miami office thought to ask, they would have learned that she'd noticed two agitated men waiting at the airport. The first was a Colombian customs official. The second was the man suspected of being one of Isaac Kattan's best customers, Carlos Jader Álvarez. He was most likely asking himself why he hadn't been more patient while Isaac Kattan opened his new accounts at the Great American Bank.

The first visitor Maria Rojas received in jail was a tiny hummingbird of a woman whose Miami apartment was dominated by an enlarged photograph of her riding a horse, naked. An accounting student from the University of Miami, she would within the year inherit many of Isaac Kattan's duties. For now, her job on Álvarez's behalf was simple. She offered Rojas $300,000 from her ex-husband to see out her yearlong sentence in silence. Any hope that Maria Rojas could be flipped was short-lived. The five children she shared with Álvarez remained in Colombia, a much better guarantee of her silence than any financial incentive.

After their first win, several Greenback agents celebrated with a day's fishing. They took a boat belonging to a group supervisor down to Key Largo, close to Alligator Reef Light. Four miles off the coast, a hundred-pound bale of marijuana floated toward them. They radioed in their find, waited patiently for a Coast Guard skiff to pick it up, and then finally resumed their afternoon's fishing with the suspicion you were never far away from narcotics in South Florida. It was true. The drugs were linked to the uptick in murders, and those two Miami problems were exacerbated by the city's immigration woes. Mariel had proved how weak American immigration laws were, while the comings and goings of Colombians attested to a system that was easy to circumvent either with false documents or the abuse of private aviation. Among all the visible, rapid changes, it was hardly surprising that the group of Miamians determined to see Ferré's city hang on to its past would grow.

PART 4

PART 4

CHAPTER 24

On August 27, the anti-bilingual activist Emmy Shafer walked into the county courthouse with 44,166 signatures, almost 20,000 more than required. She said she had as many more at home if the court wished to see them. The anti-bilingual ordinance would have to be included on November's ballot. The oddly named SALAD (Spanish American League Against Discrimination) was worried. "The result of this referendum," explained its leader, "will tell us whether we have friends or not and whether we are welcome here or not. This will polarize the community even more by making Cubans more militant."

Fearing yet more unrest, the *Miami Herald* and Mayor Ferré stood behind bilingualism. On September 15, Ferré drove the vote in the commission and made the City of Miami officially bilingual, hoping to send a signal across Dade County. The Greater Miami Chamber of Commerce, never far from the influence of the Non-Group, spent $50,000 moving against Shafer. But Shafer's campaign "seemed to run itself" from the outset, spending less than $10,000, relying almost entirely on Anglo volunteers. It was unstoppable despite the lack of oxygen the media afforded it.

Eighty-five percent of whites now thought Cubans had damaged Miami. Only 44 percent of blacks agreed, but where they disagreed, the anger was just as startling. "There's so many damn rich Cubans in this town," said a forty-seven-year-old mother in Liberty City. "Why haven't we got somewhere? What have the Cubans ever done for them? Our women done lay down and had those bastard babies. We done washed their clothes . . . they go adopt some other nation. And set them free!" She'd gone for food stamps, "and there were so many Cubans and Haitians there, the American people were not getting any stamps. It looked like the foreigners were getting their stamps first." H. T. Smith, a prominent black attorney, put it simply. "The feeling is that the black community was waiting in line and now our time had come," he said. "Only it hadn't."

The anger had turned inward. Patterns of discrimination were changing quickly. Haiti, which had steadily disgorged hundreds of desperate economic migrants to South Florida on rickety boats every month throughout 1980, had increased its flow that summer, hoping to force Jimmy Carter to accept Haitian refugees as he had Cuban refugees. The only thing that the newly arrived Cubans and Haitians had in common was that they were now both greeted warily by every one of Miami's tribes. Even in predominantly black schools, the insult of choice was to call a classmate a "Haitian."

September and October saw a series of heated debates over language across local radio and television. It revealed that well after the riots, there was anger across all of Miami. Anglo Miami was resentful of the changing demographics; black Miami seethed over the justice system. Cuban Miami, still busy trying to absorb the equivalent of one new person into every household, was now waking up to the fact that their vision of themselves as invigorating entrepreneurs was not a narrative that anyone was willing to listen to except in Spanish.

SALAD had appointed telegenic Manny Diaz, Miami's future mayor, to lead the defense of bilingualism. Again and again, he battled Shafer in radio stations at two in the morning and on local afternoon television. She didn't want Spanish used in elevators or private stores. She'd arrived in America not speaking English and suffered terribly. It was what all immigrants needed to go through. Over the weeks, she began to warm to Diaz until, at the end of one vicious debate, with the microphones off, she leaned over to him and asked if he'd like to take her daughter on a date.

"I thought I had horns," said a surprised Diaz.

"You're not like the rest of them," said Shafer, and gave him an assuring pat on his arm.

———

The only shift during the summer of 1980 seemed to have been psychological. The city had become more divided, defensive, and openly paranoid. In the wake of Mariel, McDuffie, and the cocaine violence, Miami had armed itself.

The Tamiami Gun Shop, Cuban-owned, tripled sales in the weeks following the riot. They advised customers which gun was best for the home (a sawed-off 12-gauge whose pellets would be contained by walls) and which was best for work (a .38-caliber revolver that could kill a felon without damaging merchandise). Ronald Wright, the assistant medical examiner, had stopped a burglar in his house at gunpoint and advised any Miamian willing to kill to buy a gun. A homicide detective concurred. Miami was the Wild West, he said, and "people couldn't depend on the police or the courts." Even the local police union told Edna Buchanan that citizens should arm themselves because the police were spread too thin.

Only Mayor Ferré seemed to object. "That's a hell of a statement!" he told his chief of police. With its own police officers encouraging citizen militias, Miami seemed a long way from Ferré's dream as the serene Latin American capital of service, finance, and tourism.

When Edna Buchanan had referred to the Colombian vehicle at the Dadeland double murder back in 1979 as a "war wagon," it was only the beginning of the militarization of language used by Buchanan and many other *Herald* journalists. Reporters referred to Colombian gun battles on streets. Judges called for courts to unite in "a war on drug murders," while a psychiatrist Buchanan interviewed warned that the city had developed a wartime mentality and felt like "an armed camp." Murder rates were steady across all American cities, with the exception of Miami, which now had a staggering number of multiple murders, including several quadruple homicides, all related to drugs, as well as a sudden spike in murders involving Cuban refugees and a surge of potential victims shooting their aggressors during robberies, rapes, and beatings.

Covering crime and solving murders had never seemed so close. Normally there was a great separation between the two, but once a situation was viewed as a war, civil institutions set up to check one another, such as a newspaper and a police department, could suddenly have more in common than either had supposed.

The place where Buchanan's and Frank's worlds met could be found in an article she had written at the end of the summer. She had pitched the idea to her editors, asking them to let her follow an average day in a homicide bureau to show the exhaustion permeating the law enforcement community. Let it show what was really going on in the city, far from the tranquil banyan-lined streets of Coral Gables. By merely reporting on her day, Buchanan was issuing a warning to the *Herald*'s readers about the ways in which Miami was transforming into a boiling mixture of crime from three separate countries.

By ten o'clock in the morning, almost three hours into Buchanan's trailing of a pair of homicide detectives, she'd attended a natural death in Little Haiti, witnessed the arrest of a rapist in Liberty City, and then rushed to Jackson Memorial to watch detectives interview a woman whose husband had attempted to murder her with a Weedwacker in front of her three children. From the outset, it was obvious that the police now moved in an unsympathetic landscape. "Stop Killer Cops!" had been spray-painted in large letters against a wall near the northern city limits.

The first shooting of the day took place in a Cuban restaurant called El Rey de Bistec, the King of Steak. The victim, a one-legged man "grotesquely suspended atop two orange counter stools," was still dripping blood over the floor. Cause of death was easy enough: a shot to the back of the head. The waitresses were weeping. Buchanan normally squinted through windows from outside, or vaulted police tape without permission, but now she was ushered in to watch the paramedics and policemen mill about.

They'd had to wait for a bilingual detective to arrive before starting the interviews. The three killers had fled together. They'd gotten in a car and headed toward Tent City, an encampment close to Little Havana where, as of July 25, Mayor Ferré was temporarily housing hundreds of Mariel's refugees. *So this is a Mariel killing*, thought Buchanan. *So that means a warrant*, thought the detectives.

Thousands of Mariel refugees had been placed in homes around America, but many had taken the check meant to help them start a new life and bought a bus ticket straight back to Miami. Those who could not find jobs, apartments, or local sponsors ended up in Tent City, under the concrete pillars of I-95 that Ferré's family had poured twenty years before.

The manager at El Rey de Bistec was anxious for the body to be removed. He was still hoping to serve the late lunch crowd. Translated conversations buzzed on all sides of Buchanan. The dead man had been eating with a friend, who'd been dressed head to toe in white—or he *was* in all white, until the blood splatter. The friend had headed home to change. He'd be easy to spot, said a witness, since his two front teeth were missing.

Around 2:00 p.m., Buchanan followed the detectives and their five witnesses back to the station. Over the radio, another body was reported found. In a city that used to average 120 homicides a year, there were already two in a day. Edna Buchanan did the math. It was homicide number 328 for 1980, which meant that they were on course for over 500 murders in a year. Then the radio came to life again. This time, a shooting on elegant Miracle Mile.

There was no stenographer at the station. Everyone was frustrated. At 2:30, a prosecutor gave permission to conduct a lineup in Tent City. But the witnesses knew better. They were sure the killers were Colombians, since their accents were typically formal and distinct. Why would they seek cover amid Cuban refugees?

Tent City was a month into existence. Ankle-deep in dirty summer rain, it housed seven hundred strangers who existed with no walls and no jobs. Unsurprisingly, a surly reaction awaited Buchanan and the detectives. People spilled out of their tents, letting the witnesses stare at a procession of unhappy faces. No suspected killers were identified. As the traffic roared overhead on I-95 and giant freighters passed silently behind the tents down the Miami River, Buchanan and the detectives retreated.

At 4:00, they arrived at headquarters and had the witnesses leaf through books of four hundred illegal aliens from Colombia suspected of being involved in the narcotics trade. Among the deceased's wallet litter, the detectives found a photograph of the dead man with six kids and a piece of paper with phone numbers. They handed it to a Spanish-speaking officer, telling him to call down the list. The first woman to pick up was a Mariel refugee. She'd met the dead man a few days earlier and he'd promised to get her three children out of Cuba. At 8:00, they headed over to the address the woman had provided. The detectives were grumbling. One was supposed to be with his father, installing paneling. The older detective was supposed to be eating London broil, studying for his sergeant's exam that he'd take in less than forty-eight hours. Nobody answered the door. At least they now had a last name from the landlady. The "homicide headache" hit both detectives at the same time, when they remembered they'd forgotten to eat, forgotten to drink, all day long. Buchanan accompanied them to a local McDonald's at 9:00, where, in the fluorescent light, they ordered Cokes and Quarter Pounders with cheese.

And then it was 9:20, and the card they'd stuck in the witness's door just twenty minutes before was gone. Could they have missed him? Exhausted, they headed back to the station. At 9:58, the phone rang. It was the witness's lawyer. He wouldn't talk without his attorney. "Jesus," said a detective arriving early for the midnight shift, "even witnesses have lawyers?" And just before Buchanan left to go file her story at the *Herald*, a patrolman called in. He had a stab wound victim in the hospital, he told the detectives. No, not in danger. The victim had three hundred bucks on him, but now the patrolman was confronted by three women standing next to him, all claiming to be the man's wife, and they all wanted the money. What should he do?

It made for an extraordinary article for the *Herald*. Only later in life, when Buchanan reflected, did she realize what the experience was like. She wasn't covering the crime desk in the second half of 1980; she was Miami's first war correspondent, a witness to the endless grind, the fascination of violence, the questions and the breaks. That day had concerned an Irish and an Italian cop, followed around by the tiny blonde with the handbag, trying to find who shot the one-legged Latin male. All they could be certain about was that the killers were Colombian, drugs were somehow involved, and you needed fluent Spanish in Miami if you didn't want to spend half your day in translation. The restaurant's employees were from Mariel. The phone tip came from another refugee. The gunmen were from Colombia, and yet the expectation was that a homicide bureau was supposed to have a grip on criminal enterprise within Miami *and* from two foreign countries. For the moment, it was an impossible task in a city that was attempting to become the gateway to the Americas for all industries but seemed to be thriving only in one: cocaine.

CHAPTER 25

For Marshall Frank, leading the homicide bureau in such a fevered climate had presented a set of problems that were different from the ones Edna Buchanan faced as a journalist. Buchanan could work harder, sleep less, cover even more stories. And she did. A homicide captain was effectively a manager. Frank was now responsible for rebuilding a bureau that had been ravaged by the FBI's investigation of the cocaine dealer Mario Escandar. The year 1980 had seen Frank testify in the McDuffie trial but also address a congressional hearing in Washington, where he'd presented a nine-page list of victims in drug-related killings. At the same time, he had to contend with the arrival of an unknown number of murderers from Mariel while trying to pursue investigations of the killings that took place during the riots.

The only riot deaths that Frank's squads had cleared by the end of the summer were the justifiable homicides by police officers. Marshall Frank had ordered Wesolowski to send twenty-one detectives and four sergeants into the streets around the Scott Projects—a huge canvassing effort. Frank was desperate to stir up information on some of the homicides adjacent to the projects. Because the riots had been so dangerous, only one scene had been attended by a homicide squad, and that was back on May 17.

In one day, Frank's detectives knocked on almost nine hundred doors, between 6:00 p.m. and midnight. Yet the reports were almost unanimously succinct. "No response." "Out of town." "Stayed inside." "At home but saw nothing." Even the longer reports were hopeless. "Observed vehicles burning but could not identify anyone in the area." The one lead they had, from a black county paramedic, produced a statement with an open contradiction at its core. It was filled with accurate details on the way one victim had died; the time, the fire, the tag number of his car, the weapon involved. The paramedic had lived in the same neighborhood for twenty-six years. Yet he could not identify any of the killers.

Of the little they discovered, Frank's squad could discern that the riots had proved that Miami was no longer an easy place to subdivide into black and white. The opening night of the riot saw lives changing, or ending, because of snap judgments. A light-skinned Caribbean doctor was shot through the neck, his vocal cords severed. Even as he was being beaten, he could hear some of his black attackers wondering if he was Cuban, wondering if he was white. A Cuban-born butcher, mistaken for Anglo late on a Saturday night, had been beaten with rocks, stabbed with two halves of a broken rake, and then set alight in front of hundreds of witnesses.

To the furious mob, the butcher wasn't a working-class Cuban immigrant, just a light-skinned target who had fallen into their hands. The detectives had had to move so quickly in front of the rioters that they'd towed the butcher's car with his body still inside. The friction of the tireless car screeching along the street caused the fire to reignite. Those still on the streets were greeted with the hellish image of the tow truck dragging the charred remains of the butcher away from the riot zone, lit by the fire within his own vehicle.

But what had the rioters been trying to vanquish? It seemed to be as much foreignness as color, since both men were immigrants, and either unable or unwilling to speak in English. Miami's color lines and Miami's immigration issues had blurred into one seething fury that may have calmed after the riot but had not been resolved.

Marshall Frank found an even sadder coda to the butcher's fiery death. His detectives met with the man's daughter, a thirty-year-old acrobat on a cruise ship. She had kissed her father goodbye the morning of the riots.

Investigators had looked for the man's boss and had been unable to find him because he had captained a boat to Mariel. On the night of the murder, the boss had been waiting patiently in the harbor for his employee's wife and second child. The summer should have seen the reunion of father, mother, and both their children for the first time in a decade, not a daughter passing her father's dentures to homicide detectives for purposes of identification.

In order to start solving Miami's problems, its local agencies had to improvise from within. The first thing for Marshall Frank to do was recruit. The summer of 1980 would see an influx of detectives into his homicide bureau to replace those who had been indicted, fired, or transferred. For every position, there were twenty to thirty applicants: all detectives from different units within the department. Each applicant would sit facing two supervisors and Frank himself. They weren't being tested on case law; 1980s questions tipped toward ethics. You and another detective arrive at a scene. There are five hundred-dollar bills on a table. You turn around, and now there are three. What do you do?

Frank had his own favorite question. You catch a case. The body's been cleared from the scene by the ME. It's an eleven-year-old girl who shot herself in the head with her father's gun. The parents are sobbing downstairs. You find a crumpled suicide note. It reads, *"Dear Mom and Dad. You didn't want a daughter you wanted a slave. I hope you're happy now. Goodbye."* So what do you do with the note? That's what Frank would ask his prospect. Do you take it to the crime lab, where it will be fingerprinted, entered into evidence, and available for the parents to see? Or do you keep it to yourself and dispose of it? Not even the supervisors knew, but it had been a case of Frank's from over a decade before. He'd known the family, a hardworking couple, and he was certain the note would destroy them. Illegally, he'd destroyed it. There was no right answer for the applicants, only the revelation of character, and character would define Frank's recruiting choices.

Those Frank selected would be stepping into a Miami vastly different from the one Frank had found as a rookie in 1966. The murder rate was up 246 percent in under four years. Bodies seemed to be everywhere. Highways, parking lots, airports. A couple checking in to a hotel found a strangulation victim under their bed. Worst of all was South Beach, where so many of Mariel's unwanted were placed in rundown hotels, subsidized by the county. Over the last decade, South Beach had become the single poorest neighborhood in Florida, "one of the poorest in the country outside of some districts of Appalachia." It was stocked with an elderly population of Jewish retirees on fixed incomes. Still, what little money the elderly had would be withdrawn from local banks. Criminal elements from Mariel, living in the same subsidized hotels as their victims, would follow the elderly home: easy pickings.

Again and again, Frank's detectives would find refugees involved in killings. A Mariel refugee, angered after he was refused a dance by a woman, was then killed by a bartender. One refugee shot another for waking him up too early. In another bar, again Mariel provided victim and killer. The entire scene had been scrubbed clean of prints, including every glass on the counter. Someone had washed the floor so thoroughly that the body was surrounded by soapy swab marks.

Frank looked for good detectives from other units, ex-homicide detectives willing to return or Spanish-speaking detectives he could trust. After the Escandar fiasco, when cocaine had first eroded Frank's bureau, it was obvious that Cuban Americans were underrepresented. At the height of the summer, Frank made an inspired choice.

"You ever worked homicide?" Marshall Frank asked Lieutenant Raul Diaz during his interview. The deep-voiced narcotics detective in front of him seemed calm. His English was impeccable, with just a trace of his Havana birth that came through in some words but not others. Ask him to say "shit," and his low voice started with the s and dropped an octave before it hit the t.

"No," said Diaz.

"You ever process a scene?" asked Frank.

Diaz had been part of the very first Joint Terrorism Task Force in 1975 and knew how to process a *bombing* scene, to sift carefully for plastic wire, a piece of battery. But a body? "No."

"So why'd you put in for homicide?" asked Frank.

"Because your boss told me to." With a recommendation from a major in his pocket, it would have been impossible for Diaz to have been refused a position by Frank, but regardless, he warmed to the newcomer immediately.

It would have been hard to come up with a list of people Raul Diaz *didn't* know in Miami. He'd worked organized crime and taught DEA agents a specialized weapons program. He knew half their agents in Miami. McDuffie's friend, the public information officer Lonnie Lawrence? Raul called him "Agent Hawk," a nickname left over from a drug operation five years before when Lawrence had worked undercover "dressed as a pimp with big chains." Customs? He'd worked with a customs task force his first year with the county, in 1971. He even came with an infamous father-in-law, Eugenio Martinez, a Watergate burglar on the CIA payroll whom the CIA regarded as "a loyal and reliable employee." The CIA itself? Diaz counted a Miami-based agent among his closest friends. Assistant state attorneys Yoss and Adorno? Diaz had helped put together their most famous win. And Operation Greenback? Frank didn't know about it yet, but Raul Diaz did. His friend the amicable Cuban-born giant Raul de Armas was one of the IRS criminal investigators busy combing through the records of Colombian money launderers.

Diaz even had connections to Edna Buchanan. When he had begun his career as an intern with the Miami Beach police in 1969, he had watched a man miss a turn and drive straight into the canal off Indian Creek Drive. He'd dived in to drag the man out and Buchanan, back in her days at the *Miami Beach Daily Sun*, had penned a short article.

Frank brought Diaz in as lieutenant. In the PSD's homicide bureau, a lieutenant was supposedly confined to the office, eyes on rotating squads, guardian and distributor of paperwork, watching overtime, pushing rookies. Diaz was different, itchy to be on scene. With connections that covered all of Miami, he became the central node of a network of a thousand spokes. It was something recognized at once when he was approached by two of his detectives who had spent weeks attempting to interview a notorious CIA informant. The same evening, Diaz took the detectives to the Mutiny Hotel, the cocaine industry's favorite nightspot, and made the introduction.

If the world of homicide had been a business, Diaz would have been Mayor Ferré's prototype for a successful Miami entrepreneur. He was bilingual, happily moving between Anglo and Latin cultures, connecting points previously unconnected. Within his department, he understood that his own weakness was a lack of penetration into the world of Colombian enforcers, and immediately befriended another one of Marshall Frank's crew, intelligence analyst June Hawkins. Cuban American, Hawkins had begun to create a series of three-by-five cards seeking to establish the links between victims, suspects, their infinite aliases, and the cocaine trade. One of Marshall Frank's big worries during the riots had been that Hawkins's nascent datasets would go up in smoke. Fractionalized Miami, at least in the world of law enforcement, now had a chance to tie together the three worlds of Cuba, Colombia, and South Florida.

Worryingly, cocaine was the nexus. Within weeks of their arrival, many of the 4 percent of the refugees who had lived their lives as criminals in Cuba sought out work from their most likely employers, Colombians. Though there were a handful from Mariel, such as Cuba's former bicycling champion, who would make a fast fortune in the cocaine industry, most found work at the bottom end of the business, as drivers, lookouts, and enforcers working for as little as a fifth of what had been the going rate. Murder in Miami had become much cheaper almost overnight.

By September, one returning homicide detective had handled more cases in four months than in his entire two years in the mid-1970s. That included five murders in a single shift, four before lunch. It began with a murder-suicide, a gift for any detective, then two more domestics. A bloody, neat, efficient morning. Things got more complicated by the afternoon, when the detective was called out to the edge of the Everglades.

There was a body in the canal, a Latin male tied to a transmission and heaved into the water. He'd been carved from his chin down to his pubis, gutted, wrapped in chains. Once the body had decomposed, the chains loosened and up he floated like a dog at the end of his metal leash, the head just a foot under the green water. Offender: Unknown.

And that was one of the great frustrations of the summer of 1980. A decomposed body. A top medical examiner could pull a fingerprint and match it to a drug seizure, and that would lead to? Nowhere. They might suspect he was Colombian, but they couldn't pull an accurate name. Greenback, June Hawkins of the PSD, and Edna Buchanan were all coming to the same independent conclusions. Miami was filled with young men from Colombia. But were enforcers like Anibal Jaramillo flown in to do business, or did they live here? Detectives, reporters, and Greenback agents were all like butlers in a haunted Miami mansion, holding flickering candles with no idea of what lay just beyond the shadows.

Every sergeant had to train his whole squad until they were equal to him, but as Frank had admitted earlier to Edna Buchanan, he had only three detectives with more than a year of experience. His top men, including Wesolowski and Singleton, became on-the-job instructors making sure that a year from now, Frank would have experienced detectives. Wesolowski would teach his rookies to walk around the scene with their hands in their pockets. It makes you use your eyes. You remember to look up. He would patrol his own detectives, pencil tucked behind his ear, checking, rechecking reports. Because every good homicide detective isn't writing for his lieutenant or captain. The good detective is writing for his state attorney, the great one is writing for a defense attorney, presenting a case so airtight that the accused's lawyers won't dare to take the case to trial.

For those new to homicide, there was an initial natural high in reaction to the pace and the importance of the job. Every day held surprises, and most of them lay outside the office. The phone would ring and who knew where you would be sent? The more blood spilled, the less time you spent behind a desk. Always the victims' families in shock. You'd have to find the compassionate side under the cynic. And sometimes you'd have families that didn't cooperate. For the first time, detectives found families more cynical than any reporter or detective, and as inured to violence and mistrustful as the detectives themselves.

Newcomers would also have the jolt of being introduced to Doc Davis's morgue, where they brought the summer's mummifications and putrefactions as death was discovered across Dade County. Buchanan kept the running total as the rate of murder increased. Alongside Ronald Wright, she'd attended a new category of death: mules who were swallowing large amounts of cocaine. August saw the tenth dead mule of the year. Wright could always tell a mule's hotel room, not by dead bodies still running 100-degree temperatures but by the enemas, laxatives, and packages of prunes within the corpse's reach. "His last meal was worth $30,000," began one of Buchanan's articles. "And it killed him."

The airports were the hub for both drugs and money, the drugs traveling through and millions of dollars taking off from the tarmac. One detective found an unknown Colombian tied with flex cuffs, beaten, stabbed, then shot. The body had been folded, put in a television box, and marked for shipment back to Bogotá. In the parking lot the box had begun to leak, and there it was abandoned in the middle of summer. A maintenance man had spotted it, but he'd thought to leave it. If no one picked it up, he'd take the television home. A day later, when he moved it toward his van, fluids squelched from the bottom and finally he'd called the cops.

There was also the body left out in the summer sun covered head to toe in plastic wrap. That one actually melted. So many seemed to be Colombian. The midnight shift would be on scene and hear the engines of a small plane pass above and know that yet another load of cocaine was about to lead to more corpses. Once, a plane flew by a homicide scene so low that it set off car alarms. Detectives had even handled a collision of two small planes, both in the drug trade, that resulted in half a dozen dead pilots and passengers. They'd called the Coast Guard for help. In they came on the white-and-orange chopper, rushing to beat the dying sun.

"We don't fly around here at night anymore," shouted the pilot: there were far too many planes flying under the radar.

Unidentified low-flying aircraft crisscrossed South Florida as dealers paid off air traffic controllers for the schedules of any law enforcement aviation. Now that the committees in DC had revealed the extent of cocaine's penetration, now that Greenback was up and running, $7 billion of trade that couldn't be seen suddenly *was* seen. It was all around. It was the cigarette boats rumbling over Biscayne Bay with their lights off that woke Edna Buchanan in the night. It was the low-flying aircraft that set off car alarms. It was the spike in the real estate market, the car dealers accepting bricks of cash for a Rolls-Royce, and the nightclub valets inured to fifty-dollar tips.

The only thing not increasing that summer was the conviction rate. Back in the mid-1970s, only 8 percent of offenders who reached a final disposition had their charges dropped. In 1980, it hit 25 percent. Even in trials where the defendant was accused of murder in the first degree, 60 percent were convicted of lesser charges. Despite, or because of, Miami's contortions, a criminal in Miami was more likely to serve a shorter term than almost anywhere in America. Frank's squads could spend hundreds of man-hours on a killing and watch the overwhelmed courts cut a deal so lenient it would have horrified any other county in the state.

By the close of the summer, Marshall Frank's ashtray ended each day hidden under a burial mound of eighty Benson & Hedges butts. He secretly visited a psychiatrist once a week, telling only his original mentor, chief of detectives Charlie Black. The serial dater with his radio voice and aviator shades had become reclusive, impotent, and suicidal.

Frank's personal struggles with alcohol weren't created by Miami, but Miami was responsible for the current temperature, the lack of time, and the sense that its institutions could be overwhelmed at any moment. Frank still held his position in the Broward Symphony Orchestra, still relied on his violin and Tchaikovsky to calm himself, just as he had done returning home from the riots. Then, he'd felt like Nero, playing in the early morning as his city burned. On top of it all, he was still hunted by a local television news channel that, without a trace of evidence, decided that the Escandar corruption case against his homicide force must run deeper still. It didn't matter that Frank hadn't even been heading the Bureau when the FBI investigation had begun, he was still subject to Channel 10's I-Team crew pushing into his office to accuse him of corruption. An apology wouldn't arrive until 1981.

If Miami was a patient suffering from psychosis, then the local administrators were the only ones attempting treatment. Frank had a solid foundation to build on. He had Singleton and Wesolowski in charge of training, he had Diaz and his bags full of connections, and he had June Hawkins working at the edge of the unknown. At the state attorney's office, changes were also happening. Janet Reno, who had been accused by the owner of the *Miami Times* of being to blacks as Hitler was to Jews, hired ten black attorneys. Governor Graham, County Manager Stierheim, and Mayor Ferré were clear-eyed enough to see that part of the solution could begin before elections. Through appointments, they could pluck capable men and women and put them in place as judges, officials, or school board members, and they would have a chance to prove themselves before November.

Despite its reinvigoration by new recruits, Frank's homicide bureau was soon exhausted. Kidnappings remained homicide's responsibility. There were six in 1980, all relying on intensive manpower, all involving Colombians and the drug trade, and all successfully resolved. Yet not a single victim pressed charges against their Colombian kidnappers, since they were also employed in the cocaine industry. Had it been a deliberate ploy to distract and depress the homicide bureau, it couldn't have been bettered. The morale in homicide soon hit a new low. A PSD officer had been shot in Liberty City chasing robbery suspects. There was a high likelihood the same group who had ambushed him were also involved in the murder of the Cuban butcher during the riots, yet the PSD's director had ordered homicide not to investigate, fearful of starting up another disturbance.

To homicide it seemed as if their own director had decided that the city had become too volatile to police. In protest, disgusted detectives passed around a garbage can and threw their badges inside. For an hour, Marshall Frank had no homicide bureau at all. Only later were the badges grudgingly retrieved.

Buchanan visited the PSD building the following day. "There is no leadership out there at all," said one detective. "There is just no sense of direction. It's like we aimlessly wander from crisis to crisis now." Just because Buchanan was asking the questions didn't mean she wasn't apportioned part of the blame. Why was morale so low within the PSD? she asked the director. "Inflation, and low salaries," he said. "A shortage of manpower and a lack of positive recognition from the community . . . and especially the Miami news media . . . especially the *Miami Herald* and the *Miami News*."

There was a different answer. The problem wasn't catching killers. The problem was the killers themselves. How, for instance, could you even find a professional hit man like Anibal Jaramillo? Even a Cuban like Raul Diaz still had limited knowledge of Colombians. June Hawkins had heard through sources that Miami-based Colombian cocaine leader Paco Sepulveda alone ran twenty-five killers, but to arrest anyone would involve either luck on the police's behalf or sloppiness by a Colombian enforcer.

CHAPTER 26

There was no sudden turning of leaves, no rummaging for sweaters or shortening of days. Summer sat still, smothering Miami in a heat that rarely broke before Halloween. The greatest relief wasn't the first cool edge to the breeze but the approach of the official end of the hurricane season, on November 30. In 1980, at least nature had spared Miami. Criminals had not, though the pattern of murders was continuing to change.

Mariel murders were similar to one another only in their unpredictability. They were often reactive, impulsive, careless, and the perpetrators were eventually caught by Frank's squads. Murders by Colombians were often bold and preplanned, and they were almost always related to business. Mariel's crimes were committed by those sentenced to the gray area of immigration, neither accepted nor rejected by America; the Colombian killers were simply lawless. Unlike the Mariel refugees, they had never registered with customs, and were likely to have two or more identities. While Mariel's murderers could seem almost apathetic in their attempts to avoid the law, the Colombians seemed more like ghosts, even when they were seen by everyone.

Anibal Jaramillo wore black shoes, gray pants, and a blue-and-white shirt that he'd covered with a black windbreaker, despite the 78-degree weather. It was six thirty-five on the morning on November 17, moments before sunrise. Jaramillo could often be found in the driver's seat of Paco Sepulveda's Mercedes, but today he had been given a job that entailed driving an innocuous Chevy Nova. It looked like every other car on an

American road in 1980: oversize, boxy, square rear brake lights, silver bumper.

He kept the dark brown Corvette he was tailing just in view as he headed up Red Road toward the Miami International Airport. He was following twenty-four-year-old Graciella Gomez, his boss's girlfriend. Several cars ahead, Gomez was slowing down in early commuter traffic. She was easy to spot, wearing a dark turquoise two-piece satin outfit that lit up her feathered, dyed blond hair. On the empty passenger seat beside her was a bouquet of flowers. Underneath the seat was a gold-plated revolver. When the light turned red, Jaramillo eased the Nova up, squeezing between a white Mustang and Gomez's Corvette, then rolled down his window and shouted "¡Oye!" to get Gomez's attention. When she didn't look up, Jaramillo yelled, "Where're you going?"

As Gomez peered across at him, Jaramillo grabbed the blue steel Beretta from between his legs, stuck his arm through the open window, and fired once at the young woman with the feathered hair. Then he took a leisurely turn to make his way back south on Red Road. Even though he had fired his hollow-point bullet straight between Gomez's lips, she opened her door and rose to her feet. From his rearview mirror, he could see her beginning to run, panicked, along the median away from him. She hadn't even managed to put her car in park. It rolled forward and slammed into the bumper of the car in front, shattering the brake light.

There was no cover for Gomez. Nowhere for her to go. And yet the white Mustang Jaramillo had nosed in front of was suddenly thrown into reverse. The driver was backing down the three-lane road, shouting at Gomez through his window. She seemed to slow and the Mustang came to a halt. Jaramillo made another U-turn and started driving back toward Gomez.

Jaramillo accelerated, then came to a screeching halt beside the white Mustang. Stepping out of the Nova, he could see the driver of the Mustang, maybe fifty years old, standing while trying to bundle Gomez past a woman in the passenger seat. Gomez was wild-eyed, gurgling blood and struggling to squeeze past. The woman Gomez pushed past was too terrified to look directly at Jaramillo.

Walking slowly to the driver's side, where the man was now crouching by the car, Jaramillo put the muzzle of his revolver against the driver's forehead. "Fuck you," said the stranger. Jaramillo gave a slight smile, lowered the gun, and walked around the car as Gomez tried to make herself smaller, curling up in the back seat. Jaramillo stretched his arm out, brushing the gun against the female passenger in the front seat, now cowering in the footwell. Suddenly the passenger was grabbed by the driver and pulled straight across the front seats and out the driver's-side door. "Run, run, run!" the driver shouted, and the couple sprinted away from the car.

Jaramillo took a two-handed grip on his gun, leaned so close to the car that both his arms were inside, and then emptied his weapon into Graciella Gomez, shooting into her mouth again and then at the neck, through the liver, through a lung. One finger was grazed, another bullet passed through her clenched left fist. Now sure that he'd done his job, Jaramillo walked calmly back to the Nova, pulled away from the scene, drove for five minutes, and parked the car in front of a closed bar called the Lemon Twist Lounge. Leaving the murder weapon under the seat, he opened the door and stepped into the sunshine. It was still before seven in the morning.

It was done so calmly, perhaps out of Jaramillo's belief—not unusual among Colombians—that he had a decent understanding of America. Colombians had grown up on black-and-white movies featuring machine gun–toting American gangsters shamelessly riding through the streets of Chicago. They also had faith that the American legal system was entirely capitalistic—you got what you paid for. If you had money for a good lawyer, you could effectively evade the law. Together, those two complementary ideas gave men like Anibal Jaramillo a serene and undeserved confidence.

———

If you were on the other side of the equation, in Marshall Frank's position, the situation was as infuriating as ever. Wesolowski had been in charge on the scene. The Chevy Nova had already been found at the

Lemon Twist Lounge. They had a murder weapon and fingerprints. They had witnesses, even cooperative ones, and yet trying to sort their statements only revealed the magnitude of the task. The owners of the white Mustang who had tried to rescue Gomez had been close enough to the killer to have been touched by his revolver. The husband reckoned that Jaramillo was over six feet. His wife put him at five six. The killer's clothes changed depending on which of the five witnesses you talked to. By the time all statements were taken, two days after the incident, witnesses even disagreed on whether the murder had taken place in the light of day or in predawn darkness. One even swore the whole thing had happened a day later. Of the two most important witnesses, one was clearly petrified. Even as the crime was taking place, the passenger came to a conclusion. "In my panic and my fear I had acknowledged to myself I would never see and identify that man."

Frank and Wesolowski had a witness crouched two feet from a gunman, and still they knew very well that the odds of that witness identifying the murderer in a lineup were slim. *If* they could apprehend a suspect in the first place. For the moment, Gomez's murder showed every sign of slipping into the "Offender: Unknown" folder. Why not? The day before Gomez was killed, Buchanan noted another new record. Two years before, she'd followed one murder every three days. Now she wrote, "Murder Score—Six in Twelve Hours," and had refrained from counting a killing considered to be in self-defense. Gomez would only receive a tiny box in a full page devoted to the other five bodies. Between a mother framing a two-year-old for her child's murder and a heart specialist stabbed to death, it was becoming increasingly hard for many of the dead to earn ink in the *Herald*.

The bodies had another effect as the Colombian killings only aggravated the issues of immigration. Citizens who might have sympathized with Mariel's overwhelming number of ordinary refugees were constantly provoked into thinking that violent minorities *were* representative of immigrants. The issues of drugs, money, immigration, and race were connected, but the Colombians couldn't be considered representative of Miami's Latin American community. They were the opposite of the typical Mariel refugee, having no long-term interest in either the country or the city that hosted them. Ferré wanted entrepreneurs, active citizens, voters, or at least a community that would evolve into a constituency.

CHAPTER 27

The night of November 22 was busy for both Miami's legitimate and illegitimate enterprises. Mayor Ferré was shaking hands with Governor Graham at the opening of the Caribbean Conference in Key Biscayne, close to the new apartment he'd recently purchased after the sale of La Santa Maria. Bringing the conference to Miami had been a typical Ferré initiative, drawing the majority of the region's presidents and all of its business leaders north. His theory was simple. The stronger a nation's private sector, the more resistant its democracy would be against Cuba's constant attempts to export communism throughout the region. Ferré's aim for the evening was simple: let it be known that Miami should be the entrance point for Latin American goods and that Latin America should be the end point for American goods that would flow south through Miami.

The theme of the mayor's speech was obvious. Miami remained open for business, and the city's banks could still better any interest rates that lay to the south. The previous year, the *Financial Times* had insisted that Miami would have to pick one of two directions: either become similar to every other American city by seeking American investment, or wallow in a tiny local Spanish-speaking market. Ferré saw that as a false choice. You could keep what the *Financial Times* called a "Hispanic influence" and find international money that would see that Hispanic influence as a benefit. Miami may have tumbled in a public and humiliating fashion in the United States in 1980, but in Latin America, attractions were always relative.

For all the attention both Ferré and Graham paid to the bigger picture in Latin America, they also had a granular view of the city of Miami. You wouldn't have known it looking at the well-dressed governor that night at the Caribbean Conference, but Bob Graham had just spent two nights in police uniform accompanying officers in Liberty City. He'd attended robberies and assaults, encountered the worst of Mariel, and emerged determined to hire new prosecutors and build more jails for Miami. Tonight, sitting at tables covered with white tablecloths, served a preponderance of oysters, surrounded by a network of businessmen, both Ferré and Graham spoke to the cameras about the benefits of free trade in the region. You could be concerned for Miami and still be bullish.

That same evening, the third-ranked exporter of cocaine drove north past Key Biscayne, up I-95. Colombia's Carlos Jader Álvarez remained one of the DEA's most wanted men, worth an estimated half a billion dollars. Despite his wealth, Álvarez was having a terrible year. Both his ex-wife, Maria Rojas, and his business partner had been arrested in the United States in the last twelve months, while his head of transportation had been jailed in Colombia. He didn't know that Kattan, his preferred money launderer, was also under investigation. With 450 kilograms of cocaine ready for distribution, an investment with a street value of about $90 million, Álvarez made the decision to visit Miami to reorganize his operation.

The arrest of his ex-wife had taught Álvarez that it was too dangerous to move money directly through Miami's main international airport. Opa-locka Airport had been used as a CIA launch site for operations in Central America in the 1950s and for the Pedro Pan airlift that had brought in Cuban children like Lieutenant Raul Diaz in the 1960s. In 1980 it had been used briefly to house unaccompanied minors during Mariel.

The airport was, in theory, closed from 11:00 p.m. till dawn. If you chose to take off in the early morning, long before the sun rose, the place was usually empty. Tipped off to the tail number of Álvarez's airplane by the same wiretap in Colombia that had alerted Operation Greenback to his ex-wife's itinerary, agents had been following the pilots for three days.

Every afternoon, they had watched Álvarez's men haul duffel bags and suitcases out of their Mustangs and Chevy Blazers onto a twin-engine Piper Navajo at Opa-locka.

On November 22, the pilots had arranged for their plane to be fueled for a predawn departure. As night fell, agents were deployed at the far end of the runway in six vehicles. At 4:00 a.m., long after the tablecloths had been gathered at Ferré's Caribbean Conference, a white-and-tan Bronco pulled into Opa-locka. Five men began loading more boxes into the airplane. Eleven minutes later, three of the men boarded the airplane. One man walked back to the Chevy, while the second loitered outside the hangar. The engines roared to life, and the plane taxied down the ramp. As they moved from the ramp to the runway, a group of cars hurtled toward them in the dark, lit by the blue halos of their police lights. The plane slowed and stopped, immediately surrounded by a six-unit semicircle.

The Colombians were greeted by the odd sight of an IRS agent aiming a shotgun at their plane as a customs agent waved his badge at the cockpit, screaming above the roar, "Shut your engines down!" After a long minute, the engines died. With the engines off, you could hear the stillness of predawn Florida. Soon after, the hatch popped open and the three men descended onto the tarmac. Immediately, they were lined up along the airplane's wing.

"Where are you from?" asked one of Greenback's group supervisors in Spanish.

"Colombia," they said, one by one.

Agents asked for permission to search the plane. The captain nodded and began to slump, sinking to his knees. His copilot said nothing. Strangest was the lone passenger, who remained smiling the entire time. All of them were taken to the customs enforcement area, seated directly in front of a poster detailing currency reporting requirements in Spanish, and questioned individually.

It took a while to empty all the suitcases, a bag full of blue jeans, a case full of jewelry, an entire car windshield. Only when the agents heaved a large blue duffel bag onto the table did the passenger's grin disappear.

"That's not mine," he said.

"Whose is it?" asked the lead agent.

"José Martí's." It was an odd thing to say. José Martí was a Cuban national icon who died in 1895. Havana's airport was named after him. It was like questioning an American in Bogotá who suddenly claimed his luggage belonged to John F. Kennedy.

Inside the blue duffel bag were five cardboard boxes, filled with "numerous stacks of hundred- and fifty-dollar bills" wrapped tightly in tape. All three men were immediately placed under arrest.

The passenger beckoned to the customs group supervisor and asked for a quiet word. In a room reserved for interviews, he tried to explain that almost all of the bags in the plane were being carried on someone else's behalf. The agent nodded and then pulled out a photograph, placing it directly in front of the passenger. It had been taken two weeks earlier in the Bahamas by a DEA agent, showing the passenger smiling and shaking hands with Carlos Jader Álvarez.

"Do you know this man?" asked the group supervisor.

The passenger pondered the photograph. Finally, he said, "Yes." His smile was long gone now. His voice trembled.

"Didn't Álvarez give you the money in the shoeboxes?" pressed the customs agent.

Suddenly the passenger began to cry. "You don't understand," he said haltingly. "I have a wife and two daughters in Bogotá." He knew how quickly revenge could come. His nephew had been the focus of the Edna Buchanan story of the man gunned down in arrivals at Miami International Airport. The tears became full-fledged sobs. The customs agent waited patiently and, to his shock, learned that the one car that had escaped Greenback's agents that evening had been driven by Carlos Jader Álvarez himself. Greenback had come within meters of one of the DEA's top targets in the world. Finally regaining his self-control, the red-faced passenger said he'd like to see an attorney.

———

November 22 had perfectly displayed Miami's two possible futures. While Ferré and Governor Graham were trying to draw business to Miami, Álvarez and his money launderer Isaac Kattan were working on creating dependency, ravaging rather than building communities, and extracting dollars from the many for the very few.

On the morning of November 23, the three Colombians arrested in Opa-locka had their bail set at $3 million each. It was bargained down to $250,000. It didn't matter. It was soon paid. Within a month, they were back in Bogotá, flown out on false passports by Isaac Kattan's understudy. Later, a Greenback agent received information that the three Colombians had each had a family member murdered for their perceived failure.

The fact that stayed with the Greenback agents to ponder over Thanksgiving was that an organization continued to roll on, brushing aside huge consecutive confiscations of cash as well as two cocaine seizures totaling 338 kilograms. Álvarez almost lost his airplane as well. While its seizure was being signed off on in the Greenback offices in downtown Miami, the airplane was being prepared for takeoff by another set of Álvarez's pilots. Greenback agents would miss it by minutes. Worth $1.5 million, the airplane's first installment of $550,000 had been paid in cash.

After the Opa-locka arrests, Greenback's existence was acknowledged to the press for the first time. "There is an interdepartmental federal operation going on down here," announced the regional director of investigations. "Comprised of customs, DEA, IRS, and the FBI, it's an attempt to stem the large quantities of currency and monetary instruments we believe are used to perpetuate organized criminal activity." The DEA had played their role in the initial distribution of intelligence. The reference to the FBI was wishful thinking, or perhaps a warning signal to traffickers, flexing a muscle unattached to the Greenback body.

There were obvious reasons for Isaac Kattan to panic. His prime client had now been compromised twice by the IRS and customs through Greenback. Kattan had been interviewed separately by both agencies, and now he could read in the *Herald* that the agencies were working in tandem. Instead of altering his behavior, Kattan presumed he had been forgotten about. The following day was like any other, and Kattan could be found in his Citation with another million dollars in cash in the trunk.

A more cautious man would have shut down operations, but Kattan had already survived one bottleneck in 1980, thanks to the increased flow of cocaine during the boatlift. If he pulled away from his corrupted banks now, he would create an enormous backlog of thousands of kilograms of dollars in his safe houses. That could only lead to evenings like the one they had just experienced at Opa-locka, an awkward operation to move money in bulk. There was no good option for him. The more money that cocaine traffickers pushed toward Kattan, the more he benefited from keeping to already established connections within banks. Now that Greenback had claimed victories in commercial and private airports, the perimeters around Isaac Kattan were beginning to shrink.

CHAPTER 28

As disappointing as the president's underwhelming response to the boat-lift and riot had been, Maurice Ferré was still a Democrat, though he had come to think of the slow bleeds of Mariel and Iran as two central reasons why Carter would not win reelection. Carter's inner circle shared the feeling. They were relying on Ronald Reagan to destroy himself through any one of a number of outrageous statements made during his campaign. Poles, he told a rally, were so dumb they brought ducks to cockfights. Italians bet on the duck. The Mafia fixed it so the duck won. The crowd roared, but at the time, a Reagan aide had held his head in his hand and sighed, "There goes Connecticut."

Reagan was only warming up. Trees, he said, were responsible for air pollution. Fascism was behind Roosevelt's New Deal. Unemployment insurance was a "prepaid vacation plan for freeloaders." The press focused relentlessly on his lowest moments, but Reagan also presented a positive vision of the American future, hitting rhetorical highs, while Carter could only debut a petty side, calling Reagan a nincompoop, a warmonger, and a bigot.

Instead of falling in the polls, Reagan took the lead. He understood the depth of personal frustrations in an economic malaise. He under-stood Florida, even Ferré's Miami. "A national problem deserves fed-eral attention," he said about the city's inundation of refugees. And of all the things affecting the refugees, it *was* the economic malaise that now weighed the most. Honest immigrants grasped the bottom rung.

Award-winning Cuban writers now scrubbed pots on US army bases, or planted trees in Homestead for $3.35 an hour. Few refugees could afford transport, and most spent their days moving slowly to and from work across Dade's flat and heated land. The initial elation from freedom was gone. Mariel's refugees had entered the American grind, and most were off to a slow start.

Even if they sympathized with Carter, they couldn't argue with Reagan when he called out Carter for ducking the issue of Mariel and shifting the burden onto the backs of Florida voters. And the *Miami Herald* on the eve of the election? They made themselves irrelevant by backing neither Reagan nor Carter, selecting a third-party candidate who wouldn't carry a single state.

November 4 brought a crushing victory for Reagan. Dade had four times as many registered Democrats as Republicans, but even there, Reagan had beaten Carter by ten points. Carter conceded at 9:52 p.m., losing forty-four states. "If it was a prizefight," wrote the *Herald*'s Carl Hiaasen early in the evening, "it would have been stopped in the first round." Despite the efforts to force her resignation in May, Janet Reno was reelected. Not one candidate had contested her job.

The anti-bilingual ordinance passed with ease, driven by white voters and celebrated with champagne by Emmy Shafer in a red suit and a touch of blue eye shadow. Black voters had split, 55 percent to 45 percent, in favor of Miami remaining bilingual. The Cuban community was stunned by the decision. You could almost see it retract. SALAD's public statement the morning after the elections called those who'd voted against bilingualism "not only anti-Cuban but cowards too."

The national election solved nothing for Miami. It only formalized the divisions. "A person exhibiting such profound symptoms of fear, anxiety, hostility and self-destruction would have to be sedated," wrote the *Herald* about the city. The heightened paranoia from the summer had failed to subside.

Ferré still believed that the best thing he could do for Miami was continue, not adapt, his mission to turn the city south—this despite the fact that tourism had just plummeted. In the wake of the riots, numerous reservations were canceled. The Intercontinental, one of Miami's better hotels, instead made a deal with Tallahassee agreeing to house 150 state troopers sent to assist local law enforcement. When Miami's hotels were used as garrisons, the image of the city's militarization seemed to be reinforced. At least it was better than the numbers coming out of Key West. They were cataclysmic: tourism was down 60 percent, but unlike the mayor of Key West, Ferré had already prepared the city for its turn to the south rather than leaning on fickle travelers.

———

When Dresdner, the giant Hamburg-based bank, first hinted that they were interested in starting an operation in Miami, Ferré rang Alvah Chapman, CEO of Knight-Ridder and chairman of the Non-Group. Despite ongoing tension between city hall and the *Miami Herald*, Chapman agreed to help put together a lunch in Coconut Grove to entice the German bank. Ferré greeted the group, and then stepped down from the dais to allow Chapman to address the German guests. Chapman delivered some brief remarks, ending with, "Welcome to Miami, the new financial business center of Florida and the South."

Dresdner's chairman stood, took the microphone, and apologized for the misunderstanding. They weren't in Miami to look at the American South, they were in Miami looking *at South America*. Miami could be their hub. Ferré could feel the cold front break across the room. He looked around him with a mixture of relief and glee. There was no interest in Jacksonville, in Tampa or Orlando, for the Germans. Here was one of the biggest banks in Europe agreeing with what had been obvious to Ferré for years now, and yet it was a shock to the rest of the room. Miami's future was to the south in spite of its current turmoil.

If you were a long-term thinker like Dresdner, which had been investing in South America since before 1900, Miami's troubles that summer could be considered temporary. Its geography was permanent. To have Dresdner put it so candidly was like hearing the first footfall of a unified army. Within weeks, Ferré used the city's budget to seed an Insurance Exchange of the Americas, based on Lloyd's of London, then pushed to turn an island in Biscayne Bay into a tropical Tivoli Gardens. Not every idea was a good one, but while the rest of the city percolated with anger, Ferré was back to percolating with ideas.

Even downtown, where Operation Greenback was discreetly operating in the US Attorney's Office, Ferré's Miami was alive despite the passing of the anti-bilingual ordinance. English was still a rarity there. Greenback's federal prosecutors, unable to read the Spanish menus, usually just pointed to lunch in Cuban diners, after walking past newsstands filled with newspapers from Caracas and Bogotá. Cuban entrepreneurs catering to Latin visitors revived the downtown businesses that had died during the last slump in tourism in the 1970s. Ferré had encouraged that comeback, knowing that the average Latin American tourist spent twice as much as an American visitor. Despite the riots, the boatlift, and the crime, that remained true. Without Latins, said one local store owner, "we'd be dead." Ferré knew that Dresdner's interest was a vital opportunity for the city, proof that the mayor didn't have to alter his vision for Miami's revival even if it was now perceived as a pariah by America's citizens.

CHAPTER 29

A month after shooting Graciella Gomez dead in the back of the white Mustang, Anibal Jaramillo was given another job. This would be easier, insofar as it wasn't on an open road surrounded by witnesses on their morning commute. Instead it would take place on a Thanksgiving weekend in southwest Miami, a popular place for young families looking for affordable houses away from the troubles at the center of the city.

The area had undergone the same radical shift as what was now called Dade County, from six thousand years as swamp to half a century as farmland. In the last five years, a push from developers had seen an infiltration of bulldozers and dump trucks. Pits were dug, filled with water, rebranded as lakes, and surrounded by "waterfront property." Every Sunday, the *Herald* was stuffed with advertising for apartments in Somerset Lakes, Golden Lakes, and Woodbridge, which had neither a wood nor a bridge. The only vestiges of the swamp were the persistent mosquitoes. As Jaramillo and his partner drove along the street to which they'd been sent, they could see that, of the nine houses that surrounded the home they were targeting, four were still under construction.

Jaramillo stepped out of the car, a red baseball hat tight around his ears. He carried a butcher knife and a coil of rope purchased from a nearby Pantry Pride store, as well as a .45 revolver. Several minutes after he'd parked, a skinny teenager stepped from the house they were watching. Jaramillo waved him over, talked to him for several minutes, and sent him back into the house to the sound of barking. Moments later, the teenager took all three of the family's dogs into the backyard.

When thirty-six-year-old Gilberto Caicedo answered the knock on his front door, he was greeted by the sight of the red cap and a gun pointing between his eyes. He backed up from his tiled entrance farther into the house. His diminutive girlfriend, Candelaria, was steps behind him, holding a copy of a book on how to raise Alsatians. The yaps continued to come from the backyard, where the teenage nephew now cowered behind a tree with two puppies and a furious Chihuahua.

It took Jaramillo and his partner five minutes to bind the couple using the rope and then gag them with their own tops, a plaid shirt for Caicedo and a white sweater for Candelaria. Caicedo was laid facedown, but Candeleria had twisted about so that she could watch, or perhaps plead with the men.

Caicedo had built a Santería shrine in his kitchen, and now Jaramillo stepped between leaves that had been scattered across the floors that morning to ward off evil. Jaramillo searched the apartment, opening drawers, throwing papers to the floor.

When Jaramillo was through, he went back toward the front door. Standing over Gilberto Caicedo, he fired three times through the back of his head. Candelaria was struggling to move away from the shots. Jaramillo walked over to her and shot her once in the neck, once in the right eye, and once in the forehead, then left the house with his partner, shutting the door behind them. The dogs were still yapping in the backyard. From behind a tree, Caicedo's terrified nephew finally tore through the back garden, running from the scene at a sprint.

It would be a full day before the nephew would return, alongside a lawyer, Marshall Frank, Singleton, Wesolowski, and Raul Diaz, to examine the 524th and 525th homicides of the year. It was not a particularly clean scene. There were fingerprints on the coil of rope and on the package the knife had come in. They had an eyewitness, albeit one shaking with fear. After a quick area search by Raul Diaz, they had, once again, a car covered in fingerprints. It was all familiar. The murdered man had told a neighbor he was Venezuelan, but there had been so much car traffic, with men leaving the house carrying brown paper bags, that the neighbor had called the DEA and had been instructed to keep note of license plates as cars came and went. It was no surprise to find that Caicedo turned out to be Colombian or that his address book included the names of the largest cocaine dealers known to the DEA. Nor, when June Hawkins ran his name against her database, was it surprising to find a family connection to Carlos Jader Álvarez.

From the point of view of the detectives, it was the casualness of the actions that remained so chilling. It would have been so easy to wipe down the weapon, to come at night, to hide the car properly. But with the assassins, as with the money launderers, there was a feeling of invulnerability. For the last eighteen months, the constant flow of cocaine, bloodshed, and drug money were increasingly open secrets in Miami, and yet not one Colombian hit man or money launderer had even been arrested, let alone convicted.

To the Anglo detectives, it was just one more example of an increasingly Latin Miami. The 1980 census had revealed almost negligible population growth in the county during the last decade. A deeper dig, however, revealed at least 100,000 Latin Americans who'd failed to fill out their surveys, balanced by the beginning of a slow march north by Anglo Miami.

Through Diaz, Marshall Frank's new detectives quickly met the heroes and villains of Cuba. They found themselves sitting at tables with men who kept newspapers folded over their right hand, covering weapons. Diaz had known who could and couldn't be trusted within the Cuban community, but Mariel had changed that. As homicide squads picked up Mariel refugees working on the edges of the Colombian drug trade, the detectives' leverage of looming prison sentences didn't seem to have the same effect. Diaz realized that recidivists dedicated to crime within a police state like Cuba were unlikely to panic or talk during PSD interrogations.

There were times when Anglo detectives could walk into a crime scene and be forgiven for questioning if they even had jurisdiction in what seemed to be a different country. That same month, one southern-born detective entered a backyard and found a fresh grave containing a chicken, marked by a basket of fruit, pastries, a can of beer, and a can of soda. Inside, the living room had been turned into a religious shrine for Chango, Santería's Lord of Fire and Lightning, complete with a cake iced in his honor. A statue of the saint adorned the fireplace, surrounded by red carnations, cantaloupes, and watermelons. On the floor lay two dead refugees from Mariel, each with multiple gunshot wounds. Standing by the door, crying and hysterical, was the twenty-eight-year-old killer, who explained he'd caught the victims stealing a necklace during the ceremony, shot them, gone to his car to reload, and shot them both again. It might have been the easiest case Frank's new detectives faced in 1980, but it was a murder that belonged to another country.

It was obvious that you couldn't do all of your job if you didn't speak Spanish. The *Herald* relied on *El Herald*. Frank relied on detectives like Diaz or Hawkins. Operation Greenback had half a dozen Spanish-speaking agents. Miami relied on Ferré and two of his commissioners. They were all public servants, all accountable. But the rest of Anglo Miami was bristling and indignant and ever more cognizant of their linguistic limitations. They refused to admit that in America you needed Spanish for a sales job at Burdines. The real affront was not that Spanish was spoken, it was that the money spoke Spanish. In 1980 Los Angeles, Spanish mowed your lawn and brought you your check when you ate out. In Miami, Spanish owned the lawn and grabbed the tab from your hand.

There was, for a moment, extraordinary malleability in agencies known for their rigidity. Yet certain information remained siloed. It wasn't that Operation Greenback hadn't considered the possibility of working closely with Frank's homicide bureau. Greenback attorney Charles Blau knew that with "twenty more attorneys, we could have dealt with the details and nuances of all those cases." There could have been a forward march in sync, where the money, the drugs, the bloodshed could be dealt with by law enforcement holistically. The fractionalized response was

Operation Greenback's greatest fear. Agencies that had refused to join, the FBI and the DEA, might end up investigating the same suspects as Greenback, and "sooner or later we were going to have a shootout with two or more of them."

What Greenback didn't want to do officially, Lieutenant Raul Diaz was prepared to do unofficially. Being Cuban-born trumped fidelity to an agency. What may have seemed treasonous in other times now made sense. The informal meetings, Diaz on whisky, Greenback's de Armas on brandy, weren't about federal secrets passed over the table but about the willingness to use each department's breadth to overcome another agency's narrowness.

When de Armas wanted a suspect's car tossed, he had no legal right. He could call Diaz, who'd order a police officer to make the stop. They'd pull the driver's license, phone or address book, copy numbers down on the scene, send the driver on his way, and relay the information over to Greenback. Diaz didn't know what it was for. He was only looking for reciprocity, the ability to call de Armas as homicide looked for links between their own cases that he could then share with his detectives.

The same went for customs agents. Uncooperative detectives at homicide scenes often frustrated agents when they tried to collect address books or papers. With Diaz in the department, he not only allowed them in, he "called to make sure somebody came." Information flowed, in Spanish, despite the walls set up between American agencies. It made perfect sense in any city, but in Miami, as different agencies closed in on murderers and money launderers, it was indispensable.

CHAPTER 30

In Cali, as a young man, Isaac Kattan had been taught by his father that "the world ran on numbers and money." Many of the first wave of Kattan's clients weren't from the street. They were similar to him. Businessmen born into hardworking entrepreneurial families who saw extraordinary opportunity, enough to turn from producing caffeine to manufacturing cocaine.

The unacknowledged movement of unacknowledged drug money held a silent threat. Kattan and his employers knew who the corrupt tellers were, which bank officers were willing to allow them in. That almost casual infiltration of Miami's banks led to a whole new threat now considered by the Treasury Department. What if drug dealers didn't just run their money through Miami's banks; what if they bought the banks? They could contaminate the entire American banking system. Greenback wasn't just a shot into the darkness of Miami, it was part of an essential diagnosis for the nation.

From 1973 to 1977, there had only been one attempt by a foreign national to buy a Florida bank. In 1979, there had been seven applications to the Florida comptroller, followed by another six in the first half of 1980, including a bid from a well-known Colombian cocaine dealer. The comptroller didn't even have a budget to fly south to Colombia to interview the prospective buyers. Again, the laws promoted by Mayor Ferré to help capital flow through Miami had also created a vulnerability within the city.

Greenback's number men rubbed their eyes at the figures they discovered. One bank in Miami that Kattan favored had a mere $37 million on deposit and should have placed approximately $13 million into the federal system the previous year. Instead, thanks to clients like Kattan, it had deposited $600 million, as one of twenty-four banks identified as having "unusual deposit patterns." Even the president of Southeast, whose chairman sat on the Non-Group, seemed clueless. In a 1980 Senate hearing about the penetration of drug money into South Florida, he had tried to convince the senators that the surge in cash was due to a mixture of tourists and horseracing, and that his own bank had a "very extensive code of ethics." It was only when specific accounts in his bank were linked directly to dealers that he grew quiet. In the same hearing, the comptroller of the state of Florida was equally stubborn, insisting that Miami's financial flood was made entirely of flight capital.

All the while, Kattan went about his business. His paper trail at the Bank of Miami could be traced to a legitimate account he'd opened in 1972. By 1978, he had four other accounts held under different names to deal with the volume of cash, but in 1980 the Bank of Miami had discovered that the IRS had questioned Kattan in New York. Their advice that he should look at other area banks had helped create the August bottleneck that had led Kattan to open his series of accounts at Great American.

In December, Greenback's federal prosecutors had, at last, signed off on a surveillance team for Great American. They'd arrived in the middle of the night and installed a hidden camera inside the transformer of a utility pole outside the bank. Sitting watching tape of the daily movements, agents were stunned by the familiarity and ease of it all. Sometimes couriers parked; sometimes they'd just pull up and wait for a guard to come help hoist boxes or suitcases onto dollies. Sometimes Kattan would be alone, sometimes he'd send two men, sometimes all three would arrive together.

The bank had to employ extra tellers to count Kattan's cash. Kattan would be encouraged to go for lunch with his couriers while three tellers spent five hours almost every day checking the numbers. What Kattan either couldn't see, or saw and found perfectly acceptable, was that the employees he dealt with quickly began to live a life that reached far beyond their paychecks. The head teller at Great American updated her wardrobe, bought jewelry, and made a deposit on a $120,000 house, all on a salary of $210 a week.

One Monday at 4:45 p.m., the monotony of watching hundreds of thousands of dollars roll in was broken. Kattan's most trusted courier had parked and entered the bank for help with his boxes of cash. Between the first and second trip, a Greenback agent parked across the street watched stunned as a man slipped into the front seat of the brand-new blue Chevy Citation and pulled out with approximately $750,000 in the back of the car.

"My car's been stolen!" screamed the courier, running out of the bank.

"Jesus!" shouted the breathless teller who'd sprinted beside him. "Let me call the police."

Kattan's courier didn't call the cops, only a taxi. He took it to the North Miami Police Department, where he reported the car stolen, along with $6,000. He claimed he'd watched from the second floor of the Great American Bank as a 320-pound Latin male entered the car and drove it away.

The stunned Greenback agents had laughed, stopped laughing, and then laughed again. It seemed preposterous. Was it a car thief? The luckiest car thief in the world? Kattan was more mistrustful. He had a strong suspicion that the Great American vice president's assistant had coordinated the theft. The assistant, unaware of Kattan's suspicion, continued his smiling greetings the following day when Kattan returned with his colleagues to drop off another deposit. He had no idea he was only a phone call away from moving from Greenback's realm to Marshall Frank's.

Although the DEA had previously shared the Álvarez wiretaps with Greenback, that had been the limit of their cooperation. To the DEA, Greenback remained amateurish diddlers. Much of the disdain came from the eternal friction between the DEA and customs. The law seemed to have been designed for conflict. If a hundred kilos of cocaine arrived in America in a sealed container, DEA had jurisdiction over the drugs, but customs could claim the container. The animosity between the agencies was so strong that, had Kattan known about the separate investigations, he might have wagered that any attempt at coordination would implode long before anybody stood a chance of convicting him.

The DEA had been tipped off to Kattan's existence by the high school friend of one of their own agents, working for the Miami branch of Donaldson, Lufkin & Jenrette (DLJ), a sober Wall Street investment bank that sat behind heavy dark wood doors and polished gold letters. He had a client by the name of Isaac Kattan who arrived daily with $800,000 to $900,000. This had been going on since July 1980, averaging $7 million every two weeks. Kattan claimed to be a money changer and a travel agent. For weeks now, he had been trailed from the investment bank by the DEA. The numbers were eye-watering, but their agents still recognized it was highly unlikely Kattan was using only one location.

DLJ was a sophisticated entity: a step up for Kattan. There Kattan would find an even quicker method of reducing money than he had at the Great American Bank. Instead of being shrunk to a check, the cash was converted by DLJ into an electron. Kattan's proceeds moved easily across the world, from terminal to terminal, lost in the faint green haze of a thousand computers in a hundred banks.

Kattan's ever-present worry was finding banks to trust. If the money wasn't in a bank, then it was sitting in one of his safe houses. He was constantly changing them, trying to stop his couriers from overfamiliarity with any one of them. The fear of a greedy teller was secondary. Fear of clients such as Álvarez was more important. And yet, as the DEA began to follow the man they'd later describe as the "Al Capone of cocaine," they, too, could only marvel at the brazenness of how he operated in Miami.

Isaac Kattan and money launderers like him had altered the moral landscape of the county. A city full of upright citizens would have identified Kattan's behavior as immoral and kept their distance. Yet for those who only adjusted their actions to comply with the rule of law, Kattan stayed within an area gray enough to encourage complicity. There was no statute that prevented a lawyer or a car dealer from accepting $100,000 in cash. If you were a citizen who stayed silent, then the money would flow toward you. If you spoke out, there wasn't a specific law you could lean on, but there were dozens of Anibal Jaramillos who might be directed your way.

Just as Greenback's federal prosecutors were preparing indictments against Kattan and his associates, their greatest fear materialized. A tow truck driver approached a Greenback surveillance vehicle lurking in the parking lot of the Great American Bank in full view of the president's windows. A DEA surveillance team had made the call. It wasn't the shootout that federal prosecutors had feared, but a provocative humiliation that led to furious Greenback agents storming into their prosecutors' offices that evening. The *fucking* DEA. At least Greenback's Charlie Blau was now aware that there wasn't just one investigation of Isaac Kattan; there were two. And they were both very much active.

When you work surveillance, it's hard to *miss* surveillance. The IRS agents had stood out because instead of the DEA's seized BMWs and Mercedes-Benzes, they were in government-issue Chevrolets. But not every DEA agent was disdainful of customs. Rather than getting into another interagency scrap, one afternoon DEA Special Agent David Wilson wandered over to a Greenback vehicle in Great American's parking lot. The window rolled down low enough for the stocky Wilson to be able to introduce himself.

"Who you watching?" he asked.

"We're watching the bank," answered a Greenback supervisor.

"Us, too. Who?"

"Isaac Kattan."

"Us, too."

Then came the words that Greenback's agents had been waiting almost twelve months to hear.

"Maybe," said Wilson, "we should sit down."

———

One full year after the DEA had been invited to join Greenback, Wilson and members of his group entered the Greenback offices to meet with their prosecutors and supervisors.

Secreted on the sixth floor in the Office of the United States Attorney, their quarters shared an elevator with the INS. Agents arriving for work walked past lines of Mariel refugees who hugged the morning shade along the sand-colored building. They were waiting to be processed, waiting to give evidence as to whom they'd been brought into the United States by—on which boat, by which captain. Inside, the elevators filled up with Mariel prisoners who had confessed to criminal records. Visitors often watched agents unchain six at a time, then squeezed into the elevator beside them as they headed up.

It was an open meeting, exactly as the Department of Treasury had intended, with the DEA providing all the information on DLJ and Treasury agents filling in the DEA on their own surveillance of the Great American Bank and the Bank of Miami. That raised questions on the part of the DEA. Prosecutors revealed information they had compiled on the Great American assistant who Kattan suspected was cheating him, and how they were sure that same assistant was behind the non-filing of CTRs.

Wilson felt that, in a shorter period of time, DEA had gotten more on Kattan than Greenback had. He also began to understand that Greenback was after not just Kattan but the bank itself. When the Greenback group supervisor in the parking lot had said he was watching the bank, he meant *the whole bank*. Kattan might be an attractive arrest to the DEA as an adjunct to the drug trade, but to Greenback's agents the Colombian was a key that might unlock the entire financial structure of the cocaine industry.

"What percentage of cocaine are you seizing?" asked Greenback's Blau of Wilson. "One percent? Two, three? What impact is the DEA really having?" Greenback, he said, could change it all. "Dealers are fungible," said the prosecutor. "They get arrested, someone else takes their place."

Wilson had been coming to the same conclusion. He knew that if you were in the presence of outrageous amounts of cash, you were staring at the aftermath of a criminal act. "If you can find the money and work backwards, instead of finding the drugs and working forwards, it's a much shorter trip," he said.

In the meeting, Wilson emphasized that he didn't want interference from Greenback on DLJ. "Please," he said, "stay away from our informant." DLJ, he explained, was on the edge of telling Kattan that they didn't want his business anymore. "We don't want him to start changing his life pattern," said Wilson, promising copies of DEA reports. In order to head off any objections, he added the details of something that one of their agents had overheard in the elevator at Great American: a frank admission between Kattan and a loan officer that Kattan's business was welcomed with open arms. To Greenback, it was a tasty morsel, exactly the type of evidence a federal prosecutor needed to move forward with a conspiracy case.

Wilson breathed out in the elevator. He'd learned something new from Greenback. In Kattan, they'd finally "grasped the tail of a very large animal." He pictured a jury, further down the road, made up of men and women making eight dollars an hour, who would "convict him so fast it'd make your head hurt." But not one agent, whether DEA, IRS, or customs, could envisage the error that Isaac Kattan would soon make. Kattan wasn't in two crosshairs anymore—just one bigger, better one.

CHAPTER 31

On December 14 in Miami International Airport, Anibal Jaramillo and a Colombian colleague took a man's purse from on top of a public pay phone. In theory, they were innocents, waiting to pick up a friend from Bogotá. They intended to take the purse to lost and found. The Jamaican owner of the purse disagreed and saw a member of the PSD only meters away. Anibal Jaramillo was charged with grand theft, carrying a concealed firearm, obstructing police, and unauthorized possession of a firearm. Down at the station, he was fingerprinted. Faced with a larceny charge, his bond was set at $2,362.50. He expected to be released before the end of the day.

With the efforts of intelligence analysts like June Hawkins, county police had become wiser during 1980. An illegal immigrant from Colombia armed in an airport raised red flags. A print check revealed he'd been arrested two years before, when he had gotten into a fight with a police officer on Biscayne Boulevard while trying to buy a friend a few minutes in the back of a car with a hooker. He'd presented a fake ID.

Jaramillo's prints were sent over to the PSD's crime lab. To the technician's shock, they matched the weapon used in a murder: the case of Graciella Gomez, the young woman with the dyed blond hair who had been shot to death in the back of the Mustang on Red Road. The latent fingerprint on the Beretta and the Chevy Nova were a match. Jaramillo was now under arrest for murder one, held without bond.

Within twenty-four hours, Marshall Frank's detectives had asked the lab to run Jaramillo's prints on their Caicedo case. It was a second match. Jaramillo's prints were on the butcher knife and rope from the double murder in South Miami. In twenty-four hours, Jaramillo had been arrested three times, the first Colombian hit man who would face the American justice system.

Marshall Frank's office liked Jaramillo for one more—from November. Another two bodies had been found in a pattern almost identical to the Caicedo double. A Colombian couple, known to be involved in the cocaine trade, had been tied up and tortured. The woman had her ear cut off, then both had been shot multiple times. Five murders, connected by fingerprints but not by witnesses. In the Caicedo murders, the nervous nephew had skipped town and had never returned from Colombia. Despite the fact that Graciella Gomez had been gunned down in the middle of Red Road, only the driver of the white Mustang was able to pick Jaramillo from a lineup, remembering not the face but "the same closed-mouth smile." Jaramillo seemed as unworried to be arrested for murder as he had been to commit it.

The only other thing that tied the three murder scenes together was cocaine. Captain Frank's squad had discovered that Gilberto Caicedo, whom Jaramillo had trussed up and executed in South Miami, had a cousin connected to Álvarez. That cousin had been arrested during a huge bust of Álvarez's cocaine that April in Miami International Airport. It proved that the twin terrors of money and blood in Miami ran in an extraordinarily small circle. Kattan may never have touched cocaine, and Jaramillo may never have laid his hands on a million dollars, but they were still linked by the likes of Álvarez's cocaine.

It was a positive way to end 1980, and a sign that the three crises of the year—the riots, Mariel, and the rising murder rate—had forced every department to innovate. Frank now held daily meetings at Finger Charlie's, the coffee shop inside the PSD building, just as shifts changed. All the squads could update each other on cases. Even better, for the first time, the US Attorney's office gave information to Frank's department rather than requesting it. The feds had their own long list of suspected

Colombian traffickers, a treasure chest for June Hawkins and her collections of three-by-five cards. It was the first signal of a possible new era in Miami's law enforcement community, the slow shift toward the sharing of information necessary to keep the city intact.

Intact would be an achievement, but intact did not mean improved. One sector of the city had been forgotten; black Miami's recovery was predicated on the city's positioning as a service sector for the Latin American economy. But whether you were African American, a third-generation Bahamian, or a newly arrived Haitian, you were excluded, not because of the color of your skin but because you didn't speak Spanish. Black neighborhoods had suffered, first covertly, at white hands, with federal highway programs and underfunded schools, and then overtly, by their own hand, during the riots. Language was a more passive way to exclude a community, though it was an exclusion from a Latin world, not an Anglo one. In Miami, you could survive with money, or by being bilingual, but it was hard to flourish without either.

An imbalance remained, even concerning the dead. Though murders committed by black suspects during the riots were now finally beginning to make their way through the justice system, no suspects had been arrested on behalf of any of the nine black victims. Even the slow-motion humiliation of Arthur McDuffie's death echoed on. There had been a spark of hope for his family later in 1980. Charles Veverka, the first officer on scene after McDuffie had pulled over, the same officer who had become an immunized witness for Reno's prosecution, was suddenly indicted on federal civil rights charges.

For months he was hounded through the courts. It was a puzzling precedent for his fellow officers to experience. A man who had cooperated was singled out for punishment at the federal level and faced twenty-six years of jail time. Again, the McDuffies had to listen to heartbreaking testimony. An arresting officer remembered how "enjoyable, exciting and fun" the chase had been, while McDuffie's beating was not so much vicious as a "tension release." Tried in Texas, Veverka was acquitted on all charges on December 18, 1980, a year to the day after the unconscious

McDuffie had first been visited by his wife in a wing at Jackson Memorial Hospital.

McDuffie's mother now lived alone, surrounded by photographs of her son. On her loneliest nights, she'd call on his brother to drive over. Frederica, McDuffie's ex-wife, said that in the year since he'd been gone, she'd yet to live a happy moment. For his nine-year-old daughter, who still remembered him clearly, the pain came in missing their trips to parks and restaurants, but mostly just in missing the sound of her father's voice. Walking through the same Miami was Officer Alex Marrero. According to the *Miami News*, he had more friends than ever. Often, he was stopped in the street by men wanting to shake his hand and commiserate on how abused he had been by the system.

CHAPTER 32

The Dade County police covered over two thousand square miles with under two thousand cops. New York used ten times the number of police to cover one tenth of the area. As a frequent visitor to New York, Isaac Kattan knew how different Miami was. Kattan was always up early. By Miami's standards, it was a beautiful, chilly winter morning, just under 60 degrees. Years of blatantly breaking laws, years of knowing that American regulations were so permissive when it came to money laundering, had lowered Kattan's guard. When you had as much as $2.2 million in cash in your trunk at any given time, Miami's relative sprinkling of law enforcement was constant comfort.

Finally, near the turn of the year, the combined power of the DEA, customs, the IRS, and federal prosecutors was concentrated on Kattan. Instead of Greenback chasing *all* of the money launderers, Kattan had moved front and center. A mechanical room in the building across the street from his apartment in the Villa Regina had been commandeered by the DEA. Kattan was tracked every morning, and every afternoon and evening. When he hit the ground floor that morning, there were three different cars filled with agents already parked in different locations along Brickell Avenue.

The most surprising moment during his surveillance wasn't when Kattan arrived at a financial institution but when he had returned home. He had entered his building and told the guard he wanted to go up to visit a different apartment. It was registered to a man named Jose Estupinan, a fact the DEA considered mind-boggling. Less than two years ago, Estupinan had been arrested in Colombia while transporting 585 kilograms of pure cocaine on behalf of Carlos Jader Álvarez. It had a street value in Miami of roughly $100 million, a world-record haul. You had, then, a block from Mayor Ferré's recently sold mansion on Brickell Avenue, a drug dealer, capable of shifting $100 million of cocaine in a day, living in the same building as a man capable of laundering at least $300 million in the same year. At a time when an office tower cost $12 million to construct, the two men could have built the entirety of Brickell's financial heart by diverting twelve months of cash flow.

Kattan exited the Villa Regina apartments carrying a large purple satchel, got into his car, and made a short drive to the parking lot of a local Holiday Inn, where he met with two Colombians. Kattan made a call from the hotel lobby, and stopped by his home, entering the garage with a pass card. This wasn't Kattan's typical morning, as three cars of tense agents immediately realized. He hadn't visited a single bank. A few minutes later, he appeared again, this time in the company of one of his most trusted couriers.

They paused for a moment in front of Kattan's building. Kattan appeared to be giving his courier directions. The man got into a 1971 Jaguar XJ6 and drove off, followed shortly by Kattan, although Kattan suddenly made a series of U-turns for no apparent purpose. To the agents' surprise, Kattan pulled in a hundred meters from the courier's car on Biscayne and NE Fourth, a short distance from his own apartment. Nearby, men had gathered to play dominoes, with a view back onto the high-rises sprouting up in Brickell. The two Colombians exited their cars but didn't acknowledge each other as Kattan stood alone in front of a bank. Did that mean anything, or was he just seeking shade in the sun? The mercury had climbed to almost 80, no winds, no clouds, no rain.

A white Chevy Citation pulled up close to the courier's car. Kattan walked over and talked to the newly arrived driver while his courier repositioned his car as close as possible to the Citation. The Citation driver opened his trunk. Kattan's courier popped his. Kattan waited seven feet away from the Citation as the courier heaved a heavy red suitcase from his car into the Jaguar's trunk. DEA agents had learned to measure the weight of a suitcase by how low the chassis sank. It looked to be forty or fifty pounds, perhaps as much as $2 million in cash if it happened to be in hundred-dollar bills. Kattan quickly shook hands with his courier before the man got back into the Jaguar.

The Jaguar drove off, followed at a distance by two DEA agents. None of this was part of Kattan's usual routine, one that Greenback's agents now knew so well. Within minutes, Kattan's courier stopped sharply in front of a Firestone tire store to pick up a second man. The courier checked his mirror once, twice, three times. The agent in pursuit picked up his radio, "We've been made."

Greenback's strength was new to the DEA. Their agents had federal prosecutor Charlie Blau live on the radio, willing to make immediate decisions on the fly. The agents had no search warrant on them. If they made a stop that a judge ruled against, then they would have ruined three months of their own investigation, as well as the DEA's efforts. Blau listened, considered the situation, breathed in, and, when asked again whether to grab the courier or not, just said, "Do it."

The Jaguar containing Kattan's courier pulled over as soon as an agent reached out and put a blue light on the roof. Immediately, a second Greenback vehicle braked hard on the courier's other side. All four agents left their cars, guns in hand. They identified themselves, ordered the passengers out of the Jaguar, and instructed them to lie facedown on the grassy median. Neither man was armed.

The DEA had gotten good at this over the last year. They had a phrase for it: "the Colombian search warrant." It involved no search warrant at all but a theory based on the belief that most Colombians in Miami's drug trade appeared to be from agricultural provinces. They didn't have the vaguest understanding of American law.

One agent pulled the keys out of the Jaguar and walked over to kneel by the courier. He asked, in Spanish, "Are these your keys?"

"Yes."

"Do I have your permission to open the trunk of your car and look inside the suitcase?"

"Yes." Had the courier said no, there was nothing the agents could have done, but, anxious to please the armed agents, the man repeated the word again. "Yes."

Greenback's agents popped the trunk, clicked open the suitcase, and began to unwrap the blocks one by one. There were twenty of them. Each weighed 1 kilogram. It wasn't money. They would later be confirmed as 98 to 99 percent pure cocaine belonging to the Álvarez organization. It had a street value of $6 million.

It made no sense. The moneymen never touched the cocaine. The dealers never touched the money. Yet here was Isaac Kattan, a man suspected of moving at least $300 million a year, getting directly involved in a cocaine deal with a client. It was better than good. It was a DEA dream. This was leverage not even the most optimistic Greenback agent had dreamed of. It was the sort of arrest that could change Miami.

Kattan's arrest on Brickell Avenue was undramatic. He was approached, cuffed, and stayed silent, but his car was filled with physical evidence. There was the $16,000 in cash jammed under his front seat. There was the $385,000 in cashier's checks in his suitcase. There was the receipt for a $1.2 million wire transfer to Switzerland. Kattan's bank accounts in Zurich, Geneva, and Bern were immediately frozen. The Swiss were coy with what they had found but sent a note over to Operation Greenback: "It's beyond your wildest dreams." They could guess. There was enough of a paper trail to suggest that Kattan's own worth could be pegged at approximately $150 million. Depending on whether you asked an agent or a prosecutor, Kattan was either "a full-service bank" or "South Florida's Al Capone."

Kattan would be held under a $10 million bond, but he wasn't the end of Greenback's desires. Greenback didn't just want Kattan. They wanted to scare South Florida's banks into submission by moving against a financial institution. In hours, Kattan would be going before a judge for his bond hearing, and Greenback would have to admit to the extensive surveillance on Great American. If they wanted to move against the bank, it had to be immediate.

The next day, twenty-seven agents, all dressed as if they might want to take out a bank loan, hit Great American at 4:15 p.m. Thoroughly confused bank customers thought they were in the middle of an elaborate heist as an agent slid over a counter into the teller's cage while others rushed to block exits. It took six hours to remove the necessary records from the bank; the agents had to push past outraged bank staff and an agitated president. They now had proof that the bank had made "several hundred million dollars' worth of transactions" on behalf of Miami's cocaine dealers.

Within hours, Greenback got irate calls from both the secretary of the treasury and the Federal Reserve. Federal prosecutor Charlie Blau had failed to let them know about the operation, leaving the Federal Reserve unprepared for a bank run. For the first time in several years, the government flew money *into* Miami. Greenback's prosecutors were chastised but hardly repentant. It took four borrowed counting machines and a day and a half to total the $40 million that Kattan had "stacked floor to ceiling in his safe houses." Agents worked through the night, with armed guards at the door. The largest money launderer in the world was under arrest. The most egregiously lawless banks in Miami had just been served warrants. After a year during which federal help had been halting, finally there was reason to hope that the cocaine industry was being challenged.

The arrest of Isaac Kattan convinced the DEA that cocaine, not heroin, was the true threat. Within a week, a DEA spokesman was on CBS's *60 Minutes* lauding the work they were doing as part of Operation Greenback without any mention of the fact that they'd spent almost a year refusing to participate. Kattan's arrest had also let them understand the nature of Greenback's work. Until Greenback, they had no accountants with the ability to weaponize bank records. From Kattan onward, the DEA was a willing participant inside Greenback, avid students of narco-accountancy.

Kattan's lawyer would win a suppression hearing on the legality of the "Colombian arrest warrant" and then lose the appeal and watch his client head south to a medium-security prison in Homestead to await his trial. The first time Greenback's Blau visited, he had explained to Kattan that he would soon be heading for a maximum-security prison. If Kattan was willing to explain how he ran his business, said Blau, then perhaps he could help direct Kattan's placement within the federal prison system.

Specifics, Blau knew, would get Kattan's family in Colombia killed. Slowly, Kattan began to talk. He walked Blau through the peso exchange, explaining that there were an enormous number of legitimate Colombian businessmen eager to have US dollars inside the United States. As long as the cocaine producers were willing to accept a similar amount in pesos in accounts in Colombia, then life was easy. Especially for Kattan, who would establish the rates of exchange, tearing a small piece off either end of the deal. It usually ended up a total of 7 percent. Blau tried to do the numbers in his head. Kattan, he estimated, might have cleared $40 million in 1980 alone. The average executive compensation for a CEO in the largest 350 American companies that year was $1.6 million.

Blau spent a month going back and forth, learning Kattan's worries, strengths, and weaknesses. The secret, explained Kattan, was simple. He had to find secure financial institutions and pay them well to ensure their cooperation. Any money that was lost, he personally had to make up. But once he could reduce his daily or weekly holdings to an electron, he could move them freely around the world.

His biggest worry, he said, had been security; he was always afraid that another group or someone unconnected to him would discover his safe houses brimming with cash. That left Kattan in a constant battle to establish links to trustworthy bankers. Sometimes the connections had failed him, and he'd move money out in bulk on freighters and airplanes. Customs, Kattan had explained, had missed large boats that carried *only* dollars. Those were sleepless days for Kattan. What if a pilot or a captain disappeared, a plane crashed, a ship sank? It was Kattan's responsibility until the dollars were handed over.

Keeping immaculate books, Kattan would reconcile his balances once a month, transfer the balance over to fresh books, and burn the old evidence. What he never had, he explained, was the luxury of time. Every day meant a wave of cash crashing against him. He explained the multiple accounts, the cashier's checks, the methods he'd used at the investment bank DLJ. Some banks demanded he leave cash in accounts longer than others so they could make their money off of his. He kept dormant accounts in banks all around Dade County. They would spark into life with huge deposits, get heavy use for four months, then be shut down again.

"Was it hard to find a bank?" Blau asked.

"They fell over themselves," said Kattan, acknowledging a city awash in cash.

Over a three-year period in Miami, $220 million had been spent on cars alone. Another $153 million had been paid to lawyers in cash, both ten times the average of other American cities. And yet, in those two regards, at least, Kattan had been discreet. Perhaps it was fortunate for both Kattan and the city that his arrest hadn't come earlier. Miami had been so vulnerable in the summer of 1980 that it would have been much more difficult for the city to have forged a path out of the fires. The draining of narco-dollars during the boatlift and the McDuffie riots may well have sucked the city into a fatal spiral. Ferré now saw it clearly. "Money doesn't know that it comes from cocaine," he said. "It's terrible, it's illegal, and it's Miami's salvation," an invaluable resource between the city's implosion and its stabilization.

Perhaps the most extraordinary thing about Kattan was the sangfroid with which he went about his business. He was laundering for Medellín, he was laundering for Cali. He laundered for business associates, he laundered for men and women attempting to murder one another. Within the world's most dangerous industry, Kattan was a civilized man, running an effective, honest business. Blau sat across from the warm, well-educated Colombian and thought, *If I was going to launder money, I'd want him to do it for me.*

Blau knew of his ties to Álvarez, but once the DEA and Greenback delved into Kattan's papers, they were shocked at the final tally. He had eighty-eight clients who had been convicted of drug trafficking. Using the knowledge Blau collected from Kattan, Greenback's agents began to approach bank tellers directly who identified dozens of regular couriers. It was like the first time van Leeuwenhoek had placed a droplet of water under a microscope three hundred years before: seemingly pure water was teeming with bacteria. With roughly twenty banks clustered near the Greenback offices, agents would get a call from a friendly teller, run two blocks to the bank, follow the suspect down the street until they got into a car. The first time, they'd take the tag number. The second time, they'd follow the car, then set up further surveillance on warehouses down south in Kendall, slowly piecing together a broader picture of the interaction between dealers, safe houses, couriers, banks, and moneymen. Soon Greenback doubled in size, a year of patient work resulting in a bounty of convictions and cash seizures.

Kattan's arrest had an effect. Agents would watch grainy video images of couriers with boxes and duffel bags as they paused in front of banks to read warnings that they were required to report any transaction over $10,000 using government-issued identification. Despite Emmy Shafer's best efforts, the signs were posted in both English and Spanish. The couriers would stare, consider, and retreat. The apprehension of Isaac Kattan wasn't the end of money laundering, any more than the arrest of Anibal Jaramillo was the end of bloodshed. It was the beginning of sophisticated money laundering. The days of an amiable middle-aged man driving a Chevy Citation bulging with money were gone. With aggressive federal programs appearing across South Florida, drug money seeped quietly west to California, Texas, and Mexico. Greenback had changed, but not won, the game.

At trial, Kattan would be given thirty years for cocaine possession, to be served concurrently, with five years for falsely filing currency transaction reports. The jury's decision came quickly, as the DEA's Wilson had once predicted. Kattan's lawyer had only just ordered lunch in a nearby restaurant when he stood up and hurried back hungry to watch his client receive a record sentence for a money launderer.

CHAPTER 33

Homicide captains are judged by clearance rates, not death tolls. Marshall Frank had tried to rebuild a fractured bureau in the middle of the greatest spike in the history of the nation's homicide rates. The national average in 1980 for clearing homicides was 72 percent. In Dade County, when you measured only criminal homicides, the clearance rate was 51 percent.

Frank had loved being a homicide detective. It was one of the few jobs that cut across Miami's divides, from race to riches, criminals to innocents. He had witnessed so many changes in the city since he arrived in 1947. Back then, he'd taken a downtown tram and passed Seminoles in their bright red, yellow, and blue cottons. When he was a young man in uniform, he'd thrilled at the arrival of those who would not stand for Castro's Cuba. The injection of life and vibrancy into Miami was obvious. Only later would he reflect on the embedded divisions of his adopted city, and on the fact that, until he had left the state and joined the marines, he'd never shaken a black man's hand.

Frank's mistake, he came to recognize, was stepping upward in the PSD. Captains were caught in the swirl of politics. Frank lasted until the end of 1981. In his two years in charge of homicide, no superior had ever knocked on his door, advised him, or congratulated him for keeping afloat in a hurricane. Instead, when his mentor Charlie Black was demoted, Frank was pushed sideways into the Civil Process Bureau. From there his movement was always sideways, far from homicide. On the way to his pension, Frank went through staff inspections, the transit police, and two more marriages. Night after night, Tchaikovsky remained his "personal therapy for maintaining sanity."

Frank's support of Raul Diaz would prove crucial. Diaz had been raised in Miami Beach without the assumptions of an insider, had worked Liberty City, Little Havana, and downtown. At the end of 1980, he became increasingly troubled by the bureaucratic walls that he felt kept the county homicide bureau from being efficient. When he and June Hawkins sat down to write the proposal for the creation of a special homicide squad called CENTAC 26, it was an odd reflection of Operation Greenback, a hybrid built for the streets. It would be made up of detectives from various homicide bureaus in South Florida, contain intelligence analysts such as Hawkins, and include DEA agents in the squad.

With Ronald Reagan turning his attention to the drug trade, Diaz's timing was perfect. By late 1981, Diaz and Hawkins headed north to Washington to look for funding. Within weeks, money was forthcoming, and the wall that separated county and federal agencies fell temporarily. Three days after its foundation, Diaz's new team had survived two shootouts and arrested their number-one target. CENTAC 26 was expanded. Eventually, that would include the recruitment of Frank's most trusted detective, Al Singleton. In 1980, the clearance rate for murdered Colombians had been 19 percent. Within a month, CENTAC 26 had a clearance rate of well over 100 percent, only possible when capturing one murderer leads to the solution of cases long considered cold.

For a year, CENTAC 26 churned through the Miami underworld, until what had raised Diaz so high took him low. Despite support from the DEA, the IRS, the county, customs, and city officials, Diaz's aggressive and unorthodox methods worried the FBI. For every agent who was convinced that Diaz had found the right concoction to fight the drug trade, there were others who believed "that he made up his own laws and selectively enforced them." They spread whispers of corruption. By the summer of 1982, Diaz was under secret investigation by the FBI. Never charged, he was tossed from CENTAC 26 and sentenced to patrolling the airport. Six months later, he quit the force.

During 1981, Mariel refugees showed up on Doc Davis's tables with what he considered "mind boggling, astronomical" regularity—five times the rate of any other group. The average Mariel corpse, he said, was someone who had been shot multiple times, had elaborate tattoos, and had been stripped of their few belongings. And yet there was a quieter truth. A year after the havoc at Key West, most refugees had settled and secured jobs, while hovering uncomfortably within Carter's invented designation of "status pending." Within three years, 95 percent of Mariel immigrants had either found or created work. Their children were in schools learning English. If it hadn't been for Castro's gift of his prison system and asylums, the statistics of the Mariel exodus would have been entirely typical of any immigrant group.

In 1981, Edna Buchanan would witness the final uptick in Miami's murder rate, as it rose by another thirty-eight bodies. More than ever, Buchanan was reduced to the literary equivalent of Doc Davis's stacking of corpses: "A 76 year old migrant shot and killed a friend who asked him for money, two Rastafarians killed a man in a downtown bar, a woman gunned down her boyfriend, a Miami man was savagely stabbed in his bed and a young couple returning from their first date surprised a burglar and killed him, according to police who investigated six slayings in a violent 24 hour period ending Sunday." The year 1979's articles had shrunk to 1980's paragraphs. In 1981, Buchanan often captured murders between commas.

Race was all-consuming in 1980. But just as homicide detectives were among the few Miamians to go back and forth across all the city's boundaries, so were crime reporters. Reading through the hundreds of articles Buchanan produced in that turbulent time, it's striking how the woman who loved details often omitted race. She liked oddities, coincidences, sentiments, and the grotesque. Race could be a part of that. She couldn't resist the story of a police supervisor caught trying to rob a jai alai betting parlor while wearing blackface. How could she, when he was a former Officer of the Month? Rarely had a reporter gathered as much color as Buchanan did but cared so little for race.

Buchanan's work would be noticed. It was her colleague Gene Miller who would eventually bring her to the Pulitzer Prize committee's attention. He had called a friendly feature writer at the *New Yorker*, who wrote a knowing, glowing piece about her. Within a year the Pulitzer was hers. It was a Miami dichotomy: the ultimate decoration of respectability for a first-class reporter abetted by the ignoble side of the city she covered.

Isaac Kattan would serve ten of his thirty-year sentence and then be deported to Colombia. To the small, proud Jewish community of Cali, he was an embarrassment. He doesn't appear again in the annals of law enforcement until 1995, when a warrant was issued by Peruvian police accusing him of acting as the money launderer for a group attempting to export cocaine worth $200 million to Europe in a single shipment.

Operation Greenback had done the country an extraordinary service. Not only did Greenback imitators pop up all over America, but the art and power of forensic accountancy was acknowledged across federal law enforcement agencies. In 1980, the combined budgets of every government agency fighting the drug trade came to under a billion dollars. It wasn't until the government coordinated efforts in Florida in 1982 after a quiet push from the Non-Group that the fight against cocaine became more evenly matched when US armed forces arrived to assist law enforcement agencies. With the knowledge gathered chasing Isaac Kattan and other launderers, Charlie Blau would eventually be called to Washington, DC, to help write America's first statutes against money laundering.

Even after Anibal Jaramillo was sentenced to death in Florida for the Caicedo double murder, his boss, Paco Sepulveda, would visit their lawyer to see if there were ways he might assist the prisoner. Once, Sepulveda arrived in his lawyer's office in knee-high boots, sunglasses, and shaggy hair, looking like the bassist from a psychedelic rock group. He never looked exactly the same, growing and shaving off beards, dyeing his hair, wearing wigs, and visiting plastic surgeons, but the clothes were always flamboyant. This time, he placed a briefcase with $250,000 on the lawyer's table while suggesting that they attempt to bribe the justices on

Florida's Supreme Court. Only months after his conviction, Jaramillo's lawyer launched an appeal based on a recovered memory. Jaramillo now alleged he *had* been at Caicedo's house the night before his murder, helping the man's nephew tidy up a messy garage. That explained his fingerprints on the knife, packaging, and rope.

The seven members of Florida's Supreme Court not only reversed Jaramillo's conviction but ordered his immediate discharge. The Miami judge forced to release Jaramillo was so disgusted she threw his papers from her bench to the floor. The only arrest of a Colombian hit man from 1980 had been overturned. His lawyer was sure of only one thing: Jaramillo wasn't even his client's real name. A year after returning to Colombia, he was reported murdered.

As Carter's domestic policy adviser would write, "It is difficult to conjure up a more catastrophic final year in any American president's term of office than 1980, Carter's last year in the White House." It wasn't just cocaine. There was Mariel and Iran, Afghanistan and inflation, the doubling of oil prices, a primary challenge, and a humiliating debate against Reagan. The next president had listened to Carter delve into the minutiae of policy and sighed, "There you go again."

If 1980 was a diagnostic test for America, Miami was the biopsy. It revealed the coming contamination of cocaine, the complications of a sudden burst of immigration, and the potential triangulation of race. Miami had simmered, exploded, and survived on its own. Nineteen eighty had accelerated, not created, changes; but every short-term threat had a long-term upside. Cocaine corruption would leave behind enough money to help strengthen a city. The same went for immigration. It had looked like an overwhelming tide, but it was eventually absorbed. The true effect was found in Miami's demographics. Miami had changed in 1980 from a city split relatively evenly between three tribes to a city most definitively Latin.

Miami would continue to struggle—that was clear from Buchanan's or Frank's perspective on the exorbitant murder rate. Equally important, optimists like Governor Graham or Mayor Ferré hadn't given up on the city, even when it seemed President Carter had. Graham was born there. Ferré was never going to leave. They were confident that geography trumped difficulty. Cocaine didn't contradict the argument, it reinforced it. A foreign business scaled in South Florida could spread successfully across the nation.

Ferré called the drug trade "a depravity of the human soul," but he also said that "from an economic point of view, once that money goes into the bank and gets deposited, and is loaned out to build more condominiums, well, money is money." Drugs had brought blood to Ferré's city. They'd also provided roughly 25,000 legitimate jobs in banking, real estate construction, and service industries. An extra $400 million in sales tax receipts bolstered Dade County. In Brickell, more than twenty skyscrapers were rising from the marriage of good and bad money as the city's accountants became masters of concealment in response to Operation Greenback. Delaware corporations were established, owned by offshore companies with anonymous directors. It was almost impossible to tie ownership of a Miami asset to the person using it.

Unsurprisingly, Miami's tourism industry had suffered in 1980, down a shocking 23 percent from the previous year. Early in 1981, Ferré winkled contributions out of the city commission, Alvah Chapman, and the Miami Chamber of Commerce and financed a junket for fifty journalists from around the world. Instead of pinning them to pool chairs and whipping them through the Everglades in airboats, Ferré made Miami's torturous year of 1980 the central attraction.

The correspondents first gathered at City Hall to be greeted by the mayor. He looked, wrote a journalist, "like a Kennedy who had wandered south" as he gave a speech that roamed from the city's early history to the McDuffie trial. It was typical brusque Ferré, directly addressing Mariel, racism, and the riots. "Are we over that?" he asked. "No, we still have the same problems we had last May. Poverty. Unemployment. You'll see it, I'm sure." At the same time, Ferré knew that behind tourism, his strategy of encouraging trade was already working. The year 1980 had seen an incredible 20 percent increase in imports and exports with Latin America.

Despite the combination of local and geopolitical problems thrown at Miami, despite record numbers of immigrants, of murders, of drug seizures, despite muted federal help, Miami had actually thrived at the exact time American journalists were preparing to toll funeral bells throughout the city.

The foreign journalists spent their days crossing Dade County, pausing near where Tent City had stood until late September, when federal officials had paid relief agencies $2,000 per refugee to find alternative housing. Now the journalists watched the sanitation department pick up Santería sacrifices of "chickens wrapped in red scarves" under a kapok tree. They heard bagpipers at the Calle Ocho festival play "Amazing Grace" and visited Flipper in the Seaquarium. They toured Liberty City and walked the riot zones. The editor of France's Le Monde watched the local news in his hotel room, surprised by the broadcasting of a number to call in case a citizen discovered an unidentified body. An Australian put a positive spin on Miami's good fortune to be the drug capital of America. The money, he explained, would continue to propel the city to prominence.

Most concluded that Miami was "needlessly worried about its image." The talk among the journalists was about turquoise waters, beaches, the fresh mornings, and the 80-degree afternoon on a day when New York was blasted with half a foot of snow. As the junket concluded, Ferré was there to explain once more that Miami was "in the throes" of becoming an important international city. The extraordinary thing was that it was doing so without becoming an important domestic city first.

From a Latin American perspective, Miami was a sanctuary for families and fortunes. From an American perspective, it was becoming an agitated Latin American growth on its southern tip. Domestic tourism had shuddered and slowed, but foreign tourism hadn't blinked. Even though the county's advertising budget had been reduced to zero thanks to Emmy Shafer's anti-bilingual campaign, foreign visitors had increased. By the end of 1980, 20 percent of all foreigners entering the United States were now coming through Miami.

A city viewed as highly unstable within the borders of the United States simply wasn't seen that way from abroad, where Miami's problems were viewed as winnable. Seventy-four percent of the 2.3 million international visitors to Miami came from the Caribbean or Latin America. Sixty percent returned within six months, and a quarter of those purchased condos, accounting for over half of Dade County's real estate sales.

In addition, $4 billion of flight capital came to roost in Miami. If the citizens of Miami had come close to giving up on their city, foreign money simply smelled opportunity. In late 1979, in the wake of a *Financial Times* piece on Miami's revival, a building on downtown's Flagler Street had sold for $250 a square foot. Those prices had slumped so far that now developers were willing to wade in. In late 1980, a property on Miami Avenue was bought for $50 a square foot. The *Herald* relished "the frenetic pace at which downtown Miami land is being bid up in a speculative fever that hasn't been evident since the Dade County real estate boom of the 1920s." Ferré was thrilled at the composition of that particular deal. A successful Cuban American who had arrived alone in the country as a child had gathered a group of Spanish investors interested in Miami because of its "gateway status with Latin America."

Ferré had also turned things around with local diplomats. In the mid-1970s, Latin consuls had decided that their diplomatic scene should be conducted in Spanish. Ferré had taken aside the contingent from Central America and convinced them to return to the English language. Immediately, European and Asian consuls reappeared at meetings. A *Herald* reporter found the mayor, with a light suit and "a careful tan," sitting in the corner of the Terrace Room at the Dupont Plaza Hotel with the German consul. It was the same building where Isaac Kattan had kept an office until his arrest. Five years ago, Germany was sending 15,000 tourists a year to Miami. Now, despite 1980's crises, they numbered 100,000, along with new shipping routes and banks. It could all be traced to Ferré's wooing of Dresdner Bank the previous year. There he was, not a vote to be had in a roomful of fifty consuls, still pushing his vision of what Miami could be.

———

In his twelve years as Miami's mayor, Ferré would turn a city from a 60 percent residential tax base to 60 percent commercial. Even before 1980, he had overseen $1.5 billion in construction downtown. The value of land there had tripled in 1980, and Ferré had commitments for another billion dollars of investments for each of the next three years. As the mayor pointed out, that was a larger investment in Miami than had occurred in the previous eighty-five years combined.

The air the journalists from France and Germany and England smelled on their junket wasn't always fresh. Every month, a customs agent from Operation Greenback was pulled for a day. The agent would drive to the customs office and escort kilos of cocaine and bales of marijuana out to an incinerator at the edge of the Everglades, then stand upwind and watch a crane lower the narcotics into the incinerator. Young Floridians hid downwind to catch the high. Depending on the direction of the Biscayne breezes, Miami occasionally caught the scent of its fragility.

EPILOGUE

The highway was closed for ten miles, empty in the morning rush hour except for the long line of cars following behind the hearse. All were flanked by the flashing lights and roaring throttles of a vast police motorcycle escort as Maurice Ferré's body was driven north across the concrete pillars his family had built over the city.

Ferré's hearse was carrying him acros a Miami that bore his imprint. The city had done, for the most part, what he had hoped it would do: it had grown, it had forged its own path regardless of wishes from Washington. Under Ferré, it had begun to count on Latin America just as Latin America had previously counted on Miami. That was never the end of Ferré's dream. He had wanted the spokes from Miami's hub to reach farther. They had spread to Europe and kept moving. Before his death, he could reflect on the present—there were as many Australian companies based in Florida as there were Brazilian.

Miami had become a city of international importance first, and then, and only then, did that begin to be acknowledged across the United States. It's still not fully recognized. Americans fly south, enjoy the beaches and bars just as tourists did fifty years ago, then leave without knowing they've just passed through a city running 30 million metric tons of merchandise every year to Latin America.

As Ferré's cortege passed over I-95, it was obvious that Miami's success has made it hard to see Miami's natural beauty. That's one of the city's sacrifices. Maurice Ferré raised his six children on the edge of the bay, but those homes are long gone. The loss of green space, the loss of views, was something the mayor had come to regret. Looking to the right as the hearse moved northward, you could see only the shiny stack of downtown towers that hid those turquoise waters.

The past lurked on all sides. A closed highway was an echo of a previous time in Ferré's life, when both sides of I-95 were marked by plumes of black smoke, when refugees had washed into a fractious Miami, when the mayor had been driven south to sit among local leaders and look for a solution to 1980's city on fire. Below the highway lay the ghost of Tent City, the most pathetic manifestation of Miami's inability to deal with its immigrant wave back when Mayor Ferré's friend Jimmy Carter had held tight to federal purse strings. Forty years before, when city workers had visited, they'd found men and women had plugged their ears as they struggled with the "acoustic torture chamber" of the highway traffic.

Those immigrants were absorbed into Miami. Their children are Americans who are now driven to the underpass by parents to remind them that teenage complaints need context. But the laws that allowed for special treatment of Cuban immigrants by every administration since 1960 are much weakened in recent years. Cubans who were once guaranteed asylum and a fast path to citizenship are now subject to deportation, a change in law originated under President Obama and reinforced by President Trump. Decades of malleability in South Florida immigration laws have come to an end.

After the hearse passed by the downtown towers, it reached the southern edge of Overtown, and suddenly 1980 was no longer hidden. The few patches of modern Miami's poverty are almost identical to those that once rioted. The night of the McDuffie verdict, looters had set fire to a $50 million development project in Overtown. That fire had spread to black-owned businesses until the only thing left standing on the block was the huge sign OVERTOWN – COMING ALIVE. Forty years later, Overtown is known as the hole in the donut, surrounded on all sides by growth and opportunity but mostly undeveloped. Even in fast-growing

Miami, if you were black in 2020, there was a 38 percent chance that you were living below the poverty line. No administration, including Ferré's, had managed to deliver prosperity to Overtown.

Another minute on the highway, another mile of Miami passed below. The entourage hurtled by the ramps that led to the underpass where Arthur McDuffie was beaten. Then, it was the edge of a single street called Decorator's Row. Now, with a $1.4 billion investment, it's the eastern border of Miami's Design District. December anniversaries, dates that used to be mournfully remembered in the McDuffie family, have now been replaced by parties based around Art Basel, where money meanders from gallery to gallery past polished new shops selling red-heeled shoes, gold watches, and handbags worth $10,000. One story has been laid on top of another, until some stories have been suffocated. There's not even a plaque to preserve the memory of Arthur McDuffie.

The blocks that the cortege next crossed over were the scenes of many of the five thousand violent deaths attended by Edna Buchanan during her long career. So many of those crimes were drug-related. That Miami today is no longer the epicenter of the American narcotics industry isn't so much a victory for South Florida as a loss for the rest of America. The $7 billion of cocaine cash found sloshing through Miami in 1980 has seeped across the country and is now estimated at above $34 billion. While drug-related deaths across the country have rocketed in recent years, in Miami homicide is at a fifty-year low. If Buchanan, still living in the Venetian Isles, went back to work today, she'd only be covering a murder every three days in a county whose population has doubled in size.

Finally, the hearse and the long trail of cars exited the highway and made the short drive along Seventy-Ninth Street, one of the epicenters of the 1980 riots. The funeral cortege pulled up in the slim morning shadow of St. Mary's Cathedral, and the mayor's flag-draped coffin was held aloft on six shoulders and slowly carried inside. In the cool, bright cathedral sat several rows of Ferrés, comprised of the mayor's wife, his children, his grandchildren, and great-grandchildren. There were faces from the mayor's political past dotted between mourners from Cuba, Puerto Rico, Venezuela, Colombia, Haiti, the Bahamas, and beyond.

Before the service started, you only had to listen to the mingling of accents to know that Ferré had always been right. Geography defined Miami. It was why Cubans had come in 1960 and again in 1980. It was why Bahamians had been hired to build the county's original railroad and granted land in Miami the day the city had been incorporated. It was why Miami was the recipient of so much Latin American money during decades of crises and why the city had accepted so many of the region's refugees. Geography was why Colombia's criminals had selected Miami as their gateway city to North America.

It was easy to forget that before Ferré's first administration, so many Miamians had wanted a city that mirrored and rivaled and looked to the north. But Miami was only eighty-four years old in 1980. Then, you could take a stroll down Ocean Drive and find hundreds of Floridians older than that, lugging their chairs into the sun. Florida had only 2 million citizens when Maurice Ferré was born, as opposed to today's 20 million. There wasn't even a fence law, and cows roamed free across the state. When New York City was the same age, in 1737, there was no Central Park, no Statue of Liberty, and no Stock Exchange. Miami began to grow after the centers of the nation were already established and became a news city because it was *watched* by America as it struggled, not helped. It was judged by more stable cities with their own troubled pasts who couldn't conceive of a country growing at different paces.

The mayor's eulogists at St. Mary's that September morning had a common theme: Maurice Ferré's influence over modern Miami. The surprise was that the mayor had not risen higher. With a fortune, a family behind him, a shared platform with President Carter during 1976's victorious campaign, there had been whispers of cabinet-level posts for Ferré, of a trailblazing move to Washington. Instead, Ferré remained merely a mayor, but, vitally, one who had reimagined his city's borders, then his county's and state's borders. That had allowed him to emerge as a regional, albeit unofficial, secretary of state, without ever changing his elected office.

Ferré was reelected mayor of Miami six times, until he finally lost office in 1985. By then, he knew the end was inevitable. Thanks to Mariel, Cubans had emerged as 60 percent of the city's population. As Cuban Americans continued to register to vote in greater and greater numbers, a wave formed that Ferré no longer knew how to ride. From then on it was "Cubano vota Cubano"—the pressure from Cuban American politicians that a vote for a non-Cuban such as Ferré was wasted. It pointed to the dichotomy in Ferré's legacy. He had wanted a Miami devoid of racial divides but, in his final elective victory, relied on a racial divide to create a black and white bulwark against the Cuban American vote.

The facades in Miami may now be fresh, the buildings may grow and glitter, but Miami can seem less like an American melting pot and more like a physical re-creation of a map of Latin America and the Caribbean: where neighborhoods have borders, their citizens travel and trade but don't fuse. The divisions that were so obvious in 1980 have yet to disappear. At a glance, you can see that Little Havana is entirely Latin and that Liberty City remains overwhelmingly black. Ferré was the rarest diplomat, one who traveled across local borders, and one who, in service to his city, could move between countries. Yet he never erased Miami's divides.

After the service concluded, mourners spilled out into the bright midday sun. There was none of 1980's pervasive hostility or anxiety to be felt among the cathedral crowd or in the neighborhood in which they stood. No one talked of the horrors from forty years ago and how a terrified, imploding, imperfect city had been forced to choose its own fate. That story had been laid to rest with leaders and dreamers like Maurice Ferré. Forty years ago, Ferré had given his first State of the City address in the wake of 1980's turbulent spring. It ended with a simple sentence. "Miami," he said, "has found a new direction." It was a direction of Maurice Ferré's choosing, and it still points south.

Today, no American would say that drugs, race, and immigration are issues reserved only for South Florida. The disdain with which the rest of the country viewed Miami in 1980 can seem misplaced now. It's better to think of that year in Miami as a most American experiment. A city suffered a crime rate higher than 1920s Chicago, added a wave of immigration more concentrated than turn-of-the-century New York, and then underwent a violent racial paroxysm. It had all happened in the same twelve months. Ferré knew that the city's salvation could only come about by not deviating from a course he'd already set. He understood that what so alarmed America in 1980 would, given time, attract it.

ACKNOWLEDGMENTS

For the last seven years I have lived in Miami. I owe thanks to a mixture of friends, advisers, and friendly advisers who helped guide me over the five years it took to write this book. I would like to thank those who gave generously of their time, particularly Mayor Maurice Ferré, who allowed me far too many hours at a stage when things were not easy for him. To give an author full access to decades of papers was an act of trust; to put the year 1980 into the full context of Miami was an act of patience.

I am particularly grateful to Edna Buchanan and to Marshall Frank, to Al Singleton, June Hawkins, Raul Diaz, and to David Wilson, Mike Sapsara, and Charles Blau. These men and women not only met with me for hours on more than one occasion, but fielded follow-up calls and follow-ups to the follow-ups. To Al Singleton, Arnold Markowitz, and Alberto Ibarguen for their patience in going through the manuscript, I am so grateful. They helped reduce the amount of errors lurking in this book. The remaining flaws are all mine unless they're egregious, at which point I blame Fidel Castro.

I leaned on sources from the DEA to customs, from the IRS to the INS and all across the law enforcement community. For those who wished to remain anonymous, I respect your wishes and thank you for your trust.

For those who kindly shared their time and their stories I thank Archie McKay, Aida Levitan, Alberto Tellechea, Arnold Markowitz, Bill Talbert, Bill Rose, Senator Bob Graham, Bobby Fernandez, Bob Josefsberg, Carl Hiaasen, Cesar Odio, Dave Rivers, David Kraslow, Dennis Fagan, Doug Rice, D'Wayne Jernigan, Ed Dornbusch, Eduardo Gamarra, Ed O'Donnell, Frank and Ina Wesolowski, Fred Meyers, George Knox, George Yoss, Guillermo Martinez, Howard Kleinberg, H. T. Smith, Jaime Suchliki, Jerry Green, Joe Oglesby, Jorge Rios Torres, June Hawkins, Ken Stroud, Larry Catfish Sands, Lonnie Lawrence, Louis Casuso, Maurice Ferré Jr., Manny Diaz, Marshall Frank, Marty Raskin, Marv Wiley, Marvin Dunn, Merrett Stierheim, Mike Kuhlman, Mike Wenneman, Mike Kuhlman, Mike Baxter, Patrick Malone, Peter Abalia, Pete Weitzel, Ralph Gay, Roberto Fabricio, Scott Silverman, Steve Smith, and Tim Chapman.

In the Coast Guard Archives, many thanks to Beth Crumley for all her help. At NARA in Atlanta, thanks to Robert Pease. For constant help digging through the archives at the State Attorney's, thanks to Avilio Alfonso. To the Miami-Dade public library system, many thanks for your patience. It turned out that at the time of my research the *Miami Herald* had only digitized its archives back to 1982. That meant moving back in time through microfiche, slowly reading my way through eighteen months of newspapers, not just for the *Herald* but for every newspaper in town. It was laborious and of enormous benefit. A broader picture of Miami emerged. Had the archives been digitized, I'm sure the temptation would have been to move like a magpie, picking at only the shiniest of stuff. To the HistoryMiami Museum, I am grateful for the chance to look through a vast and vital photographic archive and for their commitment to keeping South Florida's history alive. All references to weather in 1980 have been double-checked with the National Centers for Environmental Information.

Twice, when I ran into dead ends, I asked for help. Thank you first to Susan Lee, who helped track down vital files, and then to Mariana White Londoño, who helped shape a view of Isaac Kattan from within Colombia. Thank you to Lea Carpenter and GAC for the early reads and direction. Thank you to my discreet friend AC—your early advice was heeded.

Many thanks to my agent, Becky Sweren at Aevitas, who always knows the difference between my idea of a good story and an actual good story.

Thank you to Dawn Davis and to Chelcee Johns at Simon & Schuster for their wise, heavy edits that turned this book from an unwieldy behemoth into a slimmer beast.

There have been many books written about Miami over the last hundred years, though nowhere near as many as I feel should have been written. I think I've read them all, but among those that most influenced my own were Edna Buchanan's two works of nonfiction, *The Corpse Had a Familiar Face* and *Never Let Them See You Cry*. Bruce Porter and Marvin Dunn's book *The Miami Riot* is a vital building block to understanding race in Miami at the end of the 1970s. Marshall Frank's memoir *From Violins to Violence* was simply an angle I'd never seen before. For Mariel, there's Mirta Ojito's beautiful memoir, *Finding Mañana*, Alex Larzelere's *The 1980 Cuban Boatlift*, and the impressive *Florida and the Mariel Boatlift of 1980* by Hawk, Villella, and de Varona. Those seeking to know more about the fascinating conundrums of Miami's formation should turn to T. D. Allman and Jan Nijman. There is also a remarkable, forgotten record of Miami captured in a thirteen-part series the BBC shot in Miami in 1979 called *Circuit Eleven*.

Finally, I have to thank my wife, Adriana, and my children, Tomás and Eva, for the love, laughter, and support. And to Otto the Border terrier, who was always willing to listen to ideas on our beach walks.

NOTES

PROLOGUE

xiii outrun a Pontiac Grand Prix: The descriptions in the following paragraphs are all drawn from the Florida State Attorney Archives, File F79-6895.

xiv a detective sergeant in homicide for seven years: US Senate, *Organized Crime and Use of Violence, Hearings Before the Permanent Subcommittee on Investigations of the Committee on Government Operations*, 96th Cong., 2nd Sess., Part 2, May 2 and 5, 1980, 497, https://www.ncjrs.gov/pdffiles1/Digitization/72649NCJRS .pdf.

xiv the heavy stench of Florida decompositions: Marshall Frank, *From Violins to Violence* (Fortis Books, 2007), 55.

xv weapons violations and assault charges: US Senate, *Organized Crime and Use of Violence, Hearings Before the Permanent Subcommittee on Investigations of the Committee on Government Operations*, 497.

xv the worst racial disturbances of the century: Robert Sherrill, "Can Miami Save Itself? A City Beset by Drugs and Violence," *New York Times*, July 19, 1987.

CHAPTER 1

3 2.1 million international visitors a year: "Miami the New 'Capital' of Latin America," *Boston Globe*, May 15, 1981.

4 public pool, grocery store, and businesses: Interview with Lonnie Lawrence, May 27, 2016.

4 black patrolmen walking black streets: Interview with Archie McKay at the Historic Black Police Precinct Courthouse and Museum, November 17, 2015 .

5 had no power of arrest over them: Interview with Lonnie Lawrence, May 27, 2016.

5 to separate themselves from ever-blacker Liberty City: Bruce Porter and Marvin Dunn, *The Miami Riot of 1980: Crossing the Bounds* (Lexington, MA: Lexington Books, 1984), 10.

5 "Nigger go to Washington": *Eyes on the Prize II: America at the Racial Cross-*

roads, 1965–85, dir. Orlando Bagwell et al., Episode 8, "Back to the Movement" (1990).

5 an empty apartment leased to blacks: Julian M. Pleasants, ed., *Orange Journalism: Voices from Florida Newspapers* (Gainesville: University Press of Florida, 2003), 199.

5 earned the nickname "Central Negro District": Bea Hines, "At Long Last, Overtown Coming Back to Life Again," *Miami Herald*, May 1, 1980.

5 only one in five homes could afford it: Nathaniel Sheppard Jr., "Tense Miami Area Fears the Anger of Its Young," *New York Times*, July 20, 1980.

5 not one of which was black-owned: "Looking Back: How Economic Troubles Spoiled the Dreams of Blacks," *Miami Herald*, May 15, 1980.

6 and Frederica a majorette: Edna Buchanan, "Hundreds Weep at Funeral for McDuffie," *Miami Herald*, December 29, 1979.

6 a child with another woman to prove it: *Eyes on the Prize II*, interview with Frederica McDuffie, transcript.

6 They'd talked of remarriage in front of their families: Joanne Hooker and Ken Sanes, "McDuffie Case, Tragedy for All," *Miami News*, December 29, 1979.

7 five instruments, all horns: *Eyes on the Prize II*, interview with Louis McDuffie, transcript.

7 an entire white wall: Wolfson Archives, WTVJ Newstapes, Cut Stories, December 24, 1979.

7 award from his Marine Corps platoon: Edna Buchanan, "Cops' Role in Death Probed," *Miami Herald*, December 24, 1979.

7 and a pair of roller skates: Buchanan, "Hundreds Weep at Funeral for McDuffie."

7 Gas prices had doubled: US Inflation Calculator, "Gasoline Prices Adjusted for Inflation," https://www.usinflationcalculator.com/gasoline-prices-adjusted-for -inflation/.

7 with an approval rating of 61 percent: Andrew E. Busch, *Reagan's Victory: The Presidential Election of 1980 and the Rise of the Right* (Lawrence: University Press of Kansas, 2017), 59.

8 an enormous 24-point margin: "Handling of Crisis Continues to Boost Carter in the Polls," *Miami Herald*, December 17, 1979.

8 and a black motorcycle jacket: Joanne Hooker, "'Accident' Labeled Murder," *Miami News*, December 27, 1979.

8 His own car . . . and braked hard: *Eyes on the Prize II*, interview with Louis McDuffie, transcript.

9 driving back and forth to work: Edna Buchanan, Arnold Markowitz et al., "Is the Real Horror Story Still to Come?," *Miami Herald*, December 30, 1979.

9 black Americans subject to a sunset curfew: Andres Viglucci, "The 100-Year Story of Miami Beach," *Miami Herald*, March 21, 2015.

9 five blocks from the Airport Expressway: Gene Miller, "McDuffie Friend Says He Didn't Take Drugs," *Miami Herald*, May 6, 1980.

10 not even slowing for the stop signs: Edna Buchanan, "Probers: Traffic Suspect Slain," *Miami Herald*, December 27, 1979.

CHAPTER 2

11 "You go fast . . . keep an eye on the suspect": Interview with Marshall Frank, October 13, 2016.

11 It limped on after McDuffie at walking speed: "Defense: McDuffie Case Is Witch Hunt," *Miami Herald*, April 22, 1980.

12 almost indistinguishable from the night: Porter and Dunn, *The Miami Riot of 1980*, 75–76.

13 McDuffie's arms began to flail: "McDuffie Witness Asked to Check for Bullet Holes," *Miami Herald*, May 3, 1980.

13 "his entire body capacity and then some": Patrick Malone, "The Killing Blow Puzzled Probe," *Miami Herald*, December 29, 1979.

13 where hospitalized prisoners were often kept: *Eyes on the Prize II*, interview with Louis McDuffie, transcript.

14 "the entire brain was swelling uncontrollably": Malone, "The Killing Blow."

14 the only time he'd show any sign of comprehension: " 'Accident' Labeled Murder."

14 "No accident could look like this": *Eyes on the Prize II*, interview with Frederica McDuffie, transcript.

14 where her husband was based with the US Army: Patrice Gaines-Carter, "Journey to Tampa Is a Sorrowful One for McDuffie Kin," *Miami News*, May 8, 1980.

14 McDuffie's life support was unplugged: Williams, "Early Acquittals Seen Possible in McDuffie Trial," *Miami News*, May 8, 1980.

CHAPTER 3

16 while their husbands shot at the fireworks: Interview with Edna Buchanan, November 28, 2018.

16 It was a small price for the stories obtained: Interview with Edna Buchanan, November 12, 2018.

16 a tall, taciturn Dane: Paul Anderson, *Janet Reno: Doing the Right Thing* (New York: Wiley, 1994), 14.

16 "more or less a member of the department": Calvin Trillin, "Covering the Cops," *New Yorker*, February 17, 1986.

16 no looping ridges on the tips of her fingers: Interview with Edna Buchanan, November 12, 2018.

17 it usually turned out to be true: Edna Buchanan, *The Corpse Had a Familiar Face* (New York: Pocket Books, 2009), 309.

17 "He just died": Interview with Edna Buchanan, November 12, 2018.

18 "had an accident trying to outrun the police": Buchanan, *The Corpse Had a Familiar Face*, 309.

18 "didn't want to see in the daytime": Interview with Edna Buchanan, November 12, 2018.

18 40 percent of its stabbings: Porter and Dunn, *The Miami Riot of 1980*, 76.

18   it had seemed entirely logical: Interview with Edna Buchanan, November 28, 2018.

19   "retreat from his uneasiness . . . police force is increased": Ed Bradley, "CBS Reports: Miami: The Trial That Sparked the Riots," Paley Center for Media, August 27, 1980, https://www.paleycenter.org/collection/item/?q=cbs&p=35&item=T81:0148.

19   concentration camp tattoos: Interview with Edna Buchanan, November 12, 2018.

19   finally to the county: Interview with Edna Buchanan, November 28, 2018.

20   he requested the ambulance: Buchanan, *The Corpse Had a Familiar Face*, 309.

20   "sprang off the page": Buchanan, *The Corpse Had a Familiar Face*, 228.

20   there was little Buchanan could do: Buchanan, *The Corpse Had a Familiar Face*, 310.

21   next to a pool of blood: Buchanan, "Cops' Role in Death Probed."

21   "We were wondering when somebody was going to pick it up": Buchanan, *The Corpse Had a Familiar Face*, 310.

21   "all of the lights": Buchanan, *The Corpse Had a Familiar Face*, 311.

21   contemplated trying to attach the Kawasaki to her Camaro: Interview with Edna Buchanan, November 12, 2018.

21   the wider law enforcement community: Interview with Jerry Green, October 13, 2016.

21   just a couple of doors down from the morgue: Interview with Edna Buchanan, November 28, 2018.

22   into the deaths of President Kennedy and Martin Luther King Jr.: In his spare time, Dr. Davis investigated the death of Tutankhamun.

22   "brain buckets": Interview with Dave Rivers, November 6, 2017.

22   Scattered around . . . diving, guns, medicine, and cars: Edna Buchanan, "The 73,729 Deaths of Joe Davis," *Tropic Magazine*, March 22, 1981.

23   carried in by two PSD patrolmen: Interview with Jerry Green, October 13, 2016.

23   "The skull was cracked . . . at the back of the head": Malone, "The Killing Blow," *Miami Herald*, December 29, 1979.

24   on the death certificate: Yvonne Shinhoster, "Doctor Describes Six Blows Dealt McDuffie," *Tampa Tribune*, May 8, 1980.

24   "not even a curb": Buchanan, *The Corpse Had a Familiar Face*, 312.

24   a chance to console and to connect: Interview with Edna Buchanan, November 28, 2018.

24   the sound of organ music: "Holiday Cheer in the Sun," *Miami Herald*, December 23, 1979.

25   "what really happened to her son": Buchanan, *The Corpse Had a Familiar Face*, 313.

25   "Wouldn't they all be sweating by now?": Buchanan, *The Corpse Had a Familiar Face*, 234.

25   "loyal as loyal could be": Interview with Marshall Frank, October 13, 2016.

26   "more questions in less time": Frank, *From Violins to Violence*, 275.

26   "How come Homicide doesn't know about this?": Frank, *From Violins to Violence*, 282.

27   a "diminutive cave of a bar": Rebecca Wakefield, "Farewell, My Lovely," *Miami New Times*, January 17, 2002.

27   firing fake cannons: "Grinch Steals Marine Parade Audience," *Miami Herald*, December 24, 1979.

27   "too much time to fiddle with it": Wolfson Archives, Newswatch, Interview by Michael Putney, October 23, 1987.

28   when he saw the depleted numbers: "If People Won't Go to a March, Then Take the March to the People," *Miami News*, December 24, 1979.

28   concluded that they were still safe: Buchanan, *The Corpse Had a Familiar Face*, 315.

28   front lawns of Dade County that morning: Buchanan, "Cops' Role in Death Probed."

CHAPTER 4

29   during the holiday concert: Frank, *From Violins to Violence*, 286.

30   red hair turned white overnight: Ibid., 14.

31   He was definitely not in: Ibid., 78.

31   had a history in the American South: In fact, the *Miami Herald*'s Gene Miller had won the second of his two Pulitzers for one such case. He'd written most of the *Herald*'s 130 articles about one trial, rescuing two men from death row for a murder they didn't commit. Their confessions had been beaten out of them.

32   for the medical examiner to count: Edna Buchanan, "Death Machine Drove Killers to the Scene," *Miami Herald*, July 12, 1979.

32   retired his six-shot Smith & Wesson: Richard Smitten, *The Godmother* (New York: Pocket Books, 1990), 94.

32   relieved to lead the McDuffie investigation: Interview with Marshall Frank, July 3, 2018.

33   "the least tasteful thing you can do as a police officer": Interview with Alan Singleton, September 13, 2016.

33   while running backward: Interview with Marshall Frank, July 3, 2018.

33   tossed it out the window: Ibid.

33   "and you get your information": Interview with Frank Wesolowski, October 23, 2017.

33   to find a job with consequence: Interview with Alan Singleton, September 13, 2016.

34   He would be a policeman, too: Singleton's son would also become a policeman.

34   to mask the smell of decomposing bodies: Interview with Alan Singleton, September 14, 2016.

34   carried his first case to conviction: Interview with Alan Singleton, September 14, 2016.

34   a bandage on his little toe: Frank, *From Violins to Violence*, 244–246.

35 the scene had already been destroyed: *Eyes on the Prize II*, Episode 8, "Back to the Movement."

35 "I have no idea": Porter and Dunn, *The Miami Riot of 1980*, 35.

35 "Kel-Lites?" said a voice. "Oh, shit": Porter and Dunn, *The Miami Riot of 1980*, 35.

35 "only force necessary to subdue the subject": Buchanan, Markowitz et al., "Is the Real Horror Story Still to Come?"

36 had already been talking: *State of Florida v. Ira Diggs et al.*, 79-21601, Testimony of Cmdr. Dale Bowlin, 36.

36 "never worked a major case in her life": Interview with Marshall Frank, October 13, 2016.

36 "had let the officers say what they wanted": Interview with Marshall Frank, October 13, 2016.

36 the PSD was 7 percent black: Porter and Dunn, *The Miami Riot of 1980*, 184.

36 filed suit against the county: "New Sheriff Vows Change for Metro," *Miami Herald*, January 18, 1980.

37 highly resistant to change: Interview with Merrett Stierheim, May 15, 2016.

37 Lawrence received a sergeant's badge: "Three Blacks Promoted to Metro Police Commandors [*sic*]," *Miami Times*, March 20, 1980.

37 "You know the incident" . . . damned brains out: This section is drawn from three sources: the transcripts of an interview that Lonnie Lawrence gave to *Eyes on the Prize II*, my own interview with Lawrence, and a speech he gave on a panel at History Miami, "McDuffie Riots 35 Years Later: Its Legacy and Societal and Legal Impacts," on May 5, 2015.

38 and South Carolina selling policies: Joanne Hooker and Ken Sanes, "McDuffie Case: Tragedy for All."

CHAPTER 5

39 to locate the motorcycle: "Real Life Quincy Follows No Script," *Miami Herald*, January 20, 1980.

39 "it smells, it's terrible": Malone, "The Killing Blow," *Miami Herald*, December 29, 1979.

39 "certain that McDuffie was murdered": Buchanan, Markowitz et al., "Is the Real Horror Story Still to Come?"

40 "they just Wited-Out that they were there": Interview with Alan Singleton, September 13, 2016.

40 with a warrant to search the police locker room: Interview with Alan Singleton, September 13, 2016.

40 middle of her news conference: Interview with Alan Singleton, September 13, 2016.

41 placed in white boxes and entered into evidence: Wolfson Archives, WTVJ Newstapes, December 27, 1979.

41 "It's like a jigsaw puzzle": Edna Buchanan, "Charges Expected in Cyclist's Death," *Miami Herald*, December 28, 1979.

42 When other reporters ventured onto her beat: Interview with Edna Buchanan, August 20, 2018.

42 She devoured the crime section: Edna Buchanan, "How a Hopeless Kid from New Jersey Became Miami's 'Queen of Crime,'" *Forum Magazine*, Fall 2017.

42 At home, her relationship: Interview with Edna Buchanan, September 4, 2018.

42 They would never leave Miami: "The Maven of Mayhem Is Back," *Miami Herald*, March 21, 1990.

43 "I'll do it, I'll do it": Trillin, "Covering the Cops."

43 During her first interview . . . to restart their police beat: Buchanan, *The Corpse Had a Familiar Face*, 89, and a speech given by Buchanan at Miami Dade Community College during their Journalism Speakers Series on March 26, 2009 (hereinafter "Buchanan, MDCC").

43 Male editors would carp: Buchanan, MDCC.

44 he'd slide the story to Miller: Anderson, *Janet Reno*, 55.

44 "skinny, bespectacled reporter": Mike Baxter, "Freeing Pitts and Lee," *Miami Herald*, May 4, 1976.

44 it was the birth of a friendship: Buchanan, MDCC.

45 to push her stories into print: Interview with Edna Buchanan, September 4, 2018.

45 She'd had five stories published: Buchanan, MDCC.

45 strangest stories of the night: Email interview with Mike Baxter, November 9, 2017.

45 "Who wants the family?": Interview with Arnold Markowitz, August 25, 2016, and interview with anonymous source, September 15, 2016.

46 Five cops, forty-seven complaints: Wolfson Archives, WTVJ Newstapes, December 27, 1979.

46 He carried with him his first police report: Frank, *From Violins to Violence*, 287.

46 You could almost feel: Buchanan, Markowitz et al., "Is the Real Horror Story Still to Come?"

47 There would be an estimated ninety-five witnesses: Wolfson Archives, Newstapes, February 25, 1980.

CHAPTER 6

48 Like the rest of Miami: *Eyes on the Prize II*, interview with Maurice Ferré, transcript.

48 8,500 acres in Dade: "Rise, Fall of Ferré's Sprawling Dade Empire," *Miami Herald*, August 20, 1978.

48 one of the cornerstones of the city: According to an article in the *Miami Herald* on March 16, 1969, the Ferrés began buying downtown lots as early as 1954.

48 downtown would thrive: "Ferré Empire: Triumph to Travail," *Miami Herald*, September 5, 1976.

48 still barred to blacks, Latins, and Jews: Anthony P. Maingot, *Miami: A Cultural History* (Northampton, MA: Interlink, 2004), 124.

48 "the young aristocrat": "Key to Miami Growth Privately Held," *Miami Herald*, March 16, 1969.

49   as high as the presidency of the United States: "Caribbean Style Kennedy: Working His Way Up from the Top," *Tropic Magazine*, April 13, 1969.

49   put together a team . . . to say nothing of the climate: Interview with Maurice Ferré.

50   let the city keep the inconsequential salary: "Maurice Ferré Picking Up the Pieces," *Tropic Magazine*, October 28, 1979.

50   to welcome foreign banks to town: Key to this development was Ferré's previous term in the Florida legislature. Unlike many Miami politicians, Ferré also knew his way around the state capital of Tallahassee.

50   more Edge Act banks than New York: Janis Johnson, "Edge Act Builds Banking Bridge from Florida Abroad," *Washington Post*, May 3, 1981.

50   deploying money south when they wished: "Banks Bid for World Rating," *Financial Times*, October 29, 1980.

50   failed to meet their tax bills: "Maule Ordered Sold to Lone Star; Ferré Retained as a Consultant," *Miami Herald*, January 6, 1978.

50   the feted Maule Industries: "Maule Industries Files for Bankruptcy Shield," *Miami Herald*, July 23, 1976.

50   "Some men drink": "Ferré Empire: Triumph to Travail," *Miami Herald*, September 5, 1976.

51   photographed out jogging: "Ferré Finds New Freedom Without Cement Firm," *Miami News*, February 24, 1978.

51   the best home in Brickell: "Ferré Finds New Freedom Without Cement Firm."

51   He had met his neighbor . . . before either of them turned thirty: Interview with Maurice Ferré Jr., October 1, 2019.

51   too eager: "Ferré Is Right—Re-think Metro," *Miami Herald*, July 16, 1978.

51   absolutely essential to democracy: "Maurice Ferré: Picking Up the Pieces," *Tropic Magazine*, October 28, 1979.

51   handing the whole damn thing over to county: Ferré Archives, El Tiempo, October 25, 1980.

52   they were all handed over to Dade: *Eyes on the Prize II*, interview with Mayor Ferré, transcript.

53   "I wouldn't want to be black": "Leaders Find Few Surprises, Little Hope in Riot Report," *Miami Herald*, December 1, 1980.

53   "Miami's a racist city": *Eyes on the Prize II*, interview with Maurice Ferré, transcript.

53   "The truth of the matter": "Ethnic Politics Snags City Manager Search," *Miami Herald*, August 31, 1980.

53   In theory . . . without ever involving local government: Interview with George Knox, October 20, 2017.

CHAPTER 7

56   "dawdling . . . disappointment": Joe Oglesby, "Early Promise of Janet Reno Is Fading," *Miami Herald*, March 17, 1980.

57   Six black leaders in a row: Marvin Dunn, "How a Black Sees the Jones Case," *Miami Herald*, March 2, 1980. Superintendent Johnny Jones was convicted of

grand theft in 1980 but acquitted of bribery. In 1985, a district court of appeals reversed the conviction on a technicality.

58 "The brass buttons shone": Buchanan, "Hundreds Weep at Funeral for McDuffie."

58 Two church ladies . . . empty streets of Liberty City: Wolfson Archives, Channel 4 News, December 29, 1979.

58 assured the black community: These two paragraphs are also drawn from the Wolfson Archives, Channel 4 News, December 30, 1979.

59 "When all the facts are known": Joanne Hooker and Ken Walton, "McDuffie Case 'Weird,'" *Miami News*, December 29, 1979.

59 A doubling in the murder rate: "The Murder Rate in Dade County Has Grown by . . . ," UPI, December 28, 1980.

60 There had already been: William Wilbanks, *Murder in Miami* (Lanham, MD: University Press of America, UPA, 1984), 313–33.

CHAPTER 8

61 One overheard them discussing: Interview with Raul Diaz, October 6, 2017.

62 an attempt to sell jewelry: Interview with Frank Wesolowski, October 23, 2017.

62 as if to hide something: Interview with Al Singleton, September 13, 2016.

62 Instead of reassuring Singleton: Interview with Alan Singleton, September 13, 2016. Singleton would consider this the defining moment of his career. That career would be among the most storied of all Dade County detectives. It included a role leading the Miami River cops case in 1985 and overseeing the pursuit of Griselda Blanco, the "Godmother" of cocaine.

62 first caught wind of the rot: Buchanan, "Probers: Traffic Suspect Slain," *Miami Herald*, December 27, 1979.

62 where agents had their suits altered: Wolfson Archives, WTVJ News, February 1981.

62 A Cuban who had once managed: Francisco Alvarado, "A $2.8 Million Gold Heist Shows Cuban Gangs Still Rule Miami," *Miami New Times*, July 11, 2013. There's much more to the Escandar story, though no space for it here. Escandar was an associate of Mafia kingpins Santo Trafficante and Miami Beach's Meyer Lansky.

62 Escandar had fled to Miami: "Judge Is Friend of Drug Figure," *Miami Herald*, June 26, 1980.

62 using only a spoon: Andy Rosenblatt, "'Routine' Slaying Haunts Metro," *Miami Herald*, January 28, 1980.

63 In theory, the CIA's charter: Seymour M. Hersh, *Reporter* (New York: Alfred A. Knopf, 2018), 171.

63 Escandar would be a rare instance: Penny Lernoux, *In Banks We Trust* (New York: Anchor Books, 1984), 106.

63 he became an informant for the FBI: *United States of America, Plaintiff-Appellee, v. Fabio Alonso, Pedro Izaguirre, Robert Derringer, Julio Ojeda, Defendants-Appellants*, United States Court of Appeals, Eleventh Circuit, August 30, 1984.

63 parties stocked with prostitutes: "Dade Cops Told of Bribes Before FBI Began Probe," *Miami Herald*, August 7, 1980.

63 Wiretaps went up in Escandar's house: Interview with Marty Raskin, October 17, 2017.

63 as fifty-two FBI agents gathered in Miami: The FBI's top man for setting up the wiretaps was Ben Grogan, who would be shot to death in South Miami in 1986 in a gunfight with bank robbers. Among the more remarkable aspects of the FBI's enormous team was that almost all the agents were Spanish-speaking, gathered in three shifts to handle the phones.

63 Twenty stenographers: Wolfson Archives, Cocaine Cops, (Undated I-Team report . . . PLG11021.mp4). The trial transcripts alone were in seven volumes totaling more than 14,000 pages.

63 The FBI estimated that Escandar: Eventually, the FBI would know more about Escandar's family than he did. When a friend was recorded saying she'd made love four times in one night with a Cuban farmer whom she'd then watched masturbate, Mrs. Escandar had asked for his number. If the laughter inside the house amused the agents listening in, their suspicions were confirmed when homicide detectives turned out to be frequent visitors. The provision of cocaine and hookers continued.

64 "horrendous number of surreptitious tapes": *United States v. Fabio Alonso, Pedro Izaguirre, Robert Derringer, Julio Ojeda, Defendants-Appellants*, 740 F.2d 862 (11th Cir. 1984), 83-5072.

64 outstanding $2.4 million debt: Andy Rosenblatt, "Cops or Robbers?," *Miami Herald*, April 27, 1980.

64 even considered his execution: Interview with Al Singleton, September 13, 2016.

64 "the victim wasn't in an easily recognizable state": Rosenblatt, " 'Routine' Slaying Haunts Metro," *Miami Herald*, January 28, 1980.

64 Even the property room at the PSD building: *United States v. Fabio Alonso, Pedro Izaguirre, Robert Derringer, Julio Ojeda, Defendants-Appellants*.

64 signed over by another compromised detective: Andy Rosenblatt, "2 Metro Detectives Suspended," *Miami Herald*, January 31, 1980.

65 impossible to select jurors in Miami: Wolfson Archives, Newstapes, February 28, 1980.

65 "notoriety of the case": "McDuffie Trial Moved from Dade," *Miami Herald*, March 1, 1980.

CHAPTER 9

69 running errands for prostitutes: *Tono de la Voz*, interview with Héctor Sanyustiz, October 7, 2008.

69 driving an *aspirin*: "The Diary of Maria Nodarse-Perez," *Tropic Magazine*, March 30, 1980.

69 Braking hard to avoid hitting a dog: Mirta Ojito, *Finding Mañana* (New York: Penguin, 2005), 79.

70   He was released on December 17: Ojito, *Finding Mañana*, 83.

70   Three weeks later: Fabiola Santiago, "The Mariel Story That Hasn't Been Told—The Cuban Who Sparked the Exodus Breaks His Silence," *Miami Herald*, September 6, 1998.

71   let's see how they deal: "Que Se Vayan," *Granma*, April 2, 1980.

71   All Easter Sunday: Juan Casanova, "The Ordeal of a Refugee's Flight," *Miami Herald*, June 1, 1980.

72   "This country will not rest content": John F. Kennedy, "Remarks on presenting Cuban Invasion Brigade flag, Orange Bowl, Miami, Florida," December 29, 1962, JFKPOF-042-014-p0001, John F. Kennedy Presidential Library and Museum.

73   that they did not belong to the Communist Party: Calvin Trillin, *Killings* (New York: Random House, 2017), 112.

73   more splinter groups than the FBI could count: Jessica Weiss, "Forty Years Ago, Cuban Extremists Set Off Dozens of Bombs in Miami," *Miami New Times*, July 23, 2015.

73   vehicles were rigged with explosives: Joan Didion, *Miami* (New York: Vintage, 1998), 100.

74   Flagler's dream . . . via seaplane to Cuba: Les Standiford, *Last Train to Paradise: Henry Flagler and the Spectacular Rise and Fall of the Railroad That Crossed an Ocean* (New York: Three Rivers Press, 2002), 35.

74   the first city in the United States with international flights: Maingot, *Miami*, 25. As Maingot notes, for early flights between Havana and Miami, carrier pigeons were sent ahead with approximate arrival times.

74   sweeping more than two hundred: Anderson, *Janet Reno*, 22.

75   a failed tobacco crop: Wayne S. Smith, *The Closest of Enemies: A Personal and Diplomatic Account of U.S.-Cuban Relations Since 1957* (New York: W. W. Norton, 1987), 197.

75   bizarre "amateur diplomacy" began: Daniel C. Walsh, *An Air War with Cuba: The United States Radio Campaign against Castro* (Jefferson, NC: McFarland, 2011), 38.

75   Teenage girls sashayed: "Girls Tell Us Only the Right Stuff Can Free Cuba," *Miami Herald*, April 8, 1980.

75   They heard about Miami: Ojito, *Finding Mañana*, 50.

75   Two would die: Walsh, *An Air War with Cuba*, 38.

76   the actual process of application: The opening of Interests Sections in Havana and Washington, DC, came in 1977 soon after Jimmy Carter's election, with strong support from within the State Department. There was much less support from the National Security Council.

76   should have been processed: Ojito, *Finding Mañana*, 54.

76   The only exception: http://www.cubaencuentro.com/jorge-ferrer by Jorge Ferrer published on July 10, 2008.

77   Had the death of his oldest lover: Smith, *The Closest of Enemies*, 206.

77   Police sat by: Wolfson Archives, Newstapes, Channel 4 News, April 8, 1980.

77   "We have no control!": " 'Nobody's in Charge' as Calle Ocho Throbs," *Miami Herald*, April 13, 1980.

77   They swore they wouldn't eat: Interview with Cesar Odio, November 8, 2017.

78   "They can't sleep": Wolfson Archives, Newstapes, April 12, 1980.

78   "You've got to realize . . . and that's an American tradition": Wolfson Archives, TV Newstapes, April 7, 1980.

79   boiling fish bones: Casanova, "The Ordeal of a Refugee's Flight," *Miami Herald*, June 1, 1980.

79   The ambassador's cat was strangled: "Tent City—New Refugees Recall Horrors of Survival," *Miami News*, May 5, 1980.

79   and promised to pull his friend Jimmy Carter aside: Wolfson Archives, WTVJ Newstapes, April 9, 1980.

79   hidden from the asylum seekers: Casanova, "The Ordeal of a Refugee's Flight."

80   Castro wandered among the asylum seekers: "How a Trickle Turned into a Flood," *Miami Herald*, May 4, 1980.

CHAPTER 10

81   eventually numbering twenty thousand: Wolfson Archives, Channel 4 News, undated.

82   through his bimonthly trips north: Ferré Files, private library.

82   "the trouble with Cubans": "Caribbean-Style Kennedy: Working his Way Up from the Top."

82   quietly consoled homesick children: Speech given by Armando Codina at the opening of Maurice A. Ferré Park, January 31, 2019.

82   "They're welcome in South Florida": Wolfson Archives, Newstapes, April 7, 1980.

83   five neighborhood cats: *Voices from Mariel* (2011 documentary film), dir. James Carleton.

83   The Cuban government turned to a member: Guillermo Martinez had once been invited to join the Committee of 75. He begged off, protesting that he couldn't cover it from the inside.

84   Vilaboa would initiate it: Liz Balmaseda, "Exile: I Was Mastermind of Mariel," *Miami Herald*, July 31, 1989.

84   "used and mashed like a sweet potato": Balmaseda, "Exile: I Was Mastermind of Mariel."

84   Vilaboa drove to WQBA: Ojito, *Finding Mañana*, 153.

84   he was leaving for Mariel: This was all going on during memorials held both in Havana and Miami on April 17, the anniversary of the American-backed Bay of Pigs invasion. In Miami, hundreds gathered, and "women wept, children paraded and old men wore green porkpie hats." In Havana, it was a jubilant event, with tens of thousands marching, led by Castro, pointedly beginning the parade by driving in a three-vehicle convoy past the Peruvian embassy.

85   ignore the Carter administration: The first arrivals from Mariel put to sea on

the same day that Washington's attention was directed south with a new round of Cuba-based rumors. US satellites had revealed "the alarming possibility that the Soviet Union is once more preparing nuclear missile sites in Cuba." The CIA confirmed that the holes were "strikingly similar in size, shape and construction" to those that housed nuclear weapons in Russia. With MIGs operating off Cuba in the Atlantic, papers such as the *Miami Herald* opined that the Soviets had decided that Jimmy Carter was a president who could be pushed around.

85   Not until the boats arrived back: Fred Tasker and Fabiola Santiago, "Heady Days for *Herald*: Boatlift and Major Riots," *Miami Herald*, April 3, 2005.

85   "That's a good pace!": Alex Larzelere, *The 1980 Cuban Boatlift: Castro's Ploy—America's Dilemma* (Washington, DC: National Defense University Press, 2002), 124–25.

86   Graham stayed to watch it: Interview with Senator Bob Graham, October 1, 2018.

86   he'd quickly formed a crisis committee: Alfonso Chardy, "How Fidel Castro and the Mariel Boatlift Changed Lives and Changed Miami," *Miami Herald*, November 26, 2016.

CHAPTER 11

87   some of the very first refugees from Mariel: It's important to note that refugees were allowed to travel with only scant belongings. Anything of value, including the phone numbers of relatives in the Untied States, was confiscated before departure from Mariel. In Victor Andres Triay's *The Mariel Boatlift: A Cuban-American Journey* (Gainesville: University of Florida Press, 2019), this is a frequent motif (see page 98).

87   For the next eight days: Janet L. Fix, "To Get the Story, I Hid on a Boat Near Mariel," *Miami Herald*, April 3, 2005.

87   By April 26 . . . "and speaking all at the same time": Anonymous (Janet Fix), "The Wait at Mariel: An Anxious Time," *Miami Herald*, April 26, 1980.

88   They rang the Coast Guard's Miami Operation Center: VADM Benedict L. Stabile, USCG (Ret.), and Dr. Robert L. Scheina, "1980—Mariel Boatlift: US Coast Guard Operations During the 1980 Cuban Exodus," https://cgaviation history.org/1980-mariel-boatlift-u-s-coast-guard-operations-during-the-1980 -cuban-exodus/.

89   In the controlled language of the Coast Guard: Anonymous (Fix), "Storm Batters 1,500 Waiting Boats at Mariel," *Miami Herald*, April 28, 1980.

89   "grimy and industrial": "Cuba's Port of Mariel Is No Tropical Haven," *Miami News*, May 3, 1980.

89   American craft were given no choice: Triay, *The Mariel Boatlift*, 125.

89   it landed in one of the weakest agencies: David W. Engstrom, *Presidential Decision Making Adrift—The Carter Administration and the Mariel Boatlift* (Lanham, MD: Rowman & Littlefield, 1997), 72.

90   A special agent in customs: Interview with Dennis Fagan, November 16, 2017.

CHAPTER 12

91   The most extraordinary entrance: This story was covered by both the *Miami Herald* and the *Miami News*. The extortion of Jensen would be used by the Carter administration to pull all American boats from the annual Hemingway Cup fishing tournament that summer. Shocked, Cuban authorities flew the captain down to Havana, repaid him in crisp hundred-dollar bills, and announced that they were indignant that he'd suffered such a fate.

92   emptied of speedboats: "Only Imagination Limits Cuban Exodus," *Miami Herald*, April 23, 1980.

92   nautical virgins: "Cubans Flock to Bid for Rescue Boats," *Miami Herald*, April 24, 1980.

92   Ferré's office had already received a call: The mayor had also been called to help end a student-led hunger strike in front of the WQBA station, which was resolved by his friend and assistant city manager, Cesar Odio.

93   The only thing obvious: "Exiles Defy U.S. Warning on Boatlift," *Miami Herald*, April 25, 1980.

93   "not prepared to deal with this": "Exiles Defy U.S. Warning on Boatlift."

93   opera singers and poets: Kate Dupes Hawk, Ron Villella et al., *Florida and the Mariel Boatlift of 1980: The First Twenty Days* (Tuscaloosa: University of Alabama Press, 2014), 120.

93   Each refugee, once processed: "1,105 Cubans Arrive by Boatlift," *Miami Herald*, April 27, 1980.

93   He'd visited the Dominican Republic: Maurice Ferré elegy written for Horacio Aguirre, Ferré Files.

94   including Pinochet: Ferré Files, notes for unpublished Maurice Ferré book "My Miami: A Social Contract."

94   for a weeklong war game: Interview with Maurice Ferré, September 19, 2017.

94   "an untried organization": Lt. Col. Charles S. Thomas, "The Iranian Hostage Rescue Attempt," http://www.dtic.mil/dtic/tr/fulltext/u2/a183395.pdf.

94   A national security team met: Stuart E. Eizenstat, *President Carter: The White House Years* (New York: Thomas Dunne Books, 2018), 798–99.

94   "the most humiliating foul-up": "Carter Turns Newspeak into Art Form," *Miami News*, May 9, 1980.

94   he'd rushed into the president's bathroom: Eizenstat, *President Carter: The White House Years*, 803.

94   So close to Carter: Interview with Maurice Ferré, April 11, 2016.

95   fell in step . . . whispers of dissatisfaction: Interview with Maurice Ferré, February 6, 2018.

95   Returning with no help imminent: "Giant Waves, Winds Buffet Exiles Sealift," *Miami Herald*, April 28, 1980.

96   and sang the Cuban national anthem: Wolfson Archives, Newstapes, April 27, 1980.

96   "None had VHF radios": "First Victims: 2 Bodies Found," *Miami Herald*, April 29, 1980.

96   "pressed knee to knee": Interview with anonymous source, March 20, 2018.

96   "straighten out the mess": Hawk et al., *Florida and the Mariel Boatlift of 1980*, 99.

CHAPTER 13

97   The Coast Guard was playing Tom Petty's "Refugee": "Gates to Stay Open, Castro Says," *Miami Herald*, May 2, 1980.

97   Martinez studied the men . . . Cuban mental institutions: Interview with Guillermo Martinez, February 29, 2016.

98   Before they'd sailed a mile: Janet Fix and Gyllenhaal Anders, "Boat Forced to Bring Convicts and Mental Patients Reaches Fla.," *Washington Post*, May 12, 1980.

98   Another, only transvestites: Mimi Whitefield, "Mariel Memories: The Boatlift That Changed Everything," *Miami Herald*, May 19, 2012.

98   Even though Guillermo Martinez: "I Wasn't Prepared for This Huge Story," *Miami Herald*, April 3, 2005.

98   From the docks: Edward Schumacher, "Retarded People and Criminals Are Included in Cuban Exodus," *New York Times*, May 11, 1980.

98   "a bit scandalous": Glenn Garvin, "Story's Fallout Was Felt for Decades," *Miami Herald*, April 3, 2005.

99   "so they can pick up also the bums": "First Victims: 2 Bodies Found."

99   as dozens of Cuban transvestites: Interview with Aida Levitan, October 13, 2015.

99   The heaps of clothes: Triay, The Mariel Boatlift, 134–35.

99   They were taken to the Federal Correctional Institution: ". . . 100 Have Records," *Miami Herald*, April 30, 1980.

99   And then entire boatloads: "Navy Ordered to Help Move Refugee Flotilla," *Miami Herald*, May 1, 1980.

99   "tropical concentration camp": Ojito, *Finding Mañana*, 181.

99   Next to him were men: "Ex-Convict Had No Choice About Trip to U.S.," *Miami Herald*, May 2, 1980.

100   Criminals may have: "Study Provides First Estimate of Total U.S. Population with Felony Convictions," *ScienceDaily*, September 28, 2017, https://www.sciencedaily.com/releases/2017/09/170928121641.htm, citing Sarah K. S. Shannon, Christopher Uggen et al., "The Growth, Scope, and Spatial Distribution of People with Felony Records in the United States, 1948–2010," *Demography* 2017, DOI: 10.1007/s13524-017-0611-1.

100   They called Cubans "spics": "Latin Group Here Protests WNWS Talk Shows," *Miami News*, May 12, 1980.

100   WQBA sponsored their own buses: "WQBA's Role in Exodus Is 'Provocative,' " *Miami Herald*, May 2, 1980.

101   "what had been sympathetic": Elaine de Valle, "Mariel: New Leaders Were Forged in Heat of Mariel Crisis," *Miami Herald*, April 4, 2005.

101   "mocks the generosity": "A Clear Policy for the Castro Tide," *New York Times*, May 16, 1980.

101 In early May there was a demonstration: "Protesters: Send Them Elsewhere: 'They'll Take Our Jobs,'" *Miami Herald*, May 3, 1980.

101 The march was sparsely attended: "Boatlift Coverage Changed," *Miami Herald*, August 6, 1980.

101 alongside 57 percent of blacks: Richard Morin, "Dade Fears Refugee Waves, Poll Shows," *Miami Herald*, May 11, 1980.

101 Out went country's Willie Nelson: "They're Singing Blues Over WWOK's New Accent," *Miami Herald*, July 10, 1980.

102 "in the same way that Boston": Charles Whited, "Oval Office Finally Gets Message on Refugee Help," *Miami Herald*, May 8, 1980.

102 The man behind did not: Interview with Bill Talbert, January 24, 2018.

102 According to the Carter administration: The checks went from $118 for individual refugees to $143 for a family of four.

102 vast congregation for Mass: *Voices from Mariel*.

102 And yet on May 6: Eizenstat, *President Carter: The White House Years*, 873.

103 For the first time, refugees were arriving: "Controlled Chaos Rules Day 17 of 23,000-Person Cuban Exodus," *Miami Herald*, May 8, 1980.

103 "We didn't know what the policy was": "President Reverses Policy on Refugees," *Miami Herald*, May 6, 1980.

103 Local customs agents joked: Interview with Alberto Tellechea, June 13, 2018.

CHAPTER 14

104 The limited number of Colombians: Bill Curry, "Illicit Drugs Pour in via 'Crazy Colombians,'" *Washington Post*, August 13, 1979.

104 The cash that had buoyed Miami's economy: "Prime at Record 21%, Is Likely to Go Higher," *Miami Herald*, December 17, 1980. March had seen the prime rate hit 20 percent, but it wouldn't be until the end of the year that the record would rise, on the anniversary of McDuffie's beating.

105 South Florida was about transportation: Interview with David Wilson, Drug Enforcement Administration, October 19, 2017.

105 Tourism, Florida's most famous industry: *Senate Subcommittee Hearings Before the Committee on Banking, Housing, and Urban Affairs*, 96th Cong., June 5 and 6, 1980.

105 The first way to do that: "Unique Role for Miami," *Financial Times*, October 29, 1979.

106 Thanks to Graham: "Miami Drawing World's Banks," *New York Times*, December 10, 1980.

106 In the world of Washington bureaucracy: In National Archives and Records Administration documents, two of the founders of Operation Greenback were revealed to be Treasury's Robert J. Stankey Jr., adviser on financial crimes and fraud in the office of the assistant secretary for enforcement and operations, and William Nickerson, deputy assistant secretary for enforcement.

106 Puerto Rican Jorge Rios-Torres: Interview with Jorge Rios-Torres, June 7, 2018.

107   Working with Rios-Torres was a customs attorney: Interview with Alberto Tellechea, June 13, 2018.

107   "a clear and present danger": Alberto F. Tellechea, "Economic Crimes in the Capital Markets," *Journal of Financial Crime* 15, no. 2 (2008): 248. The vast number, according to Tellechea, came from the Treasury Department. It uses a multiplier based on an assumption of how much each narcotics-sale dollar generates downstream.

107   Kattan's family, Sephardic Jews . . . : Robert E. Powis, *The Money Launderers* (City: Probus, 1992), 32.

108   Kattan was responsible for many of those purchases: Joel Garreau, *The Nine Nations of North America* (New York: Avon, 1982), 190.

108   Only Kattan's home held the spoils: "A New Attack on Drugs," *Newsweek*, July 20, 1981.

108   In 1977, he formed a partnership: Robert E. Grosse, *Drugs and Money: Laundering Latin America's Cocaine Dollars* (Westport, CT: Praeger, 2001), 71.

109   The true beauty was: Interview with Pete Abalia, May 18, 2018.

109   In 1979, he carried $90 million: *United States v. The Great American Bank et al.*, 82-720-CR, Accession 88-0563.

CHAPTER 15

111   "homicide factory": Edna Buchanan, "Murders Up 61 Percent, Arrests Off," *Miami Herald*, June 6, 1980.

111   Privately, of all the incongruous thoughts: Interview with Marshall Frank, July 3, 2018.

111   There was a growing sense: James Russell, "Miami's Newfound Image of Prosperity Soiled," *Miami Herald*, May 20, 1980. In October 1979, the *Financial Times* had focused an entire issue on the extraordinary opportunities for growth around Miami. The word "cocaine" wasn't used once.

111   "The corpse had a familiar face": Edna Buchanan, "Brother of Slain 'Cocaine Cowboy,'" *Miami Herald*, April 13, 1980.

111   Another of the day's victims: Edna Buchanan, "Husband Is Murdered Year after Wife Slain," *Miami Herald*, May 8, 1980.

111   He approached the couple: Edna Buchanan, "Man Slain as Gunmen Hit Airport: Colombian with Gems Ambushed at Customs," *Miami Herald*, May 9, 1980.

112   A week later, she was arrested: This was Marlene Orejuela Sanchez, connected to Griselda Blanco, among other Colombian dealers.

112   She was tied directly: David McClintick, *Swordfish: A True Story of Ambition, Savagery, and Betrayal* (New York: Random House, 1995), 228.

112   The murder had become fodder for the dark humor of the bureau: Interview with Dave Rivers, November 6, 2017.

113   One gang, run by Miami-based Paco Sepulveda: Memorandum from June Hawkins to Marshall Frank, December 24, 1980, State Attorney's Office, Gomez homicide file, F80-24457.

113   One by one, Sepulveda's men: Interview with Louis Casuso, August 21, 2018.

114 Buchanan had arrived in time: Edna Buchanan, "Another Cocaine Cowboy Slain at Crowded Mall," *Miami Herald*, March 1, 1980.

CHAPTER 16

115 grossly overloaded: Coast Guard Archives, Immigration (Cuba), Mariel Boatlift, Box 220.

115 Even before Janet Fix had departed: "1,105 Cubans Arrive by Boatlift," *Miami Herald*, April 27, 1980.

115 "We had to take them": Janet Fix and Fitz McAden, "Survival Is Brutal for Refugees as 14 of Their Number Drowned," *Miami Herald*, May 19, 1980.

115 making final edits to a statement on Mariel: "White House Statement on Cuban Refugees," May 14, 1980, Jimmy Carter Presidential Library, https://www.jimmy carterlibrary.gov/digital_library/sso/148878/162/SSO_148878_162_05.pdf.

116 The ocean suddenly swept: Larzelere, *The 1980 Cuban Boatlift*, 170.

116 As the prow rose: Coast Guard Archives, Immigration (Cuba), Box 222, *Coast Guard News*, May 17, 1980.

117 After he had pushed a tenth child: "Death Toll at 14 in Refugee Boat Tragedy," *Tampa Tribune*, May 19, 1980.

117 Some had suffered broken arms: Larzelere, *The 1980 Cuban Boatlift*, 170.

117 The English teacher floating: Fix and McAden, "Survival Is Brutal for Refugees as 14 of Their Number Drowned."

118 Five days before: Coast Guard Archives, Immigration (Cuba), Box 224.

118 One man had managed to lash himself: LCDR Paul Ibsen, "United States Coast Guard Aviation History: Rescue of Cuban Refugees on the *Olo Yumi*," https:// cgaviationhistory.org/hangar-flying/rescue-of-cuban-refugees-on-the-olo -yumi/.

119 "All that was left": "Deadliest Day Claims 10 Lives," *Miami Herald*, May 18, 1980.

119 Children, their stomachs filled with salt water: Stabile and Scheina, "Coast Guard Operations During the 1980 Cuban Exodus."

119 The dead were delivered directly to Key West by helicopter: Coast Guard Archives, Immigration (Cuba), Box 231, May 17, 1980, SITREP.

119 There were shiny leather gun belts: "High Seas, Wind Rip at Flotilla," *Miami Herald*, May 3, 1980.

119 The next day . . . "She doesn't look like my sister": Robert Rivas, "Sepultan en Cayo Hueso a toda la familia de Ibis Guerrero," *El Miami Herald*, May 20, 1980.

120 "was the result of American greed": Joe Morris Doss and Walker Percy, *Let the Bastards Go: From Cuba to Freedom on* God's Mercy (Baton Rouge: Louisiana State University Press, 2003), 90.

120 Docking before the sobering news: *Tono de la Voz*, interview with Héctor Sanyustiz.

120 It would be eighteen years: Ojito, *Finding Mañana*, 273. The *Miami Herald* interviewed Sanyustiz in 1998 after he had suffered a heart attack. He had

ended up living quietly in Winter Garden, near Orlando, driving a construction truck.

120   The Coast Guard saved all 200: Coast Guard Archives, Immigration (Cuba), Box 222, May 19, 1980, SITREP.

121   In total, eighty-three boats: Stabile and Scheina, "U.S. Coast Guard Operations During the 1980 Cuban Exodus."

121   delivering the boatlift its 51,000th refugee: "Refugee Wave Passes 51,000," *Miami Herald*, May 18, 1980.

CHAPTER 17

125   The *Miami News* had described him: "Lawyers Starring in Otero Sequel," *Miami News*, January 17, 1977.

125   As Yoss described the final moments: Wolfson Archives, Newstapes, Channel 4 News, April 18, 1980.

126   Yoss paused: "Prosecutor: McDuffie Yelled, 'I Give Up,'" *Miami Herald*, April 19, 1980.

126   immunized against Marshall Frank's advice: Interview with Marshall Frank, July 3, 2018.

127   The prosecution, no less conspicuously: "In McDuffie Case, Lawyers Are Still the Judges," *Miami Herald*, April 2, 1980.

127   It was a city with a distinct Anglo majority: "Black Leaders Fear McDuffie Trial in Tampa," *Miami Herald*, March 13, 1980.

128   What was he on trial for: Interview with Ed O'Donnell, August 28, 2017.

128   Gene Miller, awarded two Pulitzer Prizes: Interview with Ed O'Donnell, August 28, 2017.

129   There was a notable absence . . . keep her from the stand: Buchanan, *The Corpse Had a Familiar Face*, 328–29.

129   She sat at her desk: Buchanan, *The Corpse Had a Familiar Face*, 88.

129   In Judge Nesbitt's words: "McDuffie Trial Moved from Dade."

130   She'd known her source: Buchanan, *The Corpse Had a Familiar Face*, 330. The real source in the McDuffie trial was Fran Griscom, the wife of Sherwood Griscom, a police officer Buchanan considered a legend in Miami Beach. An unpublished poet, he had shot several criminals; the shootings had been investigated and had been ruled justified. He'd also rescued drowning swimmers and delivered a baby at a bus stop.

130   On the first day of his testimony . . . "As hard as I could": Yvonne Shinhoster, "Ex-Policeman Says Actions Were Justified," *Tampa Tribune*, May 14, 1980.

131   Again, "No, sir": "Ex-Officer: Cops 'Gang-Tackled' McDuffie," *Miami Herald*, April 23, 1980.

131   Despite the testimony, Yoss was worried: Interview with George Yoss, October 27, 2017.

131   And how, in the aftermath: Wolfson Archives, Newstapes, April 23, 1980.

131   "Weren't you calling him a nigger that night?": "Ex-Cop Withstands Defense Pounding," *Miami Herald*, April 25, 1980.

132 Gene Miller's dislike: Gene Miller, "Ex-Cop: I Lied to 'Look Good,'" *Miami Herald*, May 13, 1980.

132 In the station later that morning: "Chronology of Case No. 369-7432-Z," *Miami News*, May 18, 1980.

133 The defense attorneys went at Hanlon: Miller, "Ex-Cop: I Lied to 'Look Good.'"

133 Again and again, Hanlon couldn't explain: "Defense Rakes Over State Witness," *Miami News*, April 30, 1980.

133 He read disbelief: Interview with George Yoss, October 27, 2017.

133 The largest-ever building project: "Dream of a New Overtown Now Lies in Ashes,'" *Miami Herald*, May 20, 1980.

133 He would appoint the first black city attorney: The full-time city manager position lay empty for part of 1980. Howard Gary wouldn't step into it until April 1981.

CHAPTER 18

135 The officer testified that he'd muttered: Verne Williams, "Ex-Miami Cop Says McDuffie Was Last Straw; He Quit," *Miami News*, May 2, 1980.

135 The witness knew Alex Marrero: Verne Williams, "Cop Confuses Beating Case," *Miami News*, May 1, 1980.

136 Neither, it turned out: Yvonne Shinhoster, "Witness' Credibility Labeled in 'Serious Condition,'" *Tampa Tribune*, May 2, 1980.

136 Black people . . . "may just do themselves a favor by expecting the worst out of Tampa": "Too Many Unexplained Twists in McDuffie Trial," *Miami Times*, April 24, 1980.

136 Yoss knew they didn't: Interview with George Yoss, October 27, 2017.

136 "Where'd you get that?": Interview with Ed O'Donnell, August 28, 2017.

136 If O'Donnell hadn't seen Miller there: O'Donnell's confusion wasn't unwarranted. Of Miller's sixty-four paragraphs on the Hanlon testimony, only five were related to the brutal cross-examination that the *Miami News* thought might swing the trial.

137 had saved the outspoken Wright: Verne Williams, "Early Acquittals Seem Possible in McDuffie Trial."

137 As the defendants sat solemnly: Buchanan, *The Corpse Had a Familiar Face*, 329.

137 One officer alone: "Metro's Meanest? A Look at 9 Officers," *Miami Herald*, July 23, 1979.

137 "Concrete," replied Wright: Gene Miller, "Wright: McDuffie Hit with Force of 4-Story Fall," *Miami Herald*, May 8, 1980.

138 When a defense attorney kept asking: Williams, "Early Acquittals Seen Possible in McDuffie Trial."

138 Though Wright had privately admitted: Interview with Carl Hiaasen, December 12, 2017.

138 He'd watched the McDuffie beating: Buchanan, Markowitz et al., "Is the Real Horror Story Still to Come?"

138 They'd printed and distributed: Buchanan, *The Corpse Had a Familiar Face*, 322.

139 More often than not, the same cops: Trillin, "Covering the Cops."

139 After that blow, McDuffie stopped moving: Yvonne Shinhoster, "Ex-Policeman Says Actions Were Justified," *Tampa Tribune*, May 14, 1980.

140 "No, sir," said Marrero. "I feel badly this man is dead": Gene Miller, "Marrero: McDuffie Grabbed Gun," *Miami Herald*, May 14, 1980.

140 As he'd finished with his witness: Interview with Ed O'Donnell, August 28, 2017.

140 "I didn't have a Kel-Lite": Verne Williams, "Marrero Testifies to Fighting McDuffie and Using Nightstick," *Miami News*, May 14, 1980.

141 "Would it refresh your memory": Verne Williams, "Marrero Testifies to Fighting McDuffie and Using Nightstick," *Miami News*, May 14, 1980.

141 Use of force was entirely justified: Yvonne Shinhoster, "McDuffie Beating Called 'Justifiable Force,'" *Tampa Tribune*, May 16, 1980.

141 One attorney wept openly: Wolfson Archives, Newstapes, May 15, 1980.

141 The defense had tried to portray McDuffie: Gene Miller, "Cops Meted Out 'Street Justice' State Charges," *Miami Herald*, May 17, 1980.

141 "He was only concerned with inflicting anguish": Yvonne Shinhoster, "Prosecutor: McDuffie Got 'Street Justice,'" *Tampa Tribune*, May 17, 1980.

142 "And who would have believed McDuffie?": Shinhoster, "Prosecutor: McDuffie Got 'Street Justice.'"

143 waiting for Adorno to rush back from the airport: Interview with Ed O'Donnell, August 28, 2017.

143 Marrero would be spared the murder-two count: Verne Williams, "Prosecution Case Crumbled Like Hotel in a 'Cane,'" *Miami News*, May 18, 1980.

143 Marrero banged his hands on the table: Yvonne Shinhoster, "McDuffie Jury: 4 White Ex-Police Officers Are Innocent of Beating to Death Black Miamian," *Tampa Bay Tribune*, May 18, 1980. The fifth officer had been acquitted in the middle of the trial. He had never participated in the beating and was the last of all the officers present to arrive on the scene.

143 In a brief news conference: Gene Miller, "Cops Freed in McDuffie Case," *Miami Herald*, May 18, 1980.

CHAPTER 19

144 Instead it had become a home: Joe Oglesby, "A Dream Fades into Despair," *Miami Herald*, March 5, 1980.

145 "What extraordinarily talented jurors": Joe Oglesby, "Blacks Can't Cure Travesty with Rioting," *Miami Herald*, May 19, 1980.

145 Reno had just been alerted: "The Lawyers," *Miami News*, May 18, 1980.

145 Lawrence whispered to Bobby Jones: Interview with Marvin Wiley, February 12, 2017.

145 In the car, on the way back to the PSD building: Interview with Lonnie Lawrence, May 27, 2016.

146 They opted to increase their manpower: Interview with Jerry Green, September 16, 2016.

146 Squad leaders were told: Interview with anonymous source, September 8, 2016.

146 The royal poinciana trees: Marvin Dunn, *Black Miami in the Twentieth Century* (Gainesville: University Press of Florida, 2016), 245.

146 "Our Safe Streets officers": Randall Kennedy, *Race, Crime and the Law* (New York: Vintage, 1998), 115–16.

146 "this guy is so dense": Interview with Edna Buchanan, September 4, 2018. Buchanan knew that the pressure on the black community had been mounting slowly. The coming violence was the result of the McDuffie verdict, but she'd broken other stories that had played out in similar arcs. It was a police informant who'd led her to the case of a highway patrolman who'd molested an eleven-year-old black girl in the back of his car. He'd been spared a criminal record. The girl had been promised psychiatric care that had then been withheld. She also knew all about a black motorist, shot to death by a white off-duty policeman while Heath was urinating against a warehouse wall. No criminal charges were pressed there or in the case where an innocent schoolteacher had been beaten in a wrong-house raid.

147 Before five o'clock: Buchanan, *The Corpse Had a Familiar Face*, 331.

147 The photo desk editor: Interview with Edna Buchanan, August 20, 2018.

147 The photographers were trapped: "Miami Riots, May 1980—After Action Report," Miami Police Department, May 1980, 7, http://www.ncjrs.gov/App/pub lications/abstract.aspx?ID=75626.

147 As they emerged bleeding: Buchanan, *The Corpse Had a Familiar Face*, 332.

147 The chief of security made a run: Interview with Edna Buchanan, August 20, 2018.

148 Michael Kulp was hit: Nathaniel Sheppard Jr., "It Was a Wrong Time and Wrong Place to Be White," *New York Times*, May 31, 1980.

148 Her right leg was severed: Porter and Dunn, *The Miami Riot of 1980*, 51.

148 "Get the crackers!": Inter-Office Memorandum to Janet Reno, State Attorney, from Jeffery Raffle, Assistant State Attorney, July 2, 1980, State Attorney Archives, F81-21021, Box 2/4.

149 Surrounded by the large crowd: "Random Acts of Revenge," *Miami Herald*, May 19, 1980.

149 shot several times: "Suspect Admits Kicking Kulp, Says He Saved Girl," *Miami Herald*, October 26, 1980.

149 When he walked on blocks: Interview with Joe Oglesby, March 8, 2016. Oglesby had moved from Liberty City, frustrated by the endless police stops.

149 Then, even more slowly: "Suspect Admits Kicking Kulp, Says He Saved Girl."

150 "The crowd cheered and yelled": Earni Young, "Bodies of Two White Men in Street . . . and a Car Drove Over One of Them," *Miami Herald*, May 19, 1980.

150 He watched a black man: Inter-Office Memorandum to Janet Reno from Jeffery Raffle, July 2, 1980.

150 Just before eight: Young, "Bodies of Two White Men in Street . . . and a Car Drove Over One of Them."

151 Finally, the first officer: Porter and Dunn, *The Miami Riot of 1980*, 60. Incredibly, Michael Kulp would survive and in October testify against the men who beat him. He wore a black patch over his eye as he prepared for another operation, during which part of his skull would have to be replaced. The officer responsible for Kulp's rescue, Sergeant Patrick Burns, had grown up in Miami before seeing six months of combat in Vietnam as a marine.

151 saw the van race east: Young, "Bodies of Two White Men in Street . . . and a Car Drove Over One of Them."

151 As the Kulp brothers . . . "Oh, shit": "Looking Back on the McDuffie Riot," *History Miami*, May 17, 2016.

152 "orderly expression of hostility": Interview with George Knox, October 20, 2017.

152 Lawrence watched the crowd: Interview with Lonnie Lawrence, May 27, 2016.

152 The gunshot that scared the nurse: "Looking Back on the McDuffie Riot," *History Miami*, May 17, 2016.

153 She worried that the McDuffie trial: Joe Oglesby and Charles Whited, "Blacks in Miami Continue to Bleed," *Miami Herald*, March 9, 1980.

153 Anger had to be displayed: Interview with H. T. Smith, May 19, 2016.

153 Lonnie Lawrence felt that he was no different: "Looking Back on the McDuffie Riot," *History Miami*, May 17, 2016.

153 From up high, Lawrence watched: Porter and Dunn, *The Miami Riot of 1980*, 64.

154 And the vets, they took cover: Ibid., 63–64.

154 I could be a half-naked black man: "Looking Back on the McDuffie Riot," *History Miami*, May 17, 2016.

155 *Just let me get home*: Interview with H. T. Smith, May 19, 2016.

155 Nearby, Capt. Marshall Frank: Interview with Marshall Frank, October 13, 2016.

156 With his three lines of officers: "How Police Recaptured Justice Building," *Miami Herald*, May 18, 1980.

156 He was handcuffed: "How Police Recaptured Justice Building."

156 It would take two hours: Porter and Dunn, *The Miami Riot of 1980*, 94.

157 Coordination between city: "Miami Riots, May 1980—After Action Report," 2.

157 Some buildings were set on fire: "Miami Riots, May 1980—After Action Report," 2.

CHAPTER 20

158 By daybreak on Sunday: Porter and Dunn, *The Miami Riot of 1980*, 66.

158 How would he deal with it?: "When Asked about Present, Ferré Talks of Past," *Miami Herald*, May 19, 1980.

159 The PSD would receive: "Damage Toll: $100 Million," *Miami Herald*, May 20, 1980.

159 The incidents ranged from a triple murder . . . an attempted murder charge: State Attorney Archives, F81-21021, Box 2, incident reports including "Master Case" of the riot.

160 Inside the boardroom: "Leaders Squabble as Parts of Dade Burn," *Miami Herald*, May 19, 1980.

160 Reno didn't mention: Anderson, *Janet Reno*, 80.

160 There were conferences: "Trade Fair Salvages Best of Interama," *Miami Herald*, March 7, 1978.

160 Who else but Ferré: Maurice Ferré's introduction of Roslyn Carter at Trade Fair of the Americas, Ferré Archives.

160 He stopped and talked: "Leaders Squabble as Parts of Dade Burn."

161 There was an untouched Harley store: Interview with Jerry Green, October 13, 2016.

161 Close by, at a Woolworth's: "Jones House Burns, but Blacks, Whites Battled to Save It," *Miami News*, May 18, 1980.

161 A parade of cars: Interview with Jerry Green, October 13, 2016.

161 The looting wasn't all peaceful: "Cop Goes Home; Gunman Sought," *Miami Herald*, May 25, 1980. All three survived.

161 "Arguably the worst race riot of the century": Robert Sherrill, "Can Miami Save Itself?; A City Beset by Drugs and Violence," *New York Times*, July 19 1987.

162 A police officer on the corner: "Night Patrol: Riots or No Riots, Cops Have Strange Pride," *Miami Herald*, May 22, 1980.

162 Latins now comprised: "War of Words—Petition Drive May Force Dade to Watch Its Tongue," *Miami Herald*, August 3, 1980.

162 Black Miami had resorted: Interview with H. T. Smith, May 19, 2016.

CHAPTER 21

164 One editor declared: de Valle, "Mariel: New Leaders Were Forged in Heat of Mariel Crisis."

164 By the time the riots hit: "If It Happens Here, They Tell the World," *Miami Herald*, August 23, 1980.

164 After a difficult beginning: de Valle, "Mariel: New Leaders Were Forged in Heat of Mariel Crisis."

164 Moscow covered Miami's problems: "Moscow Radio Says Racists Caused Riot," *Miami Herald*, May 20, 1980.

165 The counter was a measly: Hubert Burkholz, "The Latinization of Miami," *New York Times*, September 21, 1980.

165 After that vote: "$6 Million Riot-Relief Plan OK'd," *Miami Herald*, June 8, 1980.

165 Cuban businessmen reported to the Orange Bowl: "New Refugees Taught ABCs of Life in USA," *Miami Herald*, May 22, 1980.

166 Before the end of July, Shafer had collected: Joanne Omang, Philip J. Hilts, and Kathy Sawyer, "Election 80/National," *Washington Post*, November 5, 1980; Sara Rimer, "How Anti-Bilingualism Crusade Began," *Miami Herald*, October 26, 1980.

167 "How can we have communication at home": "Anti-Bilingualism Referendum Passed in 1980," *Miami Herald*, December 19, 2011.

167   When interviews ran longer: Omang, Hilts, and Sawyer, "Election 80/National."

167   Moments later, another blond woman: *Latino Americans*, Episode 6, "Peril and Promise (1998–2000)," PBS, Fall 2013.

167   The odium also ricocheted: "'Bilingual' Death Threat Investigated," *Miami News*, August 5, 1980.

167   the same anti-Castro group: "Cuban U.N. Attaché Shot to Death in N.Y.," *Washington Post*, September 12, 1980.

167   A *Miami Herald* poll: "Black Rage Runs Deep, Survey Shows," *Miami Herald*, June 22, 1980.

167   Carter would refer to the black vote: Joe Oglesby, "Carter's Black Secret Weapon May Backfire," *Miami Herald*, August 16, 1980.

167   A pamphlet passed out: "Miami Riots, May 1980—After Action Report," 1.

167   He would meet the city leaders: "Miami Riots, May 1980—After Action Report," 3.

168   could feel the agitation building: Interview with Lonnie Lawrence.

168   "We can't get justice here!": "Polite, Mostly Quiet Crowds Turn Surly," *Miami Herald*, June 10, 1980.

169   It was followed by a barrage of soda cans: *Eyes on the Prize II*, Episode 8, "Back to the Movement."

169   Hustling over to the crowd: Interview with Lonnie Lawrence, May 27, 2016.

169   Inside the limousine: Interview with Maurice Ferré, February 6, 2018.

169   It was hard not to feel despair: "Aid May Be in Works Despite Carter Silence," *Miami Herald*, June 10, 1980.

169   The bill had also come before Congress: Editorial Op-ed, "Solutions to Miami's Problems Must Be Found Right Here," *Miami Herald*, July 1, 1980.

170   But Governor Graham: Governor Graham had been highly aware of the lack of Cuban representation at county level. He appointed both judges and school board members. Ferré had appointed Knox as his city attorney. Stierheim promoted Cuban American Sergio Pereira to his assistant county manager in the wake of Mariel.

CHAPTER 22

172   Five foot seven: "Cuban Finds Death at Journey's End," *Miami News*, June 12, 1980.

172   In four days: Edna Buchanan, "Fleeting Reunion, Death Greeted New Cuban Exile," *Miami Herald*, June 12, 1980.

173   Finally, the Toledos were united: Ibid.

173   A doctor quickly explained: "Miami Police Officer Cleared in Immigrant's Death," *Tampa Tribune*, February 8, 1984.

175   In July, the city and the county: "US: Cuban Refugees in Good Health," *Miami Herald*, May 22, 1980.

175   By June, no boats: Eizenstat, *President Carter: The White House Years*, 874.

175   though small numbers: "Sealift Sailing to Calm Conclusion," *Miami News*, June 12, 1980.

175   "It's a mess," said President Carter: Eizenstat, *President Carter: The White House Years*, 874.

175   A week before the riots: "FBI Identifies Cubans as Spies," *Miami Herald*, May 8, 1980.

175   Eventually the government: "FBI Identifies Cubans as Spies."

CHAPTER 23

177   With his fortunes at an ebb: "IRS Places $22,000 Lien on Ferré Property," *Miami Herald*, September 5, 1980.

178   Washington estimated an extra billion dollars: Letter from Admiral Costello to Palmieri, Coast Guard Archives, Immigration (Cuba), Box 229, July 31, 1980.

178   After betting heavily: Ron Chepesiuk, *Crazy Charlie: Revolutionary or Neo Nazi* (Rock Hill, SC: Strategic Media Books, 2016), 24.

178   It made no difference to Isaac Kattan: McClintick, *Swordfish*, 299.

179   Kattan had once ended up: *United States v. The Great American Bank et al.*, Affidavit by Special Agent Mike Hammert.

179   One August day: Ibid.

180   They'd found cocaine in bicycle tubes: Jane B. Baird, "The Source," *Tropic Magazine*, March 23, 1980.

180   hidden by models in their luggage: Interview with Louis Casuso, August 21, 2018.

180   authorities had seized 137 kilograms: McClintick, *Swordfish*, 128.

180   seizure of 200 kilograms: *United States v. Maria Lilia Rojas*, 80-350-Cr., Accession No. 021880382, Boxes 65, 66, Location No. B0801321SAN.

181   In a year of struggle: Agis Salpukas, "General Motors Reports '80 Loss of $763 Million," *New York Times*, February 3, 1981.

181   Rojas was followed up: "Mission: Murder Assassination Kit Guns Seized at Miami Airport," *Miami Herald*, August 1, 1980.

182   Was she taking more than: *United States v. Maria Lilia Rojas*.

182   There had been nineteen skyjackings: wikipedia.org/wiki/List_of_aircraft_hijackings #1970s.

182   forced onto boats to Key West: "Aviation Officials Worry About Soaring Hijack Rate," *Miami Herald*, August 13, 1980.

182   you became fair game: Interview with Charles Blau, September 13, 2017.

183   There she was informed: *United States v. Maria Lilia Rojas*.

183   Women's clothes: Ibid.

183   The same thought: Interview with Dennis Fagan, November 16, 2017.

183   A quick bundle count: "No Questions Asked," *60 Minutes*, March 2, 1981, Wolfson Archives, WTVJ.

183   The missing Monopoly boards: McClintick, *Swordfish*, 130.

183   She rose from her seat: *United States v. Maria Lilia Rojas*.

184   The supervisor quietly pointed out: Ibid.

184   The Greenback agents found: Ibid.

184 At the Greenback office: At this point, Greenback had no public information officer, because it was believed they'd be more effective if they moved quietly. Maria Rojas's arrest wasn't publicly admitted as part of Operation Greenback until April 9, 1981, when the *Miami Herald* ran an article Andy Rosenblatt headlined "Operation Drains Dollars from Drug Business."

184 had to itemize: Interview with Charles Blau, September 13, 2017.

184 Rojas was detained: *United States v. Maria Lilia Rojas.*

184 Despite the success: Ibid.

184 The second was the man: Interview with Mike Kuhlman, December 5, 2017.

185 Any hope that Maria: It would be a cruel year for Maria Rojas. Three of her and Álvarez's children were kidnapped by guerrilla fighters and taken to the mountains. The following April, they were all murdered.

185 The five children: *United States v. Maria Lilia Rojas.*

185 They radioed in their find: Interview with Fred Meyers, December 16, 2017.

CHAPTER 24

189 The oddly named SALAD: "Bilingual Foes Upset Latins," *Miami News*, August 27, 1980.

189 Fearing yet more unrest: "Commission Makes City Bilingual in response to Referendum Bid," *Miami Herald*, September 16, 1980.

189 never far from the influence: James Crawford, ed., *Language Loyalties: A Source Book on the Official English Controversy* (Chicago: University of Chicago Press, 1992), 179.

189 But Shafer's campaign: "Latins Fight New Language Law in Court," *Miami Herald*, November 6, 1980.

189 the anger was just as startling: Porter and Dunn, *The Miami Riot of 1980*, 126.

190 H. T. Smith, a prominent black attorney: Interview with H. T. Smith, May 19, 2016.

190 Even in predominantly black schools: Madeleine Blaise, "At Nobody's Mercy," *Miami Herald*, April 13, 1980.

190 SALAD had appointed: SALAD employed not only Manny Diaz but also Eduardo Padrón, the future head of Miami Dade Community College. These were two of the city's most prominent positions.

190 Over the weeks: Interview with Manny Diaz, November 11, 2017.

191 The Tamiami Gun Shop: Porter and Dunn, *The Miami Riot of 1980*, 150.

191 Even the local police: Edna Buchanan, "Angered Citizens Taking the Law into Own Hands," *Miami Herald*, September 6, 1980.

191 Only Mayor Ferré seemed to object: "City Looking for a Few (150) Good Cops," *Miami Herald*, October 10, 1980.

191 Judges called for courts: Buchanan, "Angered Citizens Taking the Law into Own Hands."

191 Murder rates were steady: Edna Buchanan, "1980 Dade's Deadliest Year—362 Homicides," *Miami Herald*, September 6, 1980.

192 Cause of death was easy enough: Wilbanks, *Murder in Miami*, 345.

192 Buchanan normally squinted: Interview with Edna Buchanan, August 20, 2018.

193 Around 2:00 p.m.: Buchanan, *The Corpse Had a Familiar Face*, 17–22.

193 It was homicide number 328 for 1980: Wilbanks, *Murder in Miami*, 345.

194 He had three hundred bucks on him: Edna Buchanan, "Detective's Fate: Homicide Headache," *Miami Herald*, September 7, 1980. This article, combined with Buchanan's longer version in her book *The Corpse Had a Familiar Face*, plus an interview she granted to the author, provide the meat of this chapter.

195 she was Miami's first war correspondent: Journalism Speaker Series, Wolfson Archives, March 26, 2009.

CHAPTER 25

196 The year 1980 had seen Frank testify: US Senate, *Organized Crime and Use of Violence, Hearings Before the Permanent Subcommittee on Investigations of the Committee on Government Operations*, 96th Cong., 2nd Sess., Part 2, May 2 and 5, 1980.

197 A Cuban-born butcher: State Attorney Archives, F81-21021, Box 4/4.

197 Those still on the streets: State Attorney Archives, F81-21021, Box 4/4, Trial Testimony of Sgt. John Spiegel, PSD Homicide.

198 On the night of the murder: State Attorney Archives: F81-21021: Box 2/4, PSD Supplementary Report on Munoz.

198 The summer should have seen: "Families Plan Funerals, Friends Mourn," *Miami Herald*, May 20, 1980.

198 For every position: Interview with Dave Rivers, November 6, 2017.

198 Frank had his own favorite question: Interview with Marshall Frank, July 3, 2018.

199 The murder rate was up: Buchanan, "Dade's Deadliest Year—362 Homicides."

199 A couple checking in to a hotel: Ibid.

199 Over the last decade: Gerald Posner, *Miami Babylon* (New York: Simon & Schuster, 2009), 77.

199 angered after he was refused a dance: Edna Buchanan, "Refugee's New Life: Death After Bar Argument," *Miami Herald*, June 28, 1980.

199 One refugee shot another: Wilbanks, *Murder in Miami*, 347.

199 Someone had washed the floor: Edna Buchanan, "An Hour of Violence Pushes Homicide Toll to 308 for Year," *Miami Herald*, August 3, 1980.

200 Diaz had been part: This scene is reconstructed based on interviews with Raul Diaz, June 20, 2018, and Marshall Frank, July 3, 2018.

200 Raul called him: Interview with Raul Diaz, October 6, 2017.

200 He even came with an infamous: https://www.cia.gov/library/readingroom/docs/DOC_0000200012.pdf.

201 The same evening: Interview with Raul Diaz, October 6, 2017.

201 Though there were a handful from Mariel: Roben Farzad, *Hotel Scarface* (New York: Berkley, 2017), 112–13.

201 most found work at the bottom end: Farzad, *Hotel Scarface*, 114.

201 By September, one returning homicide detective: Interview with Dave Rivers, November 6, 2017.

202 Frank had admitted earlier: Buchanan, "Dade's Deadliest Year—362 Homicides."

202 The good detective: Interview with Marshall Frank, July 3, 2018.

203 detectives found families more cynical: When Dave Rivers first joined the force, Buchanan was starting out at the *Herald*. She'd ridden fifteen straight hours with him. But Rivers knew that in PSD homicide, Frank preferred keeping Buchanan at arm's length.

203 Wright could always tell: Edna Buchanan, "Leaky Cocaine Packets Kill Smuggler," *Miami Herald*, August 7, 1980.

203 They'd called the Coast Guard for help: Interview with David Rivers, November 6, 2017.

204 Unidentified low-flying aircraft: "Luck Alone Keeps Flying Safe in Florida," *Miami Herald*, March 8, 1981.

204 paid off air traffic controllers: "Drug Agents Claim Air Controller Gave Tips to 'Smugglers,'" *Miami Herald*, September 23, 1980.

204 Even in trials: Wilbanks, *Murder in Miami*, 64–65.

204 By the end of the summer: Interview with Marshall Frank, July 3, 2018.

204 The serial dater: Frank, *From Violins to Violence*, 277.

205 An apology wouldn't arrive: Ibid.

205 Janet Reno, who had been accused: Anderson, *Janet Reno*, 84.

205 There was a high likelihood: Over a year later, both cases would be resolved with the arrest of Ira Lee Pickett, who was tried and convicted for the murder of Emilio Munoz. In 2020, Pickett remains on death row.

206 In protest, disgusted detectives: Edna Buchanan, "Demoralized Police Feel 'Nobody Cares,'" *Miami Herald*, July 17, 1980.

206 Hawkins had heard through sources: Memorandum from June Hawkins to Marshall Frank, December 24, 1980.

CHAPTER 26

207 Anibal Jaramillo wore black shoes: The description of Gomez's murder is drawn entirely from the files at the State Attorney's Office, Gomez homicide file, F80-24457.

209 Together, those two complementary ideas: These ideas were frequently posited by retired homicide detectives when discussing the first wave of Colombian hit men to arrive in Miami. Later, expectations and understandings changed.

209 If you were on the other side of the equation: Interview with Louis Casuso. Casuso, the lawyer for Gomez's estate, was more accustomed to criminal cases and had difficulties executing his clients' wishes. He found that you couldn't ship a coffin. Bodies were returned to Colombia as standard cargo. Things got worse. The Colombian airline *Avianca* misplaced Gomez. Days later, her body was finally located in a cargo area in the Cali airport and returned to her parents in Medellín. Later, Casuso would represent Gomez's killer.

210   Even as the crime was taking place: The quote came from her deposition. The witness would eventually hire a lawyer to keep both defense and prosecution from contacting her, referring them to the psychiatrist she had begun to see in the wake of the killing.

210   Now she wrote: Edna Buchanan, "Murder Score—Six in 12 Hours," *Miami Herald*, November 16, 1980.

210   Between a mother: Edna Buchanan, "Heart Specialist Killed at Beach Hotel," *Miami Herald*, November 18, 1980; Edna Buchanan, "Gunman Kills Motorist," *Miami Herald*, November 18, 1980.

CHAPTER 27

212   Mayor Ferré was shaking hands: Wolfson Archives, WTVJ Newstapes, Cut Stories, November 23, 1980.

212   The stronger a nation's private sector: "The Caribbean Has Lost a Friend," *The Gleaner*, October 7, 2018.

212   let it be known: That summer, Ferré had also sent one of his commissioners to Argentina to press Miami's advantages at a meeting of all of Latin America's mayors.

212   Miami remained open for business: It wasn't a hard argument to win, even with high inflation. Venezuela was running 24 percent interest rates and Brazil, 42 percent.

212   Miami would have to pick one of two directions: "Unique Role for Miami," *Financial Times*, October 29, 1979.

213   He'd attended robberies: "Undercover Governor Pounds Dade Police Beats," *Miami Herald*, November 17, 1980.

213   Both his ex-wife: McClintick, *Swordfish*, 132.

213   while his head of transportation: Ibid.

213   Opa-locka Airport had been used: Alfonso Chardy, "Florida Opa-locka Field Was Once the Site of Secret CIA Base," *Miami Herald*, April 22, 2013.

214   Five men began loading more boxes: Interview with Ken Stroud, December 15, 2017.

214   The Colombians were greeted: Interview with Mike Wenneman, January 20, 2018.

214   All of them were taken: *United States v. Jaime Murcia Duarte, Eddie Joel Perez-Jaimes, Leon Manuel Arenas-Parra*, 80-CR545, January 1981.

214   Only when the agents: *United States v. Jaime Murcia Duarte, Eddie Joel Perez-Jaimes, Leon Manuel Arenas-Parra*, William Logan report to the "Hader-Moreno file."

215   inside the blue duffel: Ibid.

215   beckoned to the customs group supervisor: Ibid.

215   Suddenly the passenger began to cry: McClintick, *Swordfish*, 133.

216   On the morning of November 23: Ibid.

216   Within a month: The intermediary, Marlene Navarro, is at the center of McClintick's

excellent *Swordfish*, the story of an intricate operation launched by the DEA, inspired by Operation Greenback.

216 Later, a Greenback agent: Interview with Mike McDonald for *Frontline*'s *Drug Wars*, https://www.pbs.org/wgbh/pages/frontline/shows/drugs/interviews/mcdonald.html.

216 After the Opa-locka arrests: Wolfson Archives, Newstapes, November 23, 1980.

CHAPTER 28

218 They were relying on Ronald Reagan: "Ethnic Joke, Racial Slip-up Plagues Reagan," *Miami Herald*, February 18, 1980.

218 Unemployment insurance: Eizenstat, *President Carter: The White House Years*, 876.

218 The press focused relentlessly: Busch, *Reagan's Victory*, 113.

219 Award-winning Cuban writers: "Job Provides Food for Body but Not for Soul," *Miami Herald*, September 6, 1980.

219 Carter conceded: Busch, *Reagan's Victory*, 1.

219 "If it was a prizefight": Carl Hiaasen, "A Reagan Landslide: GOP Guns for Control of Senate," *Miami Herald*, November 5, 1980.

219 Not one candidate had contested her job: Anderson, *Janet Reno*, 86.

219 The anti-bilingual ordinance: Wolfson Archives, Newstapes, November 5, 1980.

219 Black voters had split: "Anti-Bilingualism Measure Approved in Dade County," *Miami Herald*, November 5, 1980.

219 It only formalized the divisions: "Miami: A Time for Healing," *Miami Herald*, November 3, 1980.

220 When Miami's hotels: "Crucial Tourism Business Suffering Cancellations," *Miami Herald*, May 20, 1980.

220 At least it was better: Ibid. "Aftermath of Refugee Influx: Key West Tourism Hurting," *Miami Herald*, May 25, 1980.

220 When Dresdner: Interview with Maurice Ferré, April 11, 2016.

221 Greenback's federal prosecutors . . . usually just pointed: Interview with Charles Blau, September 13, 2017.

221 after walking past newsstands: Wolfson Archives, Newstapes, October 29, 1980.

221 Ferré had encouraged: Downtown shop owners estimated that Latins provided 99 percent of business at electronics stores, 80 percent at clothing stores, and 60 percent at shoe stores.

221 Without Latins: "Without Latins, 'We'd Be Dead,'" *Miami Herald*, August 10, 1980.

CHAPTER 29

222 The area had undergone: Mark Derr, *Some Kind of Paradise* (Gainesville: University Press of Florida, 1998), 206.

222 Every Sunday: "What's in a Name? Quite a Bit, It Develops," *Miami Herald*, March 8, 1981.

222 The only vestiges: But even they weren't as bad as they used to be. In Michael Grunwald's *The Swamp* (New York: Simon & Schuster, 2007), which recounts the history of the Everglades, he tells of an entomologist who caught 365,696 mosquitoes in a single night, breaking a world record.

222 As Jaramillo and his partner drove: State Attorney Archives, Case 80-24540, aerial photographs of the Caicedo crime scene.

223 Caicedo had built a Santería shrine: This information is taken from the case file. Santería was beginning to get very negative local coverage. See, for example, "Ritual Sacrifices Turn Miami River Red," *Miami Herald*, May 30, 1981, and "8 Headless Pigs Found in Miami River," *Miami Herald*, March 28, 1981. More and more frequently, animal corpses were being pulled out of the Miami River—in one instance, eight headless pigs in one day. They were detritus from Santería rituals. The old generation of Cubans who had first arrived in Miami tended to be Catholic. Mariel brought more diverse religious representation.

224 It was no surprise to find: State Attorney Archives, Case 80-24540. This list included Griselda Blanco, the Godmother, and the Ochoas.

224 A deeper dig: "Miami Claims Count Low, Say Refugees Are Ignored," *Miami Herald*, September 27, 1980.

224 As homicide squads picked up: Interview with Dave Rivers, November 6, 2017.

224 There were times when Anglo detectives: Interview with Dave Rivers, July 17, 2018.

225 Standing by the door: "Two Slain During Cult Ceremony," *Miami News*, November 17, 1980.

225 Greenback attorney Charles Blau: Interview with Charles Blau, September 13, 2017.

226 Agencies that had refused to join: Ibid.

226 He was only looking for: Interview with Raul Diaz, June 20, 2018.

226 With Diaz in the department: Interview with Raul Diaz, October 6, 2017.

CHAPTER 30

227 In Cali, as a young man: Interview with Charles Blau, September 13, 2017.

227 From 1973 to 1977: *Senate Subcommittee Hearings Before the Committee on Banking, Housing and Urban Affairs*, 96th Cong., June 5 and June 6, 1980.

227 The comptroller didn't even have a budget: Plus, there was a loophole. Any moratorium against foreign nationals owning Florida's banks would have little effect, since an exemption had been included for any bank holding less than $100 million. That applied to 85 percent of Florida's banks.

228 Instead, thanks to clients like Kattan: *Senate Subcommittee Hearings Before the Committee on Banking, Housing and Urban Affairs*, 96th Cong., June 5 and 6, 1980.

228 It was only when specific accounts: Banks founded by Cuban Americans were at least as vulnerable. Continental Bank had been established six years before, by 250 Cuban American exiles. No one owned more than 5 percent of the stock.

Again, their strength became a weakness. They began a system of "reputational banking." American banks wouldn't give loans to businesses whose owners had no credit history, but Cuban Americans knew their own community. If you had done well in Havana in the late 1950s, someone would vouch for you. It was enormously effective in getting businesses up and running quickly, but by the late 1970s it was also totally open to infiltration. Cuban American bankers were also dragged into the Senate hearings. They were equally stubborn in their defensive stances. A leading banker, questioned about dirty money on NBC, responded, "I don't really care. You know why? Because I know the law and what I care [about] is complying with the law. Period. It's not really up to bankers to become investigators of customers." He was technically right and ethically wrong.

228 By 1978, he had four other accounts: Powis, *The Money Launderers*, 35.

228 Sitting watching tape: Interview with Charles Blau, September 13, 2017.

229 The head teller at Great American: *United States v. The Great American Bank et al.*

229 Between the first and second trip: *United States v. The Great American Bank et al.*, Hammert deposition.

229 "My car's been stolen!": Interview with Mike Wenneman, January 20, 2018.

229 He took it to the North Miami Police Department: *United States v. The Great American Bank et al.*

229 The stunned Greenback agents: Interview with Steve Smith, February 5, 2018.

229 The assistant, unaware of Kattan's suspicion: *United States v. The Great American Bank et al.*

230 The DEA had been tipped off: Wolfson Archives, Newstapes, Channel 7, February 27, 1981.

231 It wasn't the shootout: Interview with Charles Blau, September 13, 2017.

231 Rather than getting into another interagency scrap: Interview with David Wilson, October 19, 2017.

232 Visitors often watched agents unchain six: Interview with Charles Blau, September 13, 2017.

232 Prosecutors revealed information: *United States v. Hector Espinosa-Orlando*, 81-6207, United States Court of Appeals (11th Cir. May 2, 1983).

232 "What percentage of cocaine are you seizing?": Interview with Charles Blau, September 13, 2017.

233 In the meeting, Wilson emphasized: Interview with David Wilson, October 19, 2017.

233 He'd learned something new from Greenack: Interview with David Wilson, October 19, 2017.

CHAPTER 31

234 On December 14 in Miami: State Attorney Archives, 80-24540 (Caicedo).

234 Anibal Jaramillo was charged with grand theft: There was also a team of Colombian

pickpockets working in the airport. They cleared thousands a day in cash-heavy Miami. It's unclear whether Jaramillo was in the airport to supplement his work with Paco Sepulveda.

234 Faced with a larceny charge: State Attorney Archives, Case 80-24540 (Caicedo).

234 He expected to be released: State Attorney Archives, Case F80-24457 (Gomez).

235 only the driver of the white Mustang: State Attorney Archives, Case F80-24457 (Gomez): Rollnick Deposition.

235 That cousin had been arrested: State Attorney Archives, Case F80-24457 (Gomez): Nazario Deposition.

236 It was the first signal: Interview with Marshall Frank, July 3, 2018.

236 Charles Veverka, the first officer: "Veverka Trial Sent to San Antonio," *Miami Herald*, November 25, 1980.

236 An arresting officer remembered: "McDuffie Beating Not 'Unusual,' Former Cop Says," *Miami Herald*, December 11, 1980.

236 Tried in Texas: "Veverka Acquitted in Rights Case," *Miami Herald*, December 18, 1980.

237 For his nine-year-old daughter: "A Biting Pain Lingers in Their Hearts," *Miami News*, December 17, 1980.

CHAPTER 32

238 When you had as much as $2.2 million: *United States v. The Great American Bank et al.* This was Kattan's record number to deliver in one day to DLJ.

238 It was registered to a man: *United States v. Hector Espinosa-Orlando.*

239 It had a street value in Miami: "Record Cocaine Haul Seized: Car's Trunk Sags with 410 Pounds," *Miami Herald*, May 21, 1980.

239 Kattan exited the Villa Regina: *United States v. Hector Espinosa-Orlando.*

239 Did that mean anything: Interview with David Wilson, October 19, 2017.

239 A white Chevy Citation pulled up: *United States v. Hector Espinosa-Orlando.*

240 If they made a stop: Interview with Charles Blau, September 13, 2017.

240 One agent pulled the keys out: *United States v. Kattan-Kassin*, 81-83-CR-JLK, https://www.leagle.com/decision/1984715588fsupp1271678.

241 There was the receipt: Interview with Mike Sapsara, October 19, 2017.

241 Depending on whether you asked: Anders Gyllenhaal, "Drug Funds and South Florida's 'Al Capone,'" *Miami Herald*, May 24, 1981.

241 Kattan would be held under a $10 million bond: Wolfson Archives, WTVJ Newstapes, February 27, 1981.

242 They now had proof: Wolfson Archives, Wampler news conference, February 27, 1981.

242 Within hours, Greenback got irate calls: Interview with D'wayne Jernigan, April 27, 2018.

242 Federal prosecutor Charlie Blau: Interview with Charles Blau, September 13, 2017.

242 It took four borrowed counting machines: "Meet the Dallas Attorney Who Wrote the Book on Money Laundering," *Dallas Morning News*, August 10, 2013.

242 Agents worked through the night: Interview with Charles Blau, September 13, 2017.

242 After a year during which federal help: *United States v. The Great American Bank et al.* All information regarding the Great American Bank in this chapter is derived from these files.

242 Within a week, a DEA spokesman: Wolfson Archives, "No Questions Asked," March 2, 1981.

242 Kattan's lawyer would win a suppression: Interview with Bob Josefsburg, November 6, 2017.

243 The average executive compensation: Lawrence Mishel and Alyssa Davis, "CEO Pay Has Grown 90 Times Faster Than Typical Worker Pay Since 1978," Economic Policy Institute, July 1, 2015.

243 Keeping immaculate books: Interview with David Wilson, October 19, 2017.

244 "Was it hard to find a bank?": Interview with Charles Blau, September 13, 2017.

244 both ten times the average: Jan Nijman, *Miami: Mistress of the Americas* (Philadelphia: University of Pennsylvania Press, 2010), 87.

244 And yet, in those two regards: "Recession Drags Money Rates from Sky," *Miami Herald*, May 7, 1980. Cocaine had begun to flourish at one of the low points in the nation's economic history, when prime bank lending rates had risen above 20 percent.

244 Ferré now saw it clearly: Interview with Maurice Ferré, February 7, 2018.

244 Blau sat across: Interview with Charles Blau, September 13, 2017.

244 He had eighty-eight clients: *United States v. Kattan-Kassin.*

245 With roughly twenty banks: Interview with Fred Meyers, December 16, 2017.

245 The jury's decision came quickly: Interview with Bob Josefsberg, November 6, 2017.

245 Kattan's lawyer had only just ordered lunch: One of the mysteries was why Bob Josefsberg, one of the straightest arrows in Florida, would ever represent Kattan. Kattan had been presented by another lawyer as an innocent caught up in a drug sting. Josefsberg had believed Kattan all the way through until after his sentencing, when he was stunned to hear he was walking Blau through his money-laundering schemes.

CHAPTER 33

246 when you measured only criminal homicides: Wolfson Archives, Newstapes, January 5, 1981.

246 Frank had loved being a homicide detective: Interview with Marshall Frank, July 3, 2018.

246 Only later would he reflect: Marshall Frank interview, *Before They Go Untold* series, YouTube.

246 In his two years in charge: Interview with Marshall Frank, July 3, 2018.

246 From there his movement: Frank, *From Violins to Violence*, 305.

247 In 1980, the clearance rate: Wilbanks, *Murder in Miami*, 121.

247 CENTAC 26 had a clearance rate: Paul Eddy with Hugo Sabogal and Sara Walden, *The Cocaine Wars* (New York: W. W. Norton, 1988), 82.

247 By the summer of 1982: Eddy et al., *The Cocaine Wars*, 84.

248 The average Mariel corpse: "Violent Death Stalks the Boatlift Refugees," *Miami Herald*, May 31, 1981.

248 A year after the havoc: Larzelere, *The 1980 Cuban Boatlift*, 285.

248 Within three years: George Gilder, *The Spirit of Enterprise* (New York: Simon & Schuster, 1984), 102.

248 In 1981, Edna Buchanan would witness: "New York City and Miami Area Had Record Number of Murders in 1981," UPI, January 1, 1982.

248 Buchanan was reduced to the literary equivalent: Edna Buchanan, "Six Slain in Violent 24 Hours in Miami," *Miami Herald*, February 9, 1981.

248 She couldn't resist: Buchanan, *The Corpse Had a Familiar Face*, 104.

249 He had called a friendly feature writer: Interview with Joe Oglesby, March 8, 2016.

249 He doesn't appear again: Caracol Radio, June 1, 1999, http://caracol.com.co /radio/1999/01/06/judicial/0915606000_073541.html.

249 He never looked exactly the same: Memorandum from June Hawkins to Marshall Frank, December 24, 1980.

250 The Miami judge forced to release: Ellen Morphonios with Mike Wilson, *Maximum Morphonios: The Life and Times of America's Toughest Judge* (New York: William Morrow, 1991), 247.

250 His lawyer was sure of only one thing: Interview with Louis Casuso, August 21, 2018.

250 A year after returning to Colombia: State Attorney Archives, Case 80-24540.

250 As Carter's domestic policy adviser: Eizenstat, *President Carter: The White House Years*, 834.

250 There was Mariel and Iran: Ibid., 881.

251 Ferré called the drug trade: Herbert Burkholz, "The Latinization of Miami," *New York Times*, September 21, 1980.

251 In Brickell: Posner, *Miami Babylon*, 91.

251 It was almost impossible: Ibid., 93.

251 Unsurprisingly, Miami's tourism industry: "Tourism Slump Can't Be Blamed on a Single Factor," *Miami Herald*, May 22, 1980.

251 Early in 1981: Jacqueline Blais, "My Junket," *Tropic Magazine*, May 3, 1981.

251 The correspondents first gathered: "Foreign Press Learns What's True Under the Sun," *Miami Herald*, March 7, 1981.

251 1980 had seen an incredible: "Miami Bank Booster Spurs Growth," *New York Times*, December 9, 1980.

252 The foreign journalists spent their days: "U.S. Hurries to Close Tent City," *Miami Herald*, September 25, 1980.

252 Now the journalists watched: "Early Returns Mixed in Miami Media Tour," *Miami Herald*, April 12, 1981.

252 The extraordinary thing was that: Nijman, *Miami: Mistress of the Americas*, 113.

252 Even though the county's advertising budget: "International Business No. 1 in Miami," *Miami Herald*, March 23, 1980.

252 By the end of 1980, 20 percent of all foreigners: "Study Sees Florida Banks Poised for a New Boom," *Miami Herald*, June 2, 1980.

253 Sixty percent returned: "Miami the New 'Capital' of Latin America," *Boston Globe*, May 15, 1981.

253 Ferré was thrilled: "Downtown Values Triple in Year's Time," *Miami Herald*, November 30, 1980.

253 Ferré had also turned things around with local diplomats: John Dorschner, "Is Foreign Policy Actually Being Forged Over the Shrimp Bowls at the Bankers Club?," *Miami Herald*, May 31, 1981.

253 Now, despite 1980's crises: Ibid.

254 In his twelve years as Miami's mayor: Maurice Ferré would hold office from 1973 until 1985—to date, the city's longest-serving mayor.

254 Even before 1980, he had overseen: "There's No Love Lost Among Mayoral Candidates," *Miami Herald*, October 29, 1979.

254 As the mayor pointed out in the *Miami News* on March 27, 1980, there was an article about Ferré's success pushing through more projects: "'People Mover Grant OK'd,' Ferré Says." The list went on. Rolls-Royce was building an aircraft engine plant at Miami International Airport. The Miami Free Zone, opened in 1979 with a push from Ferré, would see a 95 percent rise in the number of goods it was handling. It was Ferré who'd secured a huge federal check for the city's transportation system in March. He had never doubted that Miami would survive.

254 The agent would drive to: Interview with Bobby Fernandez, December 17, 2017.

254 Young Floridians hid downwind: *Circuit Eleven Miami*, chapter 9, *Cold Turkey and Hash*, BBC, 1979.

EPILOGUE

255 Before his death . . . every year to Latin America: https://www.enterpriseflorida.com /wp-content/uploads/florida-gateway-to-latin-america-and-the-caribbean-.pdf.

256 "acoustic torture chamber": Marlise Simons, "For 750 Cuban Refugees, United States Is a Tent City Under the Expressway," *Washington Post*, September 22, 1980.

256 reinforced by President Trump: When President Obama began to lighten sanctions against Cuba and open travel, it was his administration's presumption that Cuban immigrants would soon no longer need special treatment. While President Trump has reversed the Obama-era détente with Cuba, he did not reverse the changes in immigration policy. For Cuban asylum seekers, the outcomes are equally unwelcome.

256 That fire had spread to black-owned businesses: Fred Grimm and Barry Bearak, "Dream of a New Overtown Now Lies in Ashes," *Miami Herald*, May 20, 1980.

256 Even in fast-growing Miami: http://worldpopulationreview.com/us-cities

/miami-population/.

257 Now, with a $1.4 billion investment: Rene Rodriguez, "The Coolest Miami Neighborhood You Probably Haven't Seen Is Throwing a Party. You're Invited," *Miami Herald*, February 16, 2018.

257 The blocks that the cortege: Buchanan, *The Corpse Had a Familiar Face*, introduction.

257 If Buchanan, still living in the Venetian Isles: Charles Rabin, "Miami Used to Be a Murder Capital. Now, Not So Much, as Crime Rates Hit Historic Lows," *Miami Herald*, January 9, 2019.

258 There wasn't even a fence law: Interview with Senator Bob Graham, October 1, 2018.

259 Ferré was reelected mayor: William R. Amlong, "Politics Cuban-Style Rule Miami," *Miami Herald*, May 5, 1981.

259 At a glance, you can see: https://statisticalatlas.com/neighborhood/Florida/Miami/Little-Havana/Race-and-Ethnicity.

259 It ended with a simple sentence: Robert M. Press, "Miami: A Bubbling 'Melting Pot' Looks Optimistically to the Future," *Christian Science Monitor*, September 21, 1981.

INDEX

ABOUT THE AUTHOR

Nicholas Griffin is a journalist and author of three works of nonfiction and four novels. His last book, *Ping-Pong Diplomacy*, was shortlisted for awards in both the United States and the UK. He lives in Miami with his wife, two children, and a one-hundred-year-old dog.